Phoenix

Phoenix

FASCISM IN OUR TIME

A. James Gregor

with an introduction by Alessandro Campi

Transaction Publishers
New Brunswick (U.S.A.) and London (U.K.)

Second paperback printing 2004

Copyright © 1999 by Transaction Publishers, New Brunswick, New Jersey.

All rights reserved under International and Pan-American Copyright Conventions. No part of this book may be reproduced or transmitted in any form or by any means, electronic or mechanical, including photocopy, recording, or any information storage and retrieval system, without prior permission in writing from the publisher. All inquiries should be addressed to Transaction Publishers, Rutgers—The State University, 35 Berrue Circle, Piscataway, New Jersey 08854-8042.

This book is printed on acid-free paper that meets the American National Standard for Permanence of Paper for Printed Library Materials.

Library of Congress Catalog Number: 99-20842
ISBN: 1-56000-422-3 (cloth); 0-7658-0855-2 (paper)
Printed in the United States of America

Library of Congress Cataloging-in-Publication Data

Gregor, A. James (Anthony James), 1929-
    Phoenix : fascism in our time / A. James Gregor ; with an introduction by Alessandro Campi.
        p. cm.
    Includes bibliographical references (p.) and index.
    ISBN 0-7658-0855-2 (alk. paper)
    1. Fascism. 2. Fascism—Italy. I. Title. II. Title: Fascism in our time.

JC481.G6926 1999
320.53'3' 09049—dc21   99-20842
                                                                  CIP

This volume is dedicated to the memory of Renzo De Felice—
who restored to Italy part of her history.

Contents

Acknowledgments

Everyone who fashions a manuscript for publication puts himself, or herself, in debt to any number of others and to the institutions in which they are all housed. Like everyone else, I owe an inestimable debt to the University of California, Berkeley, for providing me facilities and access to students, both of which have made my work pleasurable and stimulating. The Research Center at the United States Marine Corps University at Quantico was my host as Oppenheimer Professor for the year 1996–97 in which substantial parts of this manuscript were put together. The officers and staff of the Marine Corps University proved to be gifted and principled critics of my work.

To Professor Irving Louis Horowitz, I owe not only collegial respect, but sincere admiration. To Professor Alessandro Campi, who wrote the brief preface to this volume, I owe gratitude for having read this manuscript before its publication. As a Visiting Scholar here at Berkeley, he and his charming wife brought some light into the sometimes darkness of Berkeley. To Mr. Leonid Kil, I owe gratitude for opening vistas on the richness of Russian political thought. To my wife, Professor Maria Hsia Chang, I owe all manner of good things I cannot enumerate other than the fact that she has provided me access to the richness of Chinese political thought.

Finally, to my students I owe gratitude for their patience and their genuine interest in the subjects that have engaged my attention for so long. Whatever is good in this volume is the consequence of the influence of all these people and these institutions. Whatever is not, is solely my responsibility.

A. James Gregor
Berkeley, Winter 1998–99

Introduction

Among the scholars of international reputation studying fascism, A. James Gregor is one of the more stimulating and original. His studies on the "rational" nature of fascist ideology together with his interpretation of fascism as a "dictatorial revolutionary mass movement of development," were articulated in the sixties and seventies in books like *The Ideology of Fascism* (1969), *Interpretations of Fascism* (1974), *The Fascist Persuasion in Radical Politics* (1974), *Italian Fascism and Developmental Dictatorship* (1979), and *Young Mussolini and the Intellectual Origins of Fascism* (1979). They were works that captured the attention of research specialists. Some of the theses argued in those volumes have been the object of academic discussions, and naturally, of criticism. Whatever else they have accomplished, the discussions, and the criticism, have indicated that the theses are relevant and innovative. Gregor has argued that there is a connection between fascism and economic and industrial modernization, as well as an ideological, political, and institutional relationship between the Fascism of Mussolini and that of movements and regimes that emerged after the termination of the Second World War.

Together with a few other scholars—George L. Mosse, Juan L. Linz, Renzo De Felice, Stanley G. Payne, Eugen Weber, Ernst Nolte and Zeev Sternhell, among others—Gregor can be considered one of those authors it is necessary to consult if one wishes to adequately study the fascist phenomenon.

Phoenix: Fascism in Our Time, constitutes, in a sense, the author's return to the study of fascism after a long series of publications and research conducted during the eighties dedicated to geopolitics, and the problems attendant on the United States' security and political relations with the nations of East Asia. The peculiar political and ideological evolution manifest in the former Soviet Union, Eastern Europe, and China, after the collapse of communism, prompted the refocusing of attention.

It is Gregor's conviction, clearly expressed in the present volume, that the former communist nations, attempting a transition to an alternative political order, have experienced the rise, in their midst, of political groups and movements that share tendencies that are, in a generic sense, fascist. That is not to argue that the choice of such groups and movements is consciously mimetic. Rather, the appeal to a new single-party dictatorship, animated by a "national-communism," is the product of historic, social, and political exigencies rather than an imitation of the historic experience of Mussolini's Fascism. In other words, the evolution of the former communist nations in the direction of a "new fascism" (populist, imperialist, nationalist, statist, and militarist) is the product, not of simple imitation, but a response to specific contemporary problems.

The most modern discussions—by authors like Walter Laqueur and Richard Pipes—seem to confirm the thesis argued by Gregor more than twenty years ago. Fascism, with its mixture of nationalism and productivism, elitism and corporativism, anticipated the advent, outside of Europe, of Arab nationalism, African socialism, the Cuba of Castro, and the Libya of Colonel Ghedaffi. Today, something of the same phenomenon is to be observed among those nations in Eastern Europe and East Asia that have most recently emerged from "Marxist-Leninist" rule.

In effect, the reality of the contemporary world suggests that the expectations of analysts like Francis Fukuyama—who anticipated the universal advent of liberal democratic regimes as a consequence of the collapse of communism—were premature. We have witnessed, instead, the advent of political organizations that are "neoauthoritarian," populist and nationalist, inspired by ideas and "myths" that share clear affinities with those of "classical" Fascism.

The present volume does not rehearse the principal theses that Gregor argued more than two decades ago. Rather it gives expression to a number of other elements that warrant contemporary emphasis. In particular, there are a number of points that are essential to Gregor's thesis: (1) the acknowledgment of the relationship between historical Fascism and "development"; (2) the necessity of studying Fascist ideology in its diverse expressions; (3) the recognition of the revolutionary and "nonreactionary" character of Fascism; (4) the distinction between Fascism and conservatism and more emphatically between Fascism and the "Right"; (5) the differences between Fascism and the National Socialism of Adolf Hitler; (6) the contrast between Fascism and "neofascism"; as well as (7) the development of a "generalizing" and comparative interpretation of the fascist phenomenon.

While Gregor's earlier volumes associated Fascism's appeal to the sentiments of populations suffering the consequences of their nation's economic and industrial retardation, in the present exposition there is a specific emphasis on the profound sense of collective and individual humiliation that accompanies that retardation. That collective and individual sense of alienation and disillusion sparks the energy and sustains the revolutionary ardor of the movement and the subsequent regime. All of which suggests that Fascism not only served the ends of economic-industrial modernization, but psychosocial imperatives as well.

To satisfy all those demands, Fascism defended the more-or-less idealized established values of Italy as an historic community, as well as advancing a commitment to a program of industrialization for the peninsula. What many have considered the "contradictions" of Fascism's "conservatism" and its "futurism" finds its resolution in the recognition that Fascism could idealize the Rome of antiquity as well as exalt the industrialized modern world in order to discharge its dual revolutionary obligations.

Today, something of the same duality is to be observed in the collective psychology of a post-Soviet Russia that has suffered the humiliation attendant on Russia's fall from the rank of "super-power" to that of a "third world" community armed with nuclear weapons. Russians, suffering a traumatic sense of collective humiliation, seek a restoration of their nation to the rank of a "major power." That will require rapid increments in technological and industrial sophistication. To accomplish that might well require collective discipline and ultranationalist enthusiasm that could bring in their train antidemocratic and xenophobic sentiments that recall to mind the dangerous political and psychosocial environment of Weimar Germany.

In all of this, Fascist ideology is a matter of significant importance. Gregor was among the first to make its ideology the subject of academic study. Rather than a simple patchwork of "contradictions," Gregor has argued that the ideology of Fascism was a rational and coherent set of normative and empirical propositions designed to address the problems faced by less-developed economies in the modern world.

Studies like those of Emilio Gentile (*Le origini dell'ideologia fascista*) and Zeev Sternhell (*The Birth of Fascist Ideology*) have reinforced the importance of Fascist ideology. It is no longer possible to dismiss Fascist thought as a form of "anti-intellectualism" and "irrationalism." For that reason, Gregor's narrative exposition of the thought of Roberto Michels, Giovanni Gentile, and Sergio Panunzio is of interest and importance.

Equally significant is the discussion concerning the putative relationship between classical Fascism, "conservatism," and the "Right." Recently, there have been those who pretend that the "new right" in France, German "neo-conservatism," Latin-American military authoritarianism, and contemporary Italian populism are all forms of "neofascism." In fact, one need only consider the relationship between the *Estado Novo* of the Catholic-traditionalist Salazar and the fascists of Rolao Preto in Portugal—and that of the traditionalist General Franco and the fascists of the Falangist movement in Spain—to appreciate the distance between the "conservatives" and the "right"—and fascism.

In the interwar and postwar world, similar distinctions can be made in Latin America, in Romania and in Hungary. Fascism was, and has always been, revolutionary, antiliberal, anticonservative, and "antibourgeois." In that sense, it is possible to speak of the Front Nationale of Jean-Marie Le Pen in France as "xenophobic," "ultranationalist," "populist," or of the "extreme right," but hardly "fascist." One can speak of the Italian Social Movement or the National Alliance in Italy as "traditional" or "conservative," but certainly not "fascist."

The properties that have distinguished generic fascism in history—the unitary party, the charismatic leadership, the centralization of economic activity, the disciplined integration of youth, the employment of violence against opponents—more characterize the political system of post-Maoist "communist" China and the political aspirations of the "new nationalism" of post-Soviet Russia, than the "right" or the "conservativism" to be found in the industrial democracies.

A. James Gregor's exposition offers a manner in which classical Fascism and generic fascism might be profitably considered. His work joins that of a small group of specialists as critical to the understanding of fascism. In the search for understanding, he advances the provocative argument that Mussolini's Fascism was "a paradigmatic instance of revolution in the twentieth century…the essence of revolution in our time."

Alessandro Campi
University of Perugia, Italy

1

The Problem

For about three quarters of a century, Western intellectuals have consumed an inordinate amount of time and energy in trying to "understand fascism."[1] It has never been quite clear what that understanding might entail. More often than not, what we have been given has left us with an abiding sense of dissatisfaction.

The interpretations have come in waves. At times, fascism has been characterized as the last defense of capitalism.[2] At another time, we were told that fascism was the product of pandemic sexual disorder.[3] More recently, the preoccupation seems to be with explaining the seeming popularity of fascism—its recent "rebirth" and "rise" in a variety of places both near and far.

In fact, a case can be made that there has been an unexpected reappearance of some kind of fascism in the last decade of the twentieth century. There are political movements of varying size and importance that seem to have found fascism cognitively and emotionally appealing. Our problem arises from the incongruity that results from the insistence, urged on us by a Western academic, that to "understand" fascism, one must appreciate the "pathology" that lay "behind the hatred and destructiveness [it] unleashes."[4] We are informed by yet another that "the word *fascism* conjures up visions of nihilistic violence, war, and *Goetterdaemmerung*," together with a "world of…uniforms and discipline, of bondage and sadomasochism.…"

It seems counterintuitive to suggest that the explanation of the contemporary reappearance of fascism lies in the fact that people have suddenly come to find "nihilistic violence" and "pathological destructiveness" attractive. As a consequence, we do not immediately know how to deal with the information that "fascism" has a demonstrated "ability to appeal to important intellectuals,"[5] and those who follow them, when all the term conjures up for us is a vision of sadomasoch-

1

ism and unprecedented horrors. We are evidently left with a puzzle, "the conundrum of fascism's appeal...."[6]

In post-Soviet Russia, there are major intellectuals, who are politically influential, who show interest in Mussolini and Mussolini's Fascism.[7] In Moscow, Alexander Dugin, another of Russia's intelligentsia, reads, and translates for his audience, the literature of "neofascism." In Moldova, Bulgaria, Romania, the Czech Republic, Macedonia, Slovakia, Slovenia, Serbia, Croatia, and Lithuania, "fascist" elements have resurfaced in a "baroque, often unpredictable alchemy" of "left" and "right."[8]

What has become clear is that "fascism," however the term is understood, has an appeal for many in the contemporary, post-Soviet world. That it should have any appeal at all is a riddle. If "fascism" is typically "narcissistic and megalomanic,...sadistic, necrophiliac...[and] psychopathological," remarkable for its "sheer scale of inhumanity,"[9] it is difficult to understand its continued attractiveness to anyone, much less intellectuals, anywhere in civilized society.

All of which suggests that something is very wrong. Either Western academics have offered assessments of fascism that lack accuracy, dimension, and depth, or some portion of thinking humanity finds sadomasochism, narcissism, and necrophilism seductive. If that is the case, then the appeal of fascism is not to be explained by a scrutiny of fascism's intellectual pretentions; it is the proper subject for a textbook in abnormal psychology. Those who find fascism appealing must be left to provide case studies for psychiatrists.

Before any plausible answers can be forthcoming, it seems necessary to attempt to identify the referents of the term "fascism"—in the effort to ensure that everyone is talking about the same thing. That has been proven to be a difficult task indeed.

Fascism as a Fugitive Notion

Throughout the major part of the twentieth century, academics have sought some theoretical understanding of "fascism." At first, the concern was with the political phenomenon as it manifested itself on the Italian peninsula at the conclusion of the First World War—an effort that was not notable in its achievements.[10] With the alliance of Fascist Italy and National Socialist Germany in the 1930s, the coupling resulted in the coalescence of both into what was conceived to be a generic phenomenon. By the advent of the Second World War, Franco's Spain, Salazar's Portugal, Austria's Heimwehr, the Swiss National Front, the Falanga in Poland, the revolutionaries led by Corneliu Zelea Codreanu in Romania, the Lapua movement in Finland, and that of the Arrow Cross in Hungary—among an indeterminate host of others—were all considered "fascist."[11]

In the Far East, the Kuomintang and the Chinese Blue Shirt Society were understood to be equally "fascist."[12] In Japan, Ryu Shintaro and his New Order Movement—and sometimes the entire imperial government—were considered "fascist."[13]

In Latin America, "fascism" was to be found almost everywhere. The Brazil of Getulio Vargas and the Argentina of Juan Peron were both conceived "fascist." "Fascism" was a phenomenon that was just short of universal.

There were misgivings. At times, the "fascism" of one or another group was characterized as "conservative," or "clerical," or "authoritarian" rather than fascist. And there were times when the "fascism" of one or another movement or regime was dismissed as "false"—not a fascism at all.[14]

It was never quite clear what "fascism" was, how it was to be characterized, and how it was to be identified. By the end of the Second World War, the issue seemingly had become moot. The "War Against Fascism" had been successful.

For academics, however, victory in the War Against Fascism notwithstanding, the issues became increasingly complicated and confused. By the mid-1960s, the term "fascism" had passed into the lexicon of ordinary laymen. In general, the term had become nothing more than an expression of derogation. Not only had the terms "fascism" and "fascist" been reduced to invectives, but in 1975, Stanley Payne spoke of both as among the "vaguest of contemporary political terms."[15]

The terms had inextricably mercurial and ambiguous reference. With the passage of time, there was scant improvement. In 1995, Payne could still report that "at the end of the twentieth century *fascism* remains probably the vaguest of the major political terms."[16]

In the interim, unhappily, the issue of fascism in the modern world had taken on considerable urgency. Without any clear warning from our "Sovietologists," the Soviet Union had disappeared, and in its place more than one analyst reported the stirrings of what they could only identify as "fascism."[17] Vladimir Zhirinovsky had made his appearance and was identified as the leader of a "Russian fascism."[18] The issues had become so tendentious that when an English translation of Zhirinovsky's book, *The Final Dash South*, appeared, it was given the title, *My Struggle*[19]—a gratuitous reminder of Adolf Hitler's *Mein Kampf.*

For many academics, everything seemed to have telescoped into Hitler's National Socialism. The world appeared to lay prostrate before the threat of its revival.[20]

That was not to be the worst. Soon authors were speaking of Zhirinovsky, Serbia's Radovan Karadzic, Romania's Gheorghe Funar, and Hungary's Jozsef Torgyan as "Stalino-fascists."[21] There was talk of "Red-Brown coalitions," with former Marxist-Leninists joining forces with fascists to challenge the liberal, free market successors of a failed communism.[22]

It seemed as though everyone was testing the conceptual fungibility of language. What became eminently clear was the realization that any account of fascism, and its influence in the modern world, had become increasingly tortured and obscure. By the end of the twentieth century, scholarship gave every evidence of not understanding very much about one of the most important political phenomena of the contemporary world.

By the end of the century, it had become obvious to almost everyone charged with the responsibility of offering a comprehensive and intelligible interpretation of the political history of our time, that great confusion confounded the study of "fascism," however "fascism" was understood.

One only needed to consider the implications of the judgment of Walter Laqueur, who could argue that if fascism rather than Bolshevism had prevailed in Russia after the revolution of 1917, "it would have done what Stalin did in any case."[23] Stalinism and fascism were conceived, in some real operational sense, to be historically identical in outcome.

Had fascism prevailed in post-tzarist Russia, it would have marshalled everyone, labor and enterprise alike, to the task of making Russia a "great power." Like Stalinism, fascism would have "militarized the economy and society in general"; it would have "nationalized" heavy industry "to a significant degree." It would have persecuted "minorities" and "intellectuals" in very much the same manner as Stalin. In effect, and in substance, fascism was, for all intents and purposes, all but indistinguishable from Stalinism.

For at least half a century, we had been told that fascism was reactionary and congenitally anticommunist. Marxist-Leninists were revolutionary and intrinsically antifascist. We had been told that fascism was of the "extreme right" and Marxism-Leninism was of the left. Now we are told that "resurfacing communist leaders..." have been gravitating toward fascism, and "quite often exhibit a degree of ultranationalist prejudice we would never have expected from such past paragons of communist internationalism."[24]

Communists, in effect, have become increasingly like the fascists on the "radical right"—or perhaps they had always been of the "radical right." In any event, it would seem that we are no longer certain of anything.

If all that is not confusing enough, other academics insist that "fascism," as all "right-wing extremist groups,"[25] include "antitax," "fundamentalist religious," and "anticommunist" organizations.[26] Thus, "fascism" can be either anticommunist, or a form of Stalinism, a host for religious fanaticism, or a vehicle for tax protestors. It can be an expression of "clerical conservativism" or Islamic fundamentalism.[27] It can associate itself with the "views of Ronald Reagan" in the West, or with former communists of the defunct Soviet Union in the East.[28] More than that, politicians can explicitly renounce "all forms of racism and totalitarianism" and publicly commit themselves to "freedom, justice and democracy," and still be numbered among contemporary "neofascists."[29]

All of which can only test our tolerance of paradox. For more than fifty years, we have been told by Western analysts that right-wing "fascism" has always been "xenophobic" and "ultranationalist," while leftist Marxism-Leninism has been always "cosmopolitan" and "internationalist." But then again, we are now regularly counselled that "perhaps we have tended to misjudge the communist elites of yesterday and failed to notice their latent nationalism all along."[30] And so, it would seem that the political left, as Marxism-Leninism, may have always been nationalistic and ultranationalistic. It may never have been of the left at all. It may have always been of the right. It may have always been an anticipation of the "thought of Ronald Reagan."

Unmistakably, a forest of confusion surrounds any discussion of fascism. Some of the most responsible scholars of our time have simply rejected the notion that one might intelligently discuss a "generic fascism." Henry Ashby Turner has insisted that "Fascism as a generic concept has no validity and is without value for serious analytical purposes."[31] Renzo De Felice, one of our time's most accomplished historians of Mussolini's Fascism, all but entirely rejected any notion of a generic fascism. Fascism, for De Felice, was the movement and the regime identified with Benito Mussolini. There has been, and will be, no other.[32]

And still, there seem to be so many movements and regimes in the twentieth century that share at least some family resemblance to fascism, that political comparativists have found it difficult to do without the reference. The problem, as is the case in all family resemblances, is that it is difficult to specify fully in what way all members resemble each other.

The problem is the same with any number of political concepts. We have problems absolutely distinguishing "liberalism" and "conservatism." We have difficulty absolutely distinguishing "democracies" from "authoritarianisms." The one almost invariably shades off into the other. The concepts are, as they say in social science, "porous."

More emphatically than the rest, "fascism" appears to have no fixed core of meaning for Western academics. As a consequence we have seen a veritable thrashing about for some semblance of meaning that might confidently be assigned to the term. By the end of the century, one other attempt was made to divine the meaning of "fascism" for our time and in the clumsiness of our academic language.

Fascism and the "Radical or Extreme Right"

Perhaps the most uninspired effort to understand "fascism" has been that which attempts to identify it as "right-wing." After the end of the Second World War, there has been a systematic effort to associate "fascist" and "neofascist" political phenomena with the "radical or extreme right" as though all were logically and demonstrably related.

If right-wing extremists include anyone who objects to unrestricted immigration, is "overly conservative," uses "hate speech," is "intolerant" of other people's religious beliefs, holds "stereotypical" views concerning those of other races, gender, age, degree of handicap, and/or sexual life-style,[33] he or she may be identified, under one or another definition, as "radical right-wing," but hardly "fascist."

There are obvious cautions that recommend themselves to those who would associate the "extreme right" with fascism. While there seems to be singular eagerness to make the association,[34] some of those, similarly disposed, are prepared to acknowledge that however "fascistic" the contemporary "extreme right" may be, it displays "glaring differences from inter-war fascist movements."[35]

That, in itself, would seem to recommend caution. If the "extreme right" is "glaringly different" from interwar fascism, how can we be expected to know that it is really "fascist" or "neofascist"?

Thus, we are informed that the "radical right" in the United States includes "racists," anticommunists, antistatist libertarians, tax-protestors, survivalists, and those who object to the unqualified right to abortion. The "radical right" includes opponents of the welfare state. It includes Christians who see salvation only through Christ. It includes those who advocate a defense of wilderness property rights against federal environmental regulation, or who advocate the devolution of federal power to the states. The radical right thus includes celebrities like G. Gordon Liddy and Rush Limbaugh as well as prominent members of the post-1992 Republican opposition in Congress.[36] We are expected to accept the notion that they are all, in some intelligible sense, fascists.[37]

The "radical right" in Europe, on the other hand, seems to include all those who are "racists," nationalists, statists, antilibertarians, and the most avid supporters of "left-wing" Stalinism and communism's form of the welfare state. In Romania, the "radical right" identifies itself with the communist regime of Nicolae Ceausescu as well as with the pre-war fascist Iron Guard.[38] It is a breed of "radical right-wingers" who can be either Christian fundamentalists, atheists or agnostics, fascists or antifascists, communists or anticommunists.

It is not clear what all this means. It is not clear whether the "radical right" is "fascist" in its entirety or whether "fascists" constitute a subset of the more inclusive class. We are told that the "radical right" in Eastern Europe apparently includes the "Stalino-fascists," while the "radical right" in Central Europe "rejects both communism and liberalism." And yet, members of the "extreme right" have "much in common with some of the unrepentant communists...."[39] And while we are told that we should not be surprised by all that, it is arresting to be told that Rush Limbaugh and unrepentant communists share so much in common.

If Stalinists and libertarians, unrepentant communists and survivalists, as well as Christian fundamentalists and atheists are all fascists, it would seem we have lost all direction. If "radical right" is to be understood as an inclusive class coextensive with "fascism," we are faced with more than a few problems.

If the "radical right" is "fascist," and we are told that post-war fascism is "glaringly different" from the interwar versions of fascism, it would seem that we are twice confounded. We are told that fascism has an "almost Darwinian capacity for adaption to its environment,"[40] and can therefore appear in many, many guises—among them, as Republican congressmen, survivalists, or as tax protestors.

Since there appear to be few limits to the protean qualities of fascism, we can never be really sure that what we observe is the article sought. Does such arabesque reasoning mean that the "radical right" is, or can be, fascist—or that the "radical right" must be fascist, whatever traits it displays?

The dilation of the term "fascism" into "right-wing" or "radical right," produces an intellectual wasteland. The fact is that some of the best scholars of fascism have suggested that the attempt to characterize fascism as either left or right is unfortunate.[41] Laqueur, for example, has maintained that "the terms *right* and *left*, although not altogether useless, become more problematical as one moves away in time and space from nineteenth-century Europe."[42]

The relationship between interwar fascism and the "radical right" is, at best, problematic. The dogged attempt to associate the two confounds rather than illuminates analysis.

As a case in point, it has become standard fare among some Western academics that racism and anti-Semitism are critical, and nonsubstitutable traits of both the right-wing and fascism. Entire volumes have been written that attempt to make the connection.

"Fascism" is understood to have been all of a piece with anti-Semitic violence and biological racism.[43] Should we accept such a notion, we are left with a great puzzlement.

Any form of official anti-Semitism and racial violence was totally unknown in Fascist Italy until the mid-thirties. Anti-miscegenation laws were promulgated only after the conquest of Ethiopia in the conviction that racial intermarriage would undermine the discipline that was expected to sustain colonial rule.

Even after Mussolini succumbed to National Socialist influence, Fascism did not subscribe to biological racism. In fact, the official *Manifesto of Fascist Racism*, published in July 1938, maintained that "to say that human races exist is not to say *apriori* that there exist superior or inferior races, but only to say that there exist different human races."[44]

Official Fascist policy never committed itself to anthropological distinctions that were invidious or predictors of behavior. While there were scurrilous publications in Fascist Italy that trafficked on the vilest form of racism, the kinds of racial determinism one found in National Socialist literature was officially abjured by the regime.

More than that, official anti-Semitism was unknown in Fascist Italy until late in the 1930s.[45] Even then, it was marginal to the system.[46] In fact, Mussolini had long and enduring relationships with Jews. One of the principal ideologues of Fascism, and an intimate of Mussolini, was A. O. Olivetti. Margherita Sarfatti, Mussolini's official biographer and long-time mistress,[47] was enormously useful to the regime.[48] Aldo Finzi was a member of Mussolini's first cabinet and Guido Jung was his Minister of Finance for many years. There were Jews at the founding of the Fascist movement in March 1919 and they were overrepresented in its ranks thereafter.

In 1941, Mussolini indicated that he "could not forget that four of the seven founders of Italian nationalism were Jews,"[49] and he personally interceded with Hitler on behalf of Henri Bergson, who had been a significant influence on the philosophy of Fascism. Long after the promulgation of Fascist anti-Semitic legislation in the late 1930s, in fact, Jews continued to occupy important official and unofficial positions in Fascist Italy.[50]

Fascist anti-Semitism was the unhappy consequence of Mussolini's alliance with Hitler. It was never a central conviction of the ideology, and was almost always applied with bad conscience.[51] That anti-Semitism, or biological racism, should have been elevated to the rank of a defining attribute of Fascism reveals the measure of intellectual confusion that surrounds the entire concept of what Fascism was, or generic fascism might be.[52]

Neither biological racism nor anti-Semitism were essential to Mussolini's Fascism. That they should now have become necessary and sufficient for its identification attests to the uncertainty that today permeates most contemporary discussions of fascism. Not only are "*fascism* and *racism*...not synonyms,"[53] there is very good reason to believe that racism is not even necessary to "fascism" as a concept.

Now that we know that Josef Stalin was anti-Semitic throughout his tenure, and that anti-Semitism influenced the behaviors of the regime even after his death,[54] it seems clear that neither anti-Semitism nor biological racism can serve as defining attributes of fascism. They may be necessary, if not sufficient, to some expressions of "radical right-wing" thought, and they may have been essential to the doctrines of Hitler's National Socialism, but they are neither necessary nor sufficient to the characterization of Italian Fascism, nor as a consequence, to fascism in general.

As has been suggested, there is a credible body of scholarship that denies that fascism is of the "right." Richard Pipes has argued that "Bolshevism and Fascism were heresies of socialism,"[55] hardly an auspicious start for a "right-wing" movement. Zeev Sternhell tells us that

"Fascist ideology represented a synthesis of organic nationalism with the antimaterialist revision of Marxism"[56]—an intimation that it would not be advisable to look too far "right" in our analysis.

"Neofascism" after the Second World War

Much of the confusion that afflicts the study of fascism originates in the effort to find a fascism that survived the Second World War. In that effort, "neofascisms" are sought. Evidently, it is not at all certain what "neofascism" might be, so we find it variously identified as the "radical right," "quasi-fascism," "mimetic fascism," "nostalgic fascism," and "cryptofascism." Given the abundant choices available, we find ourselves overwhelmed by an avalanche of uncertain "neofascisms."[57]

Much of the difficulty that attends this kind of exercise turns on the use of concepts like "right-wing" and "extreme right" as though they had standard reference. If it is difficult to define historic fascism with some measure of credibility, problems are compounded by attempting to make fascism a subset of, or coextensive with, the "extreme or radical right."

In the course of our inquiry, if we wish to convey something significant about fascism after the end of the Second World War, it might be better to simply look at those individuals, and those movements, that identify themselves as fascist, and leave the analysis of the "radical right" to those having other agendas, perhaps greater skill, and certainly an infinitely broader perspective.

For the past fifty years, the safest way to trace "neofascism," the survival of fascism after the Second World War, appears to have been to follow the life-histories of the survivors of historic Fascism.[58] Thus, the most responsible studies of what gives at least the appearance of a credible neofascism are studies of the careers of unrepentant Fascists who committed themselves to political activities immediately after the Second World War. At least some of the survivors of the war and the civil strife that decimated Italians at the conclusion of that war were believing Fascists.

Some of those survivors became members of one or another of the small groups that sprang up after the war, some of the more important of which were the *Fasci d'azione rivoluzionaria*, the *Squadro d'azione Mussolini*, and the *Partito fascista democratico*. Those enthusiasts simply brought into the post-war period some of the ideas and practices with which they had become familiar during the tenure of the Fascist regime.

Most of the members of those small groups had been youthful volunteers in the Fascist militia in the brief Republic of Salò, through which Mussolini governed Northern Italy between 1943 and his death in 1945. They were "neofascists" because they were Fascists who sought to pursue Fascism in entirely new circumstances.

But there was something singular about their "neofascism." "Fascism, the defense of Fascism, and the attempt to reestablish Fascism" had been made criminal offenses in 1945—at that time by the provisional government that assumed control of Italy after the defeat of the forces of Mussolini and National Socialist Germany in April and May 1945. By 1948, any attempt to reconstitute the Fascist party had become an actionable offense in accordance with the national constitution. That could only impact on any effort to give expression to explicitly fascist sentiments.

Together with that, most of the young Fascists who joined the first, small post-war Fascist groups had very little sophistication. Most of the members of the first neofascist groups on the Italian peninsula had not experienced the twenty years of Fascist rule, nor is there any evidence that they knew anything other than superficialities about the ideology or the political ideals of Fascism. At least partly because of that, most of their activities were quixotic, and most of their tracts had very little doctrinal substance.

Rejected by the nation they had served, the survivors of the war had self-selected to give themselves over to a thankless, profitless, and hazardous effort to produce a "second Fascism" in an environment peopled by those who had just rejected the first.[59] Those who opted to join the few fascist organizations put together immediately after the war were not representative of either Italians or Fascists. They were a very, very singular group.

Alberto Giovannini called them "orphans," "political innocents," driven by the desperation of loss to pointless acts of frustration.[60] Other than a commitment to "revolution," they did not seem to be guided by any set of identifiable ideas or programs. Most of the groups to which they belonged were ephemeral, and their membership, transient.

The fact is that it is not at all clear that the neofascists of these first post-war fascist organizations had any real sense of what Fascism had been all about. As a consequence, it is not immediately evident what we are supposed to learn from them.

Almost from the very end of the Second World War, the notion of a post-war neofascism had very little coherence or integrity. As will be argued, fascism was, in large part, a product of its time and circumstance. To imagine that a "neofascism" might arise in entirely different times and circumstances—and duplicate, or tell us something significant, about the paradigm, is to expect a great deal.

The situation became increasingly perplexing when commentators began to address themselves to "neofascisms" whose programs had little, if anything at all, to do with paradigmatic Fascism. In 1946, almost immediately after the termination of hostilities, for example, a certain Guglielmo Giannini organized his *L'Uomo Qualunque*, a political organization that managed, for a time, to attract many disaffected Italian voters, including former Fascists. This seems to have qualified him, and his organization, for identification as a "neofascist."

Giannini's program was more than somewhat vague, but he did call for order and stability in an environment suffering all the disabilities of a lost war. He called everyone to return to selfless labor to restore the devastated economy. He advised a search for foreign capital investment and technological transfers from the industrialized democracies in the effort to reconstruct Italian industries and provide employment for the working population of the peninsula. In the search for stability, he advocated the retention of the monarchy. He defended private property as well as capitalism, and proposed protection for the ordinary taxpayer from a government that had become increasingly rapacious. Finally, he called for a restoration of national self-esteem after Italy's catastrophic military defeat.[61]

Given such a program, it is hard to imagine why the *Fronte dell'Uomo Qualunque* qualified as "neofascist," or why anyone would object, in principle, to its program. Giannini's views were evidently "conservative," perhaps even "traditionalist," but that he was a "neofascist" does not seem credible.

What seems evident in this instance, and it would be repeated with other illustrative examples, is the supposition that Giannini did not really make his "true" intentions known. The supposition was that he really had a clandestine agenda. He really was a neofascist, but he never told anyone. He was a "cryptofascist."

We are advised that a "cryptofascist" is one who entertains "a latent ultranationalism" and associates himself or herself with groups or political parties which "though they officially claim to be committed to liberal democracy and may explicitly dissociate themselves from interwar fascist regimes...attract fascist members and funding."[62]

Given this kind of definition of "neofascism," one can argue that many former Fascists in Italy joined Giannini—and he did talk about the "eternal values of the Motherland." He may very well have been a "latent ultranationalist."

But the fact is that more former Fascists joined the Christian Democratic and Communist parties than ever joined Giannini. Many former Fascists funded the activities of both the Christian Democrats and the Communists.[63] It is even conceivable that some Christian Democrats or Communists may have spoken of "the Motherland" and its virtues. Why all that was "cryptofascist" when undertaken with respect to Giannini's *L'Uomo Qualunque*, and not when it involved the Christian Democrats or Communists, is difficult to say.

Authors strain to make the case for Giannini's "neofascism." Some concede that *L'Uomo Qualunque* was more a "quasi-fascism"[64] than a "neofascism." Others tell us it was "only *potentially* neofascist."[65] We are really left with little more than suppositions, presumptions, and "latencies."[66] From that point on, the issue of the cognitive significance of "neofascism" for our purposes becomes increasingly debatable. By 1948, *Qualunquismo* had all but disappeared.

Of all the candidates, the most credible case for a post-Second World War neofascism is based on the fifty-year history of the *Movimento Sociale Italiano* (MSI), founded almost immediately after the war by second echelon gerarchs of the Fascist regime. Giorgio Almirante, Arturo Michelini, Giorgio Pini, Pino Romualdi, and Roberto Mieville, previously members of the small "revolutionary" groups of Fascists that survived the war, organized the *Movimento Sociale Italiano* in December 1946.

Given the criminal strictures against "reconstitution of the Fascist party," the immediate program of the MSI was not particularly Fascist. It called for a "political organization, inspired by an ethical conception of life, that has as its scope the defense of the dignity and the interests of the Italian people and to realize the social ideas that characterize their history..."[67]—none of which was intrinsically objectionable.

Nonetheless, the fact was that the members of the first meetings of the MSI referred to themselves as the "legionnaires who had fought in Spain, in Africa, in Albania, and in Russia," functionaries during the regime, simple party members, or new believers. They were almost all former Fascists.

For all that, the MSI's program was not, in any significant sense, Fascist. The MSI advocated worker participation in Italian industrial life, the organization of workers in syndicates, the protection of sovereign Italian territory, a unicameral, integrated legislature, with some representation based on producer, and not exclusively geographic, categories. It advocated a strong, directly elected executive, much like the political system that became the French Fifth Republic. More than anything else, it was "ultralegal." It was, in effect, a political party that might be spoken of as "conservative" and "rightist," but hardly "fascist."[68]

For whatever reason—the constraints of statute law, or the disrepute into which the Fascist system had fallen—it was clear that the programs of the MSI were never "fully fascist in a radical ideological sense."[69] As the years passed, and the survivors of the Second World War disappeared into their personal histories or succumbed to age, the MSI became increasingly "conservative."

Needless to say, over the years fewer and fewer Fascist hymns were sung at their gatherings. The oldsters who remembered "those days" were fewer and fewer and no longer had any serious influence over party business.

Those who search for a "neofascism" in the years after 1945 may argue that the leaders of the MSI had a "hidden agenda,"[70] but there is no real evidence that the former Fascists who led the organization did anything other than the leaders of any other political organization that sought to compete for political influence in a pluralistic environment.

By 1994, the youthful Gianfranco Fini, the most recent leader of the MSI, proposed to change its official designation to the *Alleanza nazionale*, and announced that the *Alleanza* would be "postfascist." Fini made clear that he respected both Mussolini and Italy's Fascist history—but he argued that Fascism had no immediate relevance to contemporary Italian history.

At the MSI Congress in January 1995, in which the *Alleanza nazionale* was formally founded, the representatives voted unanimously, with one exception, to commit the party to a program of "freedom, justice and democracy" and abjure "all forms of racism and totalitarianism."[71] The MSI had become a moderately right-wing, constitutional political party "modelled loosely on the lines of French Gaullism."[72]

By 1996, the urbane Fini had become one of the most popular politicians in Italy. Given all this, we are unsure how seriously we should take the suggestion that the *Alleanza* is "cryptofascist," or that Fini is a "latent ultranationalist." And we can only be unsure how much the search for "neofascism" has taught us about fascism.

Julius Evola

Among all the efforts to discover "neofascism" in post-World War

Two Italy, there is one that merits some special consideration. Most of those authors who have dealt with the subject have spent a great deal of time and energy reviewing the activities of Julius Evola (1898–1974). He continues to be considered one of the most prominent "neofascists" of the period following World War Two.

In 1970, Elisabeth Antebi informed her audience that Evola had been both the *eminence grise* behind Mussolini and the confidant of Heinrich Himmler.[73] Recently, we have been told that Evola had produced "the most original and creative body of thought to come from an Italian fascist."[74] More than that, his "fascist" work inspired an entire school of terrorists[75] as well as a cultural movement that radiated far outside the peninsula, from France to post-Soviet Russia.[76] Evola had become the undisputed father of a "fascism of the spirit."[77]

Here, evidently, was a "fascist" thinker whose ideology was neither latent nor hidden. The only difficulty was that Julius Evola had never been a Fascist—not before, during, or after the Second World War.[78]

Evola took pride in the fact that he had never been a fascist. Nationalism he found repugnant. The *squadristi*, who had been the combat soldiers of Fascism, he found plebian. The entire Fascist revolution had been "common," and "bourgeois," devoid of those elements of monarchial and aristocratic leadership that would render it truly of the "authentic right."[79]

Six years after the March on Rome that brought Mussolini to power, Evola wrote that Fascism had "lowly origins…had been born of compromise, fed on rhetoric and the petty ambitions of petty people. The state system it had fabricated [was] uncertain, ill-conceived, violent, unfree, and subject to equivocations."[80] Needless to say, Evola did not join the Fascist party.

In his retrospective on Fascism, written in the early 1960s, Evola rejected the identification as "fascist" or "neofascist." He deplored Fascism's totalitarianism, its nationalism, its corporativism, its philosophy, its unitary party, its mass-mobilization, its tutelary and pedagogical enterprise, its social policies, and its mores.[81] Evola did not like Fascism.

What Evola liked were "sacral" supranationalisms;[82] gnostic wisdom from "on high," transmitted in signs and wonders;[83] society organized in hereditary castes,[84] all subordinated to warrior-bands of men;[85]and led by "divine" rulers who represent the transcendent "light" of the world.[86] Evola liked Zen Buddhism, Tantrism, Taoism, Hinduism, and Yoga.[87] What he did not like was Fascism.

What Evola liked was the "traditional" order of Asian antiquity. He admired the imperial system of China and the caste system of ancient India. He rejected literally everything in the "modern world"—the world after the French Revolution. Evola was not a Fascist or a "neofascist." If the search for neofascism leads us to Evola, it has failed. Evola was not a neofascist by any reasonable definition of the term. He was an unmitigated, unqualified, and self-satisfied reactionary.

Evola was a minor talent who vegetated on the margins of Fascism throughout the years of the regime.[88] In his young manhood, he gave himself over to an occult "magik idealism," that Ugo Spirito, one of the most important Fascist thinkers of the period, dismissed as the product of a "mania for originality at any cost, a vain taste for novelty, and, more than anything else, an inability to endure any discipline...."[89] Giuseppe Bottai, a quintessential Fascist, founder of the major Fascist journal, *Critica fascista*, said that Evola's thought was nothing more than "an arbitrary coupling of a mass of ill-digested notions...."[90]

Evola's single accomplishment as a "Fascist thinker" was the publication, in 1941, of his volume, *Sintesi di dottrina della razza*,[91] dealing with the question of race, which was read and approved by Mussolini. It was approved by Mussolini, not because he imagined that Fascism required Evola's occult metaphysics, but because Fascism had systematically sought to avoid the subordination of Fascist doctrine to National Socialism. Fascist doctrine had always rejected biological racism. Major ideologues had made the Fascist position eminently clear.[92] Evola's book, largely by chance, supported in substance the orthodox Fascist position on race.[93]

On the other hand, what Fascist critics made equally clear was that Fascism had no need of Evola's disposition to conceive Fascism as a means to other ends—to a world of mystic musings and a "metaphysics alien to the cultural world of Fascism."[94] Fascists rejected the mummery of Evola's book on race, however useful it might be otherwise in opposing National Socialist racism.

In effect, the academic pursuit of neofascism, as it has been conducted, leads nowhere. Whatever the influence of Evola on the anti-democratic thought of Western and Eastern Europe, it cannot be classified as "fascist" or "neofascist." It is, at best, an expression of that traditional reactionary thought found among those thinkers who, in the first years of the nineteenth century, sought the restoration of a Europe that preceded the French Revolution—or, preferably, a world that preceded the Renaissance.

None of this tells us anything about Fascism.

Understanding Fascism

Since its inception, Fascism has been the object of academic scrutiny. It has been interpreted in so many mutually exclusive fashions that many have simply despaired of ever achieving a generally accepted interpretation. Each specialist has tended to pursue his or her own lights and laypersons have simply chosen whichever interpretation suits their particular prejudice.

Upon its appearance, Fascism was at first interpreted by conservatives as a movement "swayed by spiritual forces" committed to the "restoration of justice"—opposed to that Bolshevism that was "founded on hatred."[95] Throughout much of the interwar years, political conservatives (including Sir Winston Churchill) tended to consider Fascism a simple reaction to the "threat" of communism.

As late as 1929, it was still possible for some to say that Mussolini was a "man of genius, of vision, of daring, of colossal resourcefulness, [and] ideas…,"[96] and that Fascism, itself, was "a great experiment…a great idea founded on a sound theory," deserving "to be watched and studied with the very greatest sympathy and open-mindedness."[97] It could still be said that Fascist corporativism might be "the only coherent answer to the questions arising out of our new industrialism."[98]

By the early 1930s, however, an alternative consensus had settled down on the Western academic community. By that time, Fascism was conceived to be a movement of blind anticommunist reaction, a tool in the service of monied patrons.[99] By the mid-1930s, Fascism had been swallowed up by Hitler's National Socialism and both were identified with the "radical right," elitism, irrationality, inhumanity, terrorism, and unmitigated violence.

By the time of the Civil War in Spain, Fascist Italy had assumed all the features of dictatorship and hegemonic political control that made it the intractable enemy of the advanced industrial democracies. Fascism not only became inextricably identified with the counterrevolutionary "right"—it was conceived the antithesis of Marxism-Leninism and the "left."

Through much of the interwar years, the Bolshevik Revolution and Leninism were seen as humane, intellectual, essentially democratic, and life-enhancing. A swarm of Western intellectuals, ranging from John Reed to a veritable army of university leftists, emerged who were prepared to defend and elaborate on the distinction between the fascist right and the humanitarian left.

Foreign and domestic Marxist-Leninists cobbled together a comprehensive and theory-relevant interpretation of generic fascism that conceived the entire phenomenon a product of "moribund capitalism."[100] Fascism in power was understood to be "the open terrorist dictatorship of the most reactionary, most chauvinistic and most imperialist elements of finance capital."[101]

As the conscious tool of "finance capital," generic fascism was employed in the terroristic suppression of the "progressive forces of labor"—destined by history to assume the revolutionary control of industrial capitalism in decay.[102] According to the thesis, capitalism had exhausted its potential for growth (in accordance with the "general laws" of the capitalist economic system) and had entered into its "final general crisis." Generic fascism was the creature of finance capitalism, conjured up to resist the inevitable.

Charged with the task of resisting the inevitable, fascism was a monstrous obscenity, employing sadomasochistic barbarism in the futile effort to obstruct the advent of the liberating "world proletarian revolution." In its resistance to leftist "progress," fascism was drawn into an ever-tightening cycle of declining economic activity and deteriorating standards of living. Fascism had but a single recourse: war and the massacre of innocents.

The commencement of the Second World War foreclosed any further speculation on the nature of fascism. Fascism was understood to be little more than a simple barbarism—the product of evil men invoking primordial impulses at the cost of humanity in general.

Only with the advent of the cold war was a reassessment forthcoming that reopened the discussion. In 1951, Hannah Arendt published *The Origins of Totalitarianism*.[103] Whatever its disabilities, it served to reduce the distance that separated the fascist "right" and the political left. Fascism and the Marxist-Leninist systems shared obvious affinities.

"Totalitarianism," as a concept, trafficked on those obvious affinities. Once the prevailing notion of a humane and intellectually profound Marxism-Leninism was revealed to be more fiction than fact, more and more similarities between Stalinism and fascism were observed. The relationship between fascism and Marxism-Leninism was no longer seen as unilinear, but curvilinear. "Totalitarianism" became an inclusive concept in which Fascism, National Socialism, and the varieties of Marxism-Leninism all found a place.[104]

Marxism-Leninism was no longer conceived a humane system inspired by a rationally convincing and emotionally satisfying doctrine. It was characterized by political oppression, military aggression, elitism, hierarchy, single-party dominance, and systematic exploitation by a "new class." The truly liberal among Western academic leftists not only withdrew their support from Marxist-Leninist systems, but were prepared to reorganize their conceptual thinking. Fascism, National Socialism, Stalinism, and Maoism all shared substantial family resemblances.

To this day, the concept "totalitarianism" subsumes all these political systems.[105] Upon its appearance, some rejected the concept as a product of the cold war, but its evident cognitive merits prevailed over what were essentially political objections. "Totalitarianism," as part of the interpretation of fascism has survived and prospered.[106] Fascism, National Socialism, Stalinism and Maoism are all considered to share institutional and doctrinal features that now include some variant of nationalism, statism, antiliberalism, militarism, elitism, the "leadership principle," episodic mass-mobilization, ideocracy, and irredentism.

What emerged from all that was not a left/right dichotomy, but a democratic/antidemocratic distinction.[107] It was not a rational, humane and internationalist left opposing an irrational, inhumane, and ultranationalist right that provided cognitive structure and dynamic tension to political reality, it was an antidemocratic totalitarianism that opposed itself to political liberalism and representative democracy.[108] Fascism, National Socialism, Stalinism and Maoism were all species of a single genus, "totalitarianism." The resemblances they shared were cognitively more significant than the features that distinguished them.[109] More significantly, perhaps, the features that originally distinguished one totalitarianism from another gradually abated over time. By the end of the century, Marxist-Leninist systems had begun to take on some of the major species-traits of Mussolini's Fascism.

All of this attests to the futility of attempting to identify Fascism, or fascism, with the political right. Fascism was neither essentially right-wing nor intrinsically "anticommunist." Fascism was neither "anti-intellectual" nor, in principle, irrationalist. That some Western academics continue with such characterizations is testimony to the longevity of prejudice and the persistence of cognitive bias.

What Fascism Was

There are so many criterial traits, in so many permutations, that have been advanced as defining the "essence" of fascism that we are left perplexed. Among them, there are some criterial lists that have now become more or less standard in the literature.

Fascism, we are told, was antidemocratic, elitist, given to "charismatic leadership," nationalist, statist, corporativist, hegemonic, mass-mobilizing, ideocratic, terroristic, militaristic, and aggressive. But then again, so was Hitler's National Socialist Germany, Stalin's Soviet Union, and Mao's China. Such traits might just as well describe, with various degrees of faithfulness, the Korea of Kim Il Sung or the Cuba of Fidel Castro.[110]

More recently, we have been told that fascism can best be understood as "a genus of political ideology whose mythic core in its various permutations is a palingenetic form of populist ultranationalism." Then we are informed that "the Russian Revolution itself had originally been a profoundly palingenetic event"—as had been Pol Pot's Marxist-Leninist enterprise in Cambodia.[111] By the mid-1990s, everyone seemed to grant that both the Soviet Union and the Khmer Rouge had been nationalistic and both, it would seem, had been populist.

It is not certain if we are to infer from those insights that the Bolshevik Revolution and the homicidal Marxist-Leninist regime of Pol Pot were both fascist. If that is the case, it would seem that we have all misunderstood fascism. Fascism was not the "tool of finance capital," or the counterrevolution of the middle class, it was, for good or ill, the paradigmatic instance of revolution in the twentieth century. The Fascist movement captured something of the essence of revolution in our time.

What will be argued here is that Mussolini's Fascism was a form of reactive, antidemocratic, developmental nationalism that serves as a paradigmatic instance of revolution in the twentieth century. As such it featured a coherent, manifestly relevant political ideology committed to the redemption of a humiliated and retrograde people.

The necessary condition for the appearance of a reactive nationalism is an intense and protracted period of real or perceived collective humiliation. Generally, that circumstance is associated with retarded economic and industrial development in a world increasingly dominated by the technologically advanced democratic "plutocracies." When not so associated, real or fancied intense and protracted humiliation is the consequence of a lost war or political defeat of a disabling magnitude.

Mussolini's Fascism reveals all this with undiminished clarity. The humiliation suffered by Italy in Europe as a late developing nation, recently reunited after centuries of dismemberment, fueled the reactive nationalism that animated the Fascist cohorts. The ideology that gave compass to the program of Fascism was as coherent and as relevant as any in the history of modern political revolution. More than that, it was the ideology of Fascism—not that of nineteenth- or twentieth-century Marxism—that correctly anticipated the responsibilities of revolution for our time's late economic and industrial developers.

Over the years, Marxist-Leninist systems adopted and adapted more and more of the political, social, economic, and military features of Mussolini's Fascism. It was a process of "devolution" recognized and acknowledged by Fascism's major ideologues. After the collapse of the Soviet Union, as we shall see, all that was recognized and acknowledged by some of Russia's most radical intellectuals.

The argument here will be (1) that Fascism possessed an ideology that was more coherent and relevant to modern revolution than almost any other collection of ideas in the twentieth century; and (2) that the ideology of Fascism was the product of, and attuned to, the needs of the developmental and reactive nationalism that typifies many of the revolutions of our time. Neither the National Socialism of Adolf Hitler, nor the variants of Marxism-Leninism were as relevant or coherent. As a consequence, Fascism has appeared and reappeared throughout the century either in substantial form, or in caricature, among those nations on the periphery of the advanced industrial democracies.

Attempting to make the case will involve an exposition of Fascist thought as it found expression in the work of two of its most notable intellectuals—as that work grounded itself in the intellectual and political environment of reactive, developmental nationalism. An attempt will be undertaken to illustrate the significance and relevance of that type of thought, among peoples suffering an abiding sense of failure and humiliation. Finally, the emergence of a form of fascism in post-Soviet Russia affords a suggestive case study.

The argument will turn on the conviction that although "fascist ideas" may surface anywhere and at any time, fascism is a function of a collective sense of intense and protracted national humiliation. Without that pervasive and inclusive sense of humiliation, "fascist thought" has appeal to only a small minority of any population. Thus, "neofascism," however defined, has little, if any, appeal to the denizens of the advanced industrial democracies.

While some intellectuals in the advanced industrial democracies might find fascist thought interesting, fascist thought cannot serve as an ideology of mass-mobilization and national redemption without an appropriate recruitment base. Fascist thought will find consistent expression, and draw to itself the support of "masses," only in an environment of thwarted national expectations and collective humiliation. It can be expected to appear in the former Soviet Union or in China—both of which have suffered humiliation at the hands of the "imperialist" powers. It can be expected to resurface in some of the smaller nations of Eastern Europe. Whether it can survive and prosper there will be the consequence of the intersection of so many ill-defined and poorly measured variables that prediction is hazardous at best.

We have at our disposal little more than guesses about the future prospects of fascism. What we do have, at the end of the most violent century in history, is a conception of fascism that has become eminently more defensible than any entertained over the last seven decades. We have at our disposal some understanding of what historic Fascism was, some suggestion of where it might reappear, some illustrative instances of its reappearance, as well as a perspective in which all totalitarian movements of our time might be lodged.

In all of that, historic Fascist thought, as it appeared during the life of the regime, recommends itself to our consideration. Western scholarship has so long insisted that Fascism was devoid of thought and empty of intellectual substance that a reconstruction of Fascist ideology urges itself upon us. It is to that reconstruction to which we can now address our attention.

Notes

1. See A. James Gregor, *Interpretations of Fascism* (New Brunswick, N.J.: Transaction Publishers, 1997).
2. R. Palme Dutt, *Fascism and Social Revolution* (New York: International, 1934).
3. Wilhelm Reich, *The Mass Psychology of Fascism* (New York: Orgone, 1946).
4. See the account on the dustjacket of Roger Griffin, *The Nature of Fascism* (New York: Routledge, 1993).
5. Roger Eatwell, *Fascism: A History* (New York: Penguin, 1997), p. xix.
6. *Ibid.,* p. xx.
7. A. James Gregor, *The Faces of Janus: Marxism and Fascism in the Twentieth Century* (New Haven, CT: Yale University Press, in press), chaps. 6 and 7.
8. Vladimir Tismaneanu, "The Leninist Debris or Waiting for Peron," *East European Politics and Societies* 10, no. 3 (Fall 1996), p. 507.
9. Griffin, *op. cit.,* pp. 183, 229.
10. See Gregor, *Interpretations of Fascism* and *The Faces of Janus*, chaps. 2 and 3.
11. See Nicholas M. Nagy-Talavera, *The Green Shirts and the Others: A History of Fascism in Hungary and Romania* (Stanford: Hoover Institution, 1970); Mihai Fatu and Ion Spalatelu, *Garda de Fier: Organizatie terorista de tip fascist* (Bucharest: Politica, 1971); Michele Rallo, *I fascismi della mitteleuropa* (Rome:

Europa, n.d.); Stanley G. Payne, *Fascism: Comparison and Definition* (Madison: University of Wisconsin, 1980).

12. See Lloyd Eastman, "Fascism in Kuomintang China: The Blue Shirts," *The China Quarterly*, no. 49 (January-March 1972); W. F. Elkins, "'Fascism' in China: The Blue Shirts Society, 1932–1937," *Science and Society*, 33, no. 4 (1969), pp. 426-433.

13. See Miles Fletcher, *The Search for a New Order: Intellectuals and Fascism in Prewar Japan* (Chapel Hill: The University of North Carolina, 1982).

14. See Mariano Ambri, *I falsi fascismi: Ungheria, Jugoslavia, Romania 1919–1945* (Rome: Jouvence, 1980).

15. Stanley Payne, "Fascism and National Socialism," *The Forum Series* (St. Charles, Mo.: Forum Press, 1975), p. 1.

16. Stanley Payne, *A History of Fascism 1914–1945* (Madison: University of Wisconsin, 1995), p. 3.

17. See Alexander Yanov, *Weimar Russia and What We Can Do About It* (New York: Slovo-Word, 1995) and Semyon Reznik, *The Nazification of Russia: Antisemitism in the Post-Soviet Era* (Washington, D.C.: Challenge, 1996).

18. Vladimir Solovyov and Elena Klepikova, *Zhirinovsky: Russian Fascism and the Making of a Dictator* (New York: Addison Wesley, 1995).

19. Vladimir Zhirinovsky, *My Struggle* (New York: Barricade, 1996).

20. The contemporary "revival of fascism" was early anticipated. See Angelo Del Boca and Mario Giovana, *Fascism Today: A World Survey* (New York: Pantheon, 1969) and Claudio Quarantotto, *Tutti fascisti!* (Rome: Il Borghese, 1976).

21. See Tismaneanu, *op. cit.*, p. 521.

22. See A. James Gregor, "Fascism and the New Russian Nationalism," *Communist and Post-Communist Studies*, 31, no. 1 (1998), pp. 1-15.

23. Walter Laqueur, *The Dream That Failed: Reflections on the Soviet Union* (New York: Oxford University Press, 1994), p. 184.

24. *Ibid.*

25. See Leonard Weinberg, "Conclusions," in Peter Merkl and Leonard Weinberg (eds.), *The Revival of Right-Wing Extremism in the Nineties* (London: Frank Cass, 1997), pp. 274, 275.

26. See Leonard Weinberg, "The American Radical Right in Comparative Perspective," *ibid.*, pp. 231–253.

27. Walter Laqueur, *Fascism Past Present Future* (New York: Oxford University Press, 1996), pp. 147–169.

28. *Ibid.*, p. 278.

29. See Eatwell, *op. cit.*, p. 269.

30. Peter H. Merkl, "Introduction," Merkl and Weinberg, *op. cit.*, p. 8.

31. Henry Ashby Turner, "Fascism and Modernization," *World Politics*, 24 (July 1972), p. 563.

32. See the discussion in Renzo De Felice, *Fascism: an Informal Introduction to Its Theory and Practice* (New Brunswick, N.J.: Transaction Publishers, 1976), pp. 40–41, and "Il fenomeno fascista," in Ambri, *op. cit.*, pp. 5–20.

33. See Leonard Weinberg, "The American Radical Right in Comparative Perspective," in Merkl and Weinberg (eds.) *op. cit.*, pp. 231–253.

34. *Ibid.*, p. 233.

35. Peter H. Merkl, "Introduction," *ibid.*, p. 4.

36. *Ibid.*, p. 11.

37. Roger Griffin identifies a "new strand to fascist activism, namely 'survivalism'...." Griffin, *op. cit.*, p. 165. I am sure that many survivalists will be surprised to know that their activity is "fascist."

38. Henry F. Carey, "Post-Communist Right Radicalism in Romania," in Merkl and Weinberg, *op. cit.*, pp. 149, 158.
39. See Thomas S. Szyna, "The Extreme-Right Political Movements in Post-Communist Central Europe," *ibid.*, pp. 113–114.
40. Griffin, *op. cit.*, p. 146.
41. See Zeev Sternhell, *The Birth of Fascist Ideology* (Berkeley: University of California, 1994) and *Neither Right nor Left*; Renzo De Felice, *Fascism: An Informal Introduction to Its Theory and Practice* (New Brunswick, N.J.: Transaction Publishers, 1976), pp. 14–15, 67.
42. Laqueur, *op. cit.*, p. 9.
43. See the entire discussion in Glyn Ford (ed.), *Fascist Europe: The Rise of Racism and Xenophobia* (London: Pluto, 1992). In this text, the term "racist" is employed to signify those who make invidious distinctions between persons because of some ascriptive phenotypical traits. See the discussion of Fascist "racism" in A. J. Gregor, *The Ideology of Fascism: The Rationale of Totalitarianism* (New York: The Free Press, 1969), chap. 6.
44. "The Manifesto of Fascist Racism," para. 1. See Appendix A, in Gregor, *The Ideology of Fascism*, p. 383.
45. At the time of the Lateran Accords, Mussolini said that "The Jews were here in the times of prerepublican Rome.... There were fifty thousand of them in Rome at the time of Augustus and they requested permission to weep at the bier of Julius Caesar. They will remain unmolested...." Mussolini, "Relazione alla Camera dei Deputati sugli Accordi del Lateran," in *Opera omnia* (Florence: La fenice, 1953-1965), 24, p. 82. See Mussolini's comments in Emil Ludwig, *Colloqui con Mussolini* (Verona: Mondadori, 1950. Reprint of the 1932 edition.), p. 72.
46. For the best treatment of the subject, see Renzo De Felice, *Storia degli ebrei italiani sotto il fascismo* (Turin: Einaudi, 1962).
47. Margherita Sarfatti, *Dvx* (Milan: Mondadori, 1926).
48. Philip V. Cannistraro and Brian R. Sullivan, *Il Duce's Other Woman: The Untold Story of Margherita Sarfatti, Benito Mussolini's Jewish Mistress, and How She Helped Him Come to Power* (New York: William Morrow, 1993).
49. Yvon De Begnac, *Palazzo Venezia: Storia di un regime* (Rome: La Rocca, 1950), p. 643.
50. See the entire discussion in Giorgio Pisano, *Mussolini e gli ebrei* (Milan: FPE, 1967).
51. See the interesting discussion in Salim Diamand, *Dottore! Internment in Italy 1940–1945* (New York: Mosaic, 1987).
52. See the judgment of Renzo De Felice, *Interpretations of Fascism* (Cambridge, Mass.: Harvard University Press, 1977), p. 11; and the full account of Fascist "racism" in Gregor, *The Ideology of Fascism*, chap. 6.
53. Eatwell, *op. cit.*, pp. xxiv, xxv.
54. See Arkady Vaksberg, *Stalin Against the Jews* (New York: Alfred A. Knopf, 1994, and Gennadi Kostyrchenko, *Out of the Red Shadows: Anti-Semitism in Stalin's Russia* (Amherst: Prometheus, 1995).
55. Richard Pipes, *Russia Under the Bolshevik Regime* (New York: Random House, 1995), p. 253.
56. Sternhell, *The Birth of Fascist Ideology*, p. 6.
57. See, for example, Griffin, *op. cit.*, pp. 161–169.
58. A similar strategy is advised for "neo-nazism." The purpose here is to explicate the notion of "neofascist."
59. See Pier Giuseppe Murgia, *Il vento del nord* (Milan: Sugar, 1975), pp. 269–270.

60. Alberto Giovannini, "Prefazione" to Mario Tedeschi, *Fascisti dopo Mussolini* (Rome: L'Arnia, 1950), pp. 5–14.
61. See Leonard Weinberg, *After Mussolini: Italian Neo-Fascism and the Nature of Fascism* (Washington, D.C.: University Press of America, 1979), p. 14 and Eatwell, *op. cit.*, pp. 248–249.
62. Griffin, *op. cit.*, pp. 166–167.
63. See, for example, the account in Anonimo Nero, *Camerata dove sei?* (Rome: B & C, 1976).
64. Laqueur, *op. cit.*, p. 100.
65. H. Stuart Hughes, *The United States and Italy* (*Cambridge, Mass.*: Harvard University Press, 1979), p. 140.
66. See the discussion in Mario Giovana, *Le nuove camicie nere* (Turin: Edizione dell'Albero, 1966), pp. 18–26.
67. *Ibid.,* p. 48.
68. Giuseppe Mammarella, *Italy After Fascism: A Political History* (Montreal: Casalini, 1964), pp. 246–247.
69. See Eatwell, *op. cit.*, p. 250.
70. *Ibid.*, p. 264.
71. *Ibid.*, p. 269.
72. *Ibid.*, p. 269.
73. Elisabeth Antebi, *Avec Lucifer* (Paris: Calmann-Levy, 1970), as cited in Philippe Baillet, "I rapporti di Evola con il fascismo ed il nazionalsocialismo: una proposta di lettura," *Futuro Presente*, no. 6 (Spring 1995), p. 134.
74. Eatwell, *op. cit.*, p. 254.
75. See Thomas Sheehan, "Myth and Violence: The Fascism of Julius Evola and Alain de Benoist," *Social Research*, no. 48 (Spring 1981), pp. 45–73.
76. Franco Ferraresi, "Julius Evola: Tradition, Reaction, and the Radical Right," *Archives of European Sociology* 28 (1987), pp. 134–148.
77. Sheehan, *op. cit.*, p. 54.
78. "Evola was never a Fascist…and remained forever on the margin of Fascism…." Baillet, *op. cit.*, p. 134.
79. Julius Evola, *Il cammino del Cinabro* (Milan: Scheiwiller, 1963), pp. 82–83.
80. Julius Evola, *Imperialismo pagano: il fascismo dinnanzi al pericolo euro-cristiano* (Rome: Atanor, 1928), p. 11.
81. Julius Evola, *Il fascismo* (Rome: Volpe, 1964).
82. See "Rapport sur Evola a l'attention du Reichsfuehrer-SS, *Totalite*, nos. 21–22, pp. 39–41., as cited Baillet, *op. cit.*, p. 140.
83. Julius Evola, *La tradizione ermetica nei suoi simboli, nella sua dottrina, nella sua "arte regia"* (Bari: Laterza, 1948).
84. See Julius Evola, *Rivolta contro il mondo moderno* (Milan: Hoepli, 1934), part 1, chaps. 10 and 15.
85. See the discussion in Julius Evola, *Das Mysterium des Grals* (Munich: Barth, 1955).
86. See the discussion in Julius Evola, *Gli uomini e le rovine* (Roma: Dell'Ascia, 1953), pp. 51–61.
87. See Julius Evola, *La dottrina del risveglio* (Milan: Scheiwiller, 1965).
88. De Grand refers to Evola not as a Fascist, but as a "demented philosopher." Alexander J. De Grand, *Fascist Italy and Nazi Germany: The "Fascist" Style of Rule* (New York: Routledge, 1995), p. 54.
89. Ugo Spirito, *L'idealismo Italiano e i suoi critici* (Florence: le Monnier, 1930), p. 192.
90. As cited, Giovana, *op. cit.*, p. 7. It was clear that Bottai, who had served to-

with Evola in the First World War, published Evola's literary pieces with very little enthusiasm.

91. Julius Evola, *Sintesi di dottrina della razza* (Milan: Hoepli, 1941).
92. See the discussion in Gregor, *Ideology of Fascism*, chap. 6.
93. Evola recognized the reasons why Mussolini approved of his book. See Evola, *Il cammino del Cinabro*, p. 169.
94. Ugoberto A. Grimaldi, "Review of J. Evola, *Sintesi di dottrina della razza*," *Critica fascista* 9, no. 4 (February 1942), pp. 256–261.
95. H. W. Wilson, "Preface" to Sir Percival Phillips, *The "Red" Dragon and the Black Shirts: How Italy Found Her Soul* (London: Carmelite House, 1922), p. 8.
96. Milford W. Howard, *Fascism: A Challenge to Democracy* (New York: Fleming H. Revell, 1928), p. 48.
97. James S. Barnes, *The Universal Aspects of Fascism* (London: Williams and Norgate, 1929), p. 237.
98. Howard, *op. cit.*, pp. 48, 148, 152.
99. Julius Deutsch, *Die Faschistengefahr* (Vienna: Winer Volksbuchhandlung, 1923), p. 5.
100. See the account in Gregor, *Interpretations of Fascism*, chap. 5.
101. Georgi Dimitroff, *The United Front Against War and Fascism: Report to the Seventh World Congress of the Communist International, 1935* (New York: Gamma, n.d. Reprint of the 1935 First English Edition), p. 7.
102. The following account follows the text of Palme Dutt, *op. cit.*
103. Hannah Arendt, *The Origins of Totalitarianism* (New York: Harcourt, Brace and Company, 1951).
104. See Hans Buchheim, *Totalitaere Herrschaft: Wesen und Merkmale* (Munich: Koesel, 1962); Raymond Aron, *Democratie et totalitarisme* (Paris: Gallimard, 1965).
105. See, for example, Steven Paul Soper, *Totalitarianism: A Conceptual Approach* (New York: University Press of America, 1985).
106. See the discussion in Ernest A. Menze (ed.), *Totalitarianism Reconsidered* (London: Kennikat, 1981).
107. See the discussion in Carl J. Friedrich (ed.), *Totalitarianism* (New York: Grosset & Dunlap, 1964).
108. See the discussion in A. James Gregor, *Contemporary Radical Ideologies: Totalitarian Thought in the Twentieth Century* (New York: Random House, 1968), chap. 1.
109. See the discussion in Leonard Schapiro, *Totalitarianism* (New York: Praeger, 1972).
110. A quarter of a century ago, I pointed out the family resemblances between Fascism and many of the movements and regimes on the "Left." See A. James Gregor, *The Fascist Persuasion in Radical Politics* (Princeton, N.J.: Princeton University Press, 1974). The book was not warmly received. Today, many scholars have acknowledged that Fascism shared more features with Marxism-Leninism than anyone was prepared to acknowledge in the 1970s. See, for example, Pipes, *op. cit.*, chap. 5.
111. Griffin, *op. cit.*, pp. 26, 34–35, 178.

2

Paradigmatic Fascism

For more than a generation after the end of the Second World War, academics pretended to see the advent of Fascism on the Italian peninsula as the consequence of a "moral disease," an avalanche of political violence, or a final, desperate defense of moribund capitalism.[1] At best, Fascism was understood to be the mercenary and immoral protection of privilege—the reactionary resistance to progressive change.

In the process, a torrent of publications swept away any semblance of objectivity and balance in attempting to comprehend Fascism and its significance for the modern world. For Benedetto Croce, Fascism was a "parenthesis" in history, with no historic significance other than having occupied time between the First and Second World Wars. In the space of less than a decade, Mussolini, himself, had been transformed from a person "who never ceased to amaze his enemies with his broad literary background, his conversant familiarity with many forms of intellectual activity, and his ability to make proper use of the terminology of formal philosophy"[2]—to one of whom it could be said that he possessed only "limited intelligence, deficient in moral sensibility, ignorant with that fundamental ignorance which did not know and understand the elementary essence of human relationships...lacking taste in every word and gesture...."[3]

The purpose here is not to attempt to explain that transformation of collective judgment. What is of significance is the recognition that the impaired assessment of Fascism that followed the conclusion of the Second World War has left us without any real comprehension of a considerable portion of the history of the twentieth century. Mussolini's Fascism constituted a significant component of that history, and provides critical insights into the remainder.

Fascism was something more than a movement made up of a "ragbag of futurists, anarchists, communists, syndicalists, republicans,

Catholics, nationalists and liberals of various kinds."[4] While all those elements, in fact, were identifiable in the ranks of the first Fascism, they were all animated by a clutch of convictions that made of Fascism "an independent cultural and political phenomenon that was not less intellectually self-sufficient than socialism or liberalism."[5]

Years before there was a Fascist movement, Roberto Michels, as a revolutionary syndicalist, and Giovanni Gentile, as a liberal, had already given expression to the ideas that were to dominate the revolution and animate its policies. By the time Mussolini marshalled the futurists and syndicalists, the communists and nationalists, the Catholics and liberals, to the guidons of Fascism, he already had put together the critical elements of a revolutionary ideology.[6] It was an ideology that had deep roots in the political and cultural crisis that had settled down over Europe, and Italy, at the end of the nineteenth century.[7]

The First World War exacerbated that crisis, and created the furious young men who would make up the membership of the armed squads that both defeated socialism and destroyed the credibility of parliamentary government on the Italian peninsula, preparing the way for Mussolini's accession to power.[8] All of that is evident, but Fascism was not the simple byproduct of the war. The war may have provided some of the necessary conditions for its rise and success, but Fascism was far more than a function of the first world conflict.[9] The intellectual, psychological, political, social and economic circumstances that were to contribute to its rise were already maturing at the end of the nineteenth century.

Italian Nationalism at the Turn of the Twentieth Century

By the end of the nineteenth century, Italy had been newly reunited. On the peninsula, the nation had taken shape. A united Italy had made its appearance out of a history of barbarian invasions, warring city-states, and still more foreign invasions.

At the turn of the century, there was a significant minority of intellectuals who suffered a persistent and growing sense of unfulfillment. Before its reunification, Giuseppe Mazzini had spoken of the new nation as giving rise to a "Third Rome," whose civilizing mission would rank with that of the Rome of the Caesars, and the subsequent Rome of Christ.

For Mazzini, the new nation was to be "something more than an aggregation of individuals...[It was to be a] fraternity of faith [and] consciousness of a common *ideal*...." In pursuing that common ideal,

duty was to become a "holy, inexorable, dominating idea...." Duty to
the fatherland was to become the "standard of life...." It would make a
"virtue of self-sacrifice, in truth the only pure virtue, holy and mighty
in power...."[10]

For Mazzini, Italians had for centuries "dragged" themselves along,
"in abjectness and impotence....But," he went on to insist, "we want to
rise again, great and honored." He anticipated a future Italy, a "Third
Rome," as grand as the Rome of antiquity. That, he insisted, could only
be accomplished if every Italian "obeyed the commands of *duty*" to the
fatherland, a fatherland that was a living "union of all classes" committed to a single faith and a single mission.[11]

Mazzini spoke of a regenerate Italy that would accomplish the
irredentist restoration of "lost lands"—the reaquisition of the Trentino,
of Istria and Nice. He spoke of a "nation armed," in the sacred unity of
defense.[12] He anticipated an Italy that once again would enjoy primacy
in the Mediterranean in a world community of nations that would respect its national rights.[13]

Mazzini also spoke of liberty, of grandeur, of more equitable distribution of wealth, of the protection of innocents, and the succorance of
those in need. He spoke of true democracy and moral principles. He
spoke of a family of nations, united in justice and mutual respect.

The end of the century had brought none of that. There were those
who perceived very little of any of that in the Italy of their time. By
the end of the nineteenth century the world had been transformed in
ways that the revolutionaries of the beginning of the century had never
anticipated.

By that time, Great Britain stood astride the world, having colonized
almost a quarter of its surface. France and Belgium had settled vast
spaces in Africa and the French and the Dutch had reached deeply into
Asia. In the Western hemisphere, the United States had hammered together a dynamic economy, had wrested a continent away from the
aboriginals, from the Canadians and the Mexicans—and then fought
its way into the Caribbean and the Pacific to destroy the remnants of
the Spanish empire.

In the Far East, an industrializing Japan defeated Imperial China and
then turned to defeat Imperial Russia. Japanese ships of the line and the
armies of the Emperor defeated the forces of the Romanovs. Japan was
expanding into continental, littoral and insular East Asia. There was
already talk of a conflict in the Pacific between the two "young," dynamic, and expanding powers, the United States and Japan.[14]

In that rush of power and expansion, Theodore Roosevelt wrote of *The Strenuous Life*, and Friedrich Nietzsche spoke of "living danger-ously." Life in Europe and North America had become dynamic, puls-ing with the beat of internal combustion, vital with the sound of march-ing men, punctuated by the sound of both construction and cannon fire.

At the beginning of the new century, Gabriele D'Annunzio traversed industrializing Germany and was transfixed by its energy, its heavy industries and its armories. About the same time he lamented Italy's passivity, its servility, its lack of energy, its agrarian economy, and its singular lack of an entrepreneurial class. D'Annunzio wrote of Italy's future on the seas, of the necessity of a navy the equal of that of Britain or France.[15] He argued for the generation of material and spiritual power on the peninsula that would assure Italy its place among the "great nations," restoring both lost lands and dignity.

During the first decade of the new century, an entire chorus of voices raised the same themes. Enrico Corradini, and the nationalists around him, echoed the enjoinments of Alfredo Oriani, who called for a strong state that would regenerate an "inert and passive" Italy, rendering it fully capable once again of supporting the grandeur of the Rome of antiquity.[16]

The number of nationalist publications multiplied. Various national-ist intellectuals, animated by characteristically different enthusiasms about republicanism, liberalism, and socialism, and harboring emphati-cally different opinions concerning the advisability of tariff protection for domestic infant industries, the pursuit of irredentist purpose, and the merits of seeking out "vast spaces" in Africa, nonetheless collected themselves around a series of journals that appeared during the first years of the new century.

Il Marzocco of Angelo Orvieto had already appeared in 1896, to be followed by *Leonardo* in 1903, edited by Giovanni Papini and Giuseppe Prezzolini. In that same year, Enrico Corradini commenced the publi-cation of *Il Regno*. In 1909, Vincenzo Picardi began the publication of *Il Carroccio*, the same year that Mario Viana undertook the editorship of *Il Tricolore*.

Whatever their tactical differences, there was among them a com-mitment to the regeneration of the nation.[17] In the nineteenth century, the search for renewal had taken on a literary and artistic character. By the end of the first decade of the new century, however, it became mani-festly evident that Italian nationalism had begun to transform itself.

As early as 1903, Papini had written that "past nationalisms" had been largely literary and historical. They had been "histrionic and heavy with allusions to the past. They celebrated antique victories and long-ago intellectual conquests. The new nationalism," Papini went on, "was an economic nationalism, made up of statistics, founded in the present and celebratory of the forces of production...."[18] It was preeminently pragmatic, involved in the doing of things.

By the end of the first decade of the twentieth century, Papini had become the advocate of a revolutionary ideology of national regeneration. By that time, he spoke of an intense program of national development—a program that would require the concentration of all the nation's energies.

So arduous was the undertaking that one could not allow oneself the luxury of entertaining "multiple points of view, or the scepticism" so traditional among Italians. However stimulative of engaging literary production vagueness and ambiguity might be, irresolution and detachment would not serve the purposes of a demanding ideal enterprise—a national mission. What was required, instead, was a "singleness of purpose...clear and precise ideas." A people embarking on a program of rebirth needs not only motivating sentiments and precise ideas, but it must be prepared to selflessly obey, to discharge its duties, and perform its tasks.

If the nation was to regain its place in the world, Papini insisted, it must be prepared to follow a talented, self-possessed, energetic and exiguous aristocracy,[19] itself prepared to lead a community reconstituted through myth[20] and tutelage. Such a community must reconstitute itself as an assertive, goal-directed, self-affirming organism.

A leading aristocracy would be dedicated to the mobilization of all forces, proletarian and bourgeois, industrial and agrarian, in order to promote and sustain the necessary industrialization and economic growth[21] that would provide the means through which power might be projected. The nation renewed would serve as a staging area for expansion into the intensely competitive modern world of the twentieth century.[22]

In the years that followed, Enrico Corradini proceeded to weave all of these themes together to produce an ideology of reactive and developmental nationalism. It was "reactive" in that the sentiment that animated its advocates was the deep sense of personal and collective humiliation[23] that almost always afflicts denizens of an industrially and politically retrograde community—in a world of dynamic and expanding nations.

It was "developmental" in the sense that its enthusiasts prescribed the rapid industrial development of the economy.[24] Power and wealth, it was understood, was a function of industrial development and economic growth—and power and wealth was the currency of status and respect.[25]

Beneath the surface of these general empirical propositions and prescriptive notions, an entire constellation of convictions were to be found that were understood to provide the rationale of the belief system. Intricately woven together in a thousand articles and a hundred books, there was a logic to the system.

At the center of the entire structure was the conviction that human beings were essentially social animals who lived out their lives and rendered themselves humane, moral, intelligent, and creative only in communities.[26] All of human history was understood to be the history of human beings in association: in hordes, tribes, moieties, clans, families, confederations, city-states, nations, and empires.

Each individual in each such association was conceived as sustained by an abiding sense of identification with the community as a larger self. That identification generates a sense of ingroup amity that renders each member of the community prepared to sacrifice for the well-being of all. Together with that sense of collective identification with a specific community, humans living in association display a common diffidence toward outgroups that regularly, and over time, manifests itself in avoidance behavior and group conflict.[27]

Throughout history, Italian nationalists argued, the very tenuousness of life has created the group need for ready response and effective defense. However it was, and is, accomplished—through contest, heredity, or pretended democracy—each community has fashioned a governing elite for itself. Such elites have been entrusted with the security and well-being of the group.

In the modern world, in which the challenges have become so much greater, and the threat environment so much more harrowing, the demands on everyone have become increasingly exacting. The nation has become the single, most viable unity of persons seeking to survive and prevail.[28] The elites of developing nations require the support of a vigorous, authoritarian and "organically constituted" state fully capable of restoring among their populations a hierarchy of values[29] functionally adapted to the collective mission of national regeneration and renewal.[30]

Given the onerous tasks before them, developmental elites require the unqualified support of the masses, infilled with a sense of mission, and committed to an ethic of sacrifice and obedience.[31] For Corradini, all that had become particularly true by the end of the nineteenth century. It was during that period that the established "plutocracies" had created an iniquitous international environment that ensured advantage to those nations already enjoying every advantage, and imposed obstacles in the path of development for the disadvantaged.[32]

In the contest between the advantaged and disadvantaged, the poorer nations required a seamless unanimity of faith and commitment in the effort to achieve their ends. In that context, disadvantaged nations, those that were "proletarian," could not allow collective energy to be dissipated in the preoccupation with individual rights and individual privileges. The economic, political, and security circumstances in which "proletarian nations" found themselves required a disciplined[33] sacrifice of self in the service of the collectivity.[34]

Corradini spoke of the inescapable conflict between "proletarian" and "plutocratic" nations in the modern world,[35] a conflict that transposed "class warfare" to the international arena in the form of a life struggle of poor and less-developed nations against those more fortunate and ill-disposed to share the bounty of the earth.[36] The intensity of the inescapable conflicts would render the twentieth century one of the most savage in history.

In the years that immediately preceded the outbreak of the First World War, the themes that characterized Italian nationalism became increasingly emphatic and precise. Alfredo Rocco, who was to play a major role in creating the institutions of the Fascist state as President of the Chamber of Deputies and subsequently the Minister of Justice,[37]delivered a detailed treatment of the proposed policies of Italian nationalism.

The argument began with a rejection of the liberal conviction that society was to be understood as a congeries of individuals who had contracted to enter into social relations in order to further their several interests. Liberalism, Rocco argued, conceived society and its activities only in terms of "utility," affording individuals the opportunities to avoid pain and pursue pleasure.

Given such a conception of social life, it was perfectly comprehensible that the liberal state concerned itself exclusively with the distribution of benefits—wages to workers, profits to capitalists, sinecures to politicians, tax benefits to organized interest groups, and, ultimately, "entitlements" to almost everyone else.

The difficulty, Rocco argued, was that in poor countries, economically less developed and with limited resources, such a style of political life was nonviable. Industrially less- developed countries found themselves without the wherewithal to sustain such a pattern of subventionized inclusion.

More than that, given the disposition of power in the modern world, less-developed communities could never attain such a level of prosperity because the more advanced nations had preempted all the resources and accessible spaces, confining the less-developed nations to the most unpromising situations—to territories without the subsoil resources necessary for industrial development, and without sufficient support capacity to sustain a large and growing population. Still more disabling was the fact that the more advanced nations created an international trading and financial system designed to prejudice any attempt by backward nations to break out of their "underdevelopment"—an underdevelopment that was the consequence of "having arrived late" to the process of extensive and intensive industrial growth.[38]

Taking his cues from the work of Friedrich List, the mid-nineteenth-century German theoretician of nationalist economic policy,[39] Rocco gave List's views a more exacerbated expression. Rocco argued that in the more than half a century since the publication of List's *The National System of Political Economy*,[40] the problems of national economic well-being were rendered still more unmanageable by the fact that "other countries had already traversed the developmental distance Italy had only just begun."[41]

Having only just begun, Italy was burdened with a domestic political system, shaped by foreign liberal influences, that sought only to deliver individual and group welfare benefits. As a consequence, the Italian peninsula was peopled by associations of agricultural and industrial workers who sought only their personal and group advantage at the expense of the nation's critical and long-term group needs.[42]

The liberal political system of the peninsula could neither demand nor exact obedience. It could require neither sacrifice nor compliance from the major segments of the population—nor could it provide guidance for a program of accelerated growth and industrial development.[43] In the prevailing circumstances, Rocco argued that history had conspired to render it almost impossible for Italy to escape the "state of prostration in which it had languished for centuries."[44]

The style of life of the advanced industrial powers had contaminated the sense and sensibilities of Italians. Among them, there was an increasingly insistent demand for individual and group benefits. There was an erosion of traditional virtues of labor, frugality, and sacrifice. Rendered petulant and demanding, Italians would be ill-equipped to face the challenges of the new century. Because the industrialized West enjoyed every advantage, the disparities that distinguished the rich from the poor nations were becoming permanent.

For Rocco, it seemed evident that the advanced industrialized democracies had consciously or unconsciously settled on a general philosophy of international pacifism and "humanitarian" cosmopolitanism because such a world view served their purposes. They wished to avoid the possibility of any redistribution of territory, power, or benefits in the prevailing arrangements. The advanced industrial democracies sought to avoid any possible reduction of their access to markets, to investment opportunities, or to resource extraction anywhere in the world.[45]

At about the same time that J. A. Hobson was writing his *Imperialism*, a work that argued that the advanced industrial nations enjoyed market access and resource exploitation at the expense of less developed nations,[46] Italian nationalists were making the same case. As denizens of "oppressed and retrograde" nations, exploited by those that were rich and powerful, they made the argument that while political liberalism might be tolerable for economically established communities, it was fatal for those whose industrialization was either thwarted or retarded.

The advanced industrial democracies could allow themselves to succumb to political decadence, with selfishness the sole incentive for enterprise. They could tolerate antinomian behavior, the decline in overall reproductive rates, the preoccupation with pleasure and profligate wastefulness, a general slothfulness and dissipation of energy.[47] All that would be, and was, however, fatal for nations only then commencing their trajectory of economic growth and industrial development.[48]

While Hobson directed his attention to the "intrinsically exploitative nature" of industrial capitalism, Italian nationalists preoccupied themselves with a strategy calculated to lift their nation out of the servility and inferiority into which modern international economic and political circumstances had driven it. They were unconvinced that the abolition of industrial capitalism would solve their problems. Nor were they convinced that capitalism, as an economic system, had exhausted its potential.

As a case in point, they found private property and individual enterprise essential to the accelerated production of those appurtenances that afforded the nation power projection capabilities in the contemporary world.[49] As early as 1904, Giovanni Papini had chosen the United States and its entrepreneurs as developmental models. A class of producers who celebrated their power and energy in the development of their nation's productive forces—in the generation of steel mills, railroads, electricity, and the arms of war—was what was absent in the Italy of his time.[50]

Papini sought an industrial bourgeoisie that would supplant the flaccid and passive bourgeoisie of the Italy of the turn of the twentieth century. He sought an entrepreneurial class that was decisive and focused, and who would "exalt…Italian commercial and industrial life."[51] That new class would constitute the "new aristocracy of producers, the men of production, the industrialists," in whom the Italian nationalists saw the salvation of the nation.[52]

As the international crisis that culminated in the Great War of 1914–1918 matured, nationalist pleas became more insistent, emphatic, and strident. Italy was seen as somnolent and passive, devoid of purpose and energy, accustomed to negligible importance in the community of nations, and populated by tour guides, panderers, and mandolin players. It was deplored as a nation that suffered all the moral defects of the decadent plutocracies, without their history of military conquest and economic expansion. Italy was a nation without moral compass, without virtue, and without meaningful prospects. Nationalists saw Italians sunk in the sleep of the accomplishments of antiquity. The Italians of the first generation of the new century were seen by the nationalists as frivolous, inert, incompetent, venal, egoistic, sentimental, and devoid of manhood and character—forever subject to the control of peoples who were stronger.[53]

The Great War, in the eyes of the nationalists, offered Italians the opportunity of stepping on to the world stage as a serious competitor for a "place in the sun." The war was seen as the occasion of national renewal, of moral regeneration—a terrible school of sacrifice and commitment. War with all its "frightfulness and difficulties" would "scatter all the egoisms, however camouflaged, and Italy would finally become a nation."[54]

In the alchemy of war, the nationalists expected Italians to cast off the false individualism, the materialism and the easy positivism that was the fruit of that foreign liberalism that had poisoned Italian life. The duress of war would compel Italians to take up "collective, essentially ideal values. From that point of view," Rocco argued, "the war would bring to a close one era, and open another, bringing to an end the triumphant materialistic individualism of the second half of the nineteenth century"[55] and opening the epoch of a strong nation and a powerful state.

It was in all these senses that Italian nationalists saw the First World

War as the definitive moral challenge facing their new nation. It was for all these reasons that nationalists ranging from Enrico Corradini to Giovanni Gentile understood the First World War as a defining moral issue for the nation, with Fascism heir to the moral victory that intervention in that war brought in its train.

Perhaps more interesting for our concerns is the fact that the theoretical position assumed by Italy's most radical leftists, the revolutionary syndicalists, had gradually been transformed by time and circumstance into a form of nationalism, not only compatible with Italian nationalism, in general, but recognizable, in outline, as a developmental nationalism not unfamiliar to less-developed nations throughout the twentieth century.

National Syndicalism

Italian syndicalism arose out of the intellectual crisis that had settled over theoretical socialism at the close of the nineteenth century with the death of Friedrich Engels. Almost immediately after Engels' death, Eduard Bernstein had written his critique of classical Marxism. At about the same time, Thomas Masaryk's analytic "Scientific and Philosophical Crisis of Contemporary Marxism" appeared in France.[56] In Italy, F. S. Merlino published his equally searching *Pro e contro il socialismo*.

Out of that body of criticism arose an intensive reappraisal of the entire theoretical content of inherited Marxism.[57] In 1898, Georges Sorel published his *L'avenir socialiste des syndicats*, to be followed by works that were to transform both the theoretical content and the revolutionary enterprise of Marxism.

For the purposes of exposition, some of the most important constituents of Sorel's revisions of "historical materialism" included an amended role for "subjective" human factors—will, moral conviction, and determination—in any effort to explain and anticipate the pattern of economic, political, and historic events. For Sorel, phenomena were the complex products of an intersection of historic, economic, social, political, and voluntary behaviors, invariably involving human motives, dispositions, and moral choice.

Syndicalists like Enrico Leone and Arturo Labriola regularly inveighed against the "economic determinism" of what was conceived to be "orthodox" Marxism—the conviction that social change was, in some sense, the "inevitable" by-product of "ineluctable" economic developments.[58] The syndicalists argued that however one understood economic development, it would somehow have to translate itself into human aspirations, moral intentions, and collective purpose if history was to be, in any sense, explicable.

Part of the theoretical reasons for the syndicalists' decision to undertake the reform of the Marxism they had inherited, was the conviction that the entire notion of an "inevitable" course of events had rendered Italian revolutionaries passive and unresponsive. It had contributed to the disposition on the part of "reformist" socialists to accommodate themselves to, rather than dominate, events.

For Italian syndicalists, Italians were far too disposed to tolerate intolerable conditions. They tolerated poverty and humiliation. They tolerated a political system that was vastly corrupt and ineffectual. And they allowed revolution to become prisoner of an "official" socialism that waited for history to take its "ineluctable" course.

Syndicalists were to argue that there was very little in human history that was metronomic, that followed patterns prefigured in "materialistic" regularities. In fact, throughout the last half of the nineteenth century, the science of individual and collective psychology had rapidly developed among academics in the West—and the results that were obtained fueled the judgments of the most aggressive thinkers among the syndicalists.

As early as 1853, Carlo Cattaneo had presented a paper before the Royal Institute of Lombardy, devoted to the psychology of human beings in association. The issue was taken up by socialist academicians such as Enrico Ferri and Alfredo Niceforo, and by the turn of the twentieth century, the works of Gustave Le Bon, on the psychology of crowds, Scipio Sighele's *The Criminal Crowd* and his *Psychology of Sects*, Gabriel Tarde's *The Laws of Imitation*, and *Social Logic* were available to become part of the intellectual patrimony of the period.

The syndicalists, driven by a passion to shake Italians out of their lethargy, conscious of the absence of a revolutionary "Marxist theory of collective psychology," proceeded to put one together out of the available materials. In 1903, the syndicalist A. O. Olivetti published his essay on "The Problem of the Crowd," one year after the syndicalist Paolo Orano had published his treatise on *Social Psychology*.[59]

What syndicalists sought were insights into the psychological processes governing revolutionary mass-mobilization. They recognized that, like the Italians, the proletariat of Europe gave every appearance of being "conservative," "reformist," even timid —entirely at variance with what traditional Marxism had led revolutionaries to expect.

What syndicalists sought was not only an explanation of the indisposition to make revolution on the part of the working class, but some insight into how that indisposition might be overcome.

Syndicalists understood that revolution required the mobilization of masses. The work of contemporary psychologists and sociologists convinced them that the masses could be moved only by some appeal to shared and compelling sentiments. Those sentiments, precipitated by real problems that arise out of economic, social, political and historic circumstances, were understood to provide the immediate motive force for the collective political action necessary for systemic social change.

They further learned that the invocation of such pervasive sentiments could be accomplished through the employment of "social and political myths," figures of speech, and turns of phrase calculated to capture the "essence" of the critical social, economic, and political issues of each period. Syndicalists further recognized that the formulation, articulation, and effective employment of such mobilizing myths required the intercession of specially gifted leadership.

Syndicalists recognized that mobilization, itself, and the organization of masses once mobilized, required leadership and institutional skills that were exceedingly rare. That recognition forced revolutionary syndicalists to assume increasingly elitist postures, so that by the end of the first decade of our century, they identified themselves with an elitist and "aristocratic" socialism, in order to distinguish themselves from the "orthodox" socialists who pretended that revolution, mass mobilization and effective organization could be "spontaneous," "democratic" and essentially "parliamentarian."[60]

The most prominent thinkers among the syndicalists argued these themes. In one of his earliest expositions of syndicalist ideas, as a case in point, Sergio Panunzio identified syndicalism with "a new social aristocracy." He was convinced that while the popular "masses" might constitute the necessary and combustible material for successful revolution, a "vanguard elite" was required to ignite them.[61] Some of the most impressive sociological and social psychological literature of the period had said as much.

The work of Georges Sorel was critical to the interpretation, but that of Vilfredo Pareto and Gaetano Mosca[62] were no less important. By the first decade of the new century, the revolutionary syndicalists had radically modified the traditional Marxist notions of revolution.

In Panunzio's judgment, for example, the revolutionary syndicalist elite was charged with the responsibility of mobilizing passive masses to revolutionary purpose. The means by virtue of which such mobilization could be effected was through the invocation of sentiment employing suitable myths. Sentiment, once invoked, could be diffused through an entire population via mass suggestion and imitation.[63] The ultimate purpose of such an enterprise would be the generation of a "religious and heroic" sacrificial commitment among the masses—a readiness to lay down their own, and other lives, in the service of revolution.[64]

While sentiment served as a tool, it was eminently clear that for Panunzio the ultimate foundation of individual and collective behavior was to be found in the concrete individual and collective needs and interests of any given period. "Myths" gave those needs and interests generalizable expression, suitable for mass mobilization and collective mimetism.[65] But "myths" were not irrational appeals. They were calculated appeals to the half-articulated, but real, interests of the "masses."

Like most syndicalists, Panunzio understood his syndicalism to be a more modern and "pragmatic" supplement to revolutionary Marxism. It was conceived to be a supplement that was fully compatible with the original system.

Like classical Marxism, Panunzio conceived human beings as essentially social animals. He argued that human life, lived in common, beset by common needs and common interests, gives rise to group loyalties and group sentiments that find expression in group "myths." Such political myths succeed in shaping individuals to common purpose, making common life, and common enterprise, possible.

For Panunzio, and revolutionary syndicalists in general, the common needs and common interests of the early twentieth century were "proletarian." In the judgment of syndicalists, the proletariat constituted the revolutionary community that prefigured the shape of the twentieth century.

In that regard, Panunzio anticipated the decline of the politically organized nation-state. The nation-state was expected to dissolve into voluntary combinations of spontaneously organized syndicates, which would, in turn, then administer the complex needs of modern industry.[66]

With the disappearance of the nation-state, the constabulary, national borders, the defense establishment and war, itself, would all become anachronisms. Communities would be essentially anarcholibertarian in character, devoid of all coercive authority, and nations would be geographic expressions having no significance for the working class.

All of this implicitly hung on the conviction that the economy of the Italian peninsula was sufficiently mature not only to provide the masses of proletarians necessary to the revolution itself, but the economic abundance critical to the noninvidious satisfaction of postrevolutionary collective needs. It soon became increasingly evident, however, that such a notion was difficult to defend.

What became eminently clear by the end of the first decade of the new century was the realization that the Italian peninsula had only just begun the essential growth processes that Marxism required for successful revolution. Syndicalists, in general and as a consequence, became more and more convinced that industrially retrograde Italy, if it were to assume its revolutionary obligations, required an accelerated and comprehensive growth in machine production and economic output.

As early as 1911, Panunzio insisted that historic circumstances required that syndicalism emphasize industrial production—that "syndicalism represented the political economy of production...," rather than the traditional Marxist, and liberal democratic, "anti-economy of consumption."[67] It was that same year that saw syndicalism entering into yet another major intellectual crisis.

In 1911, Italy's war in the Mediterranean,[68] over its claims in Tripolitania, created deep divisions among those on the Marxist left. Whatever else it was, for many syndicalists the war fully exposed the injustices of the international system.

By the end of the nineteenth century, the advanced industrial powers had seized vast territories, and garnered for themselves the raw materials of untold spaces. Italy had been excluded from the process.

The war in North Africa was precipitated by a realistic fear that France would assume political control over the entire region—just as Great Britain had seized control of Egypt and the Sudan—and Italy would be entirely excluded from access to resources necessary for its development. Italy, without raw materials and with a population density that exceeded the support capacity of its soil, found itself guttering on the margin of Western European industrialization. The conviction was that the industrially advanced democracies had preempted the resources and the markets of Africa to the exclusion of Italy.

For Italians, it was hard to understand why the peninsula had not been able to develop its economy. It seemed clear that the injustice of the international system had contributed to the nation's industrial retardation and economic backwardness.

If the development of the productive forces of the peninsula was part of the revolutionary responsibility of the syndicalists, many of them conceived support for the war in North Africa as calculated to help "proletarian Italy" lift itself from its circumstances as an oppressed and exploited nation. Italy required natural resources and space to settle its excess population.

Given the argument, Antonio Labriola, the doyen of Italian Marxism, early granted the justice of "proletarian" Italy's expansion into North and East Africa.[69] It was therefore not totally unexpected that on the occasion of the war in 1911, Arturo Labriola, Paolo Orano, and A. O. Olivetti, all revolutionary syndicalists, opted to support their nation's "war of proletarian justice" in Tripolitania.

More significant than all that was the fact that the war of 1911 had managed to arouse large segments of the population of the peninsula out of their traditional somnolence. There was considerable popular sentiment in support of the war.

It became necessary to acknowledge that national sentiment was capable of generating the selfless enthusiasm and sacrificial disposition among sectors of the population that syndicalists had expected exclusively among proletarians.

If, as syndicalists theorized, masses responded to sentiments that reflected real interests, it seemed evident that nationalism, and national interests, were matters of real concern to an indeterminate number of Italians. The conviction that Italy required accelerated industrial development and economic growth, together with an acknowledgement that the contemporary international arrangement of rich and poor nations was not only unjust but dysfunctional to that end, created *nationalist* sentiment among the revolutionary syndicalism on the Italian radical left.

Italian syndicalism had become infused with an enthusiasm for Italian industrial development and economic growth—typified by a recognition of the role of national sentiment in the enterprise. It was elitist by conviction, transformative in intention, and prepared to defeat the antirevolutionary lethargy of "bourgeois Italy" through an appeal to myth, ritual, "moral idealism"[70] and demonstrative violence.

By the time of the Great War, national syndicalism had taken on specific intellectual character. Before leaving to die in that war, Filippo Corridoni, one of the most radical of the left-wing syndicalists could write of Italy that it remained in "economic swaddling clothes," without the minimum sense of technical and competitive efficiency. Italy was an impoverished nation, three quarters of which languished in limited industrial development.[71]

Given the standard Marxist postulate, that could only mean (1) that the enterprisory bourgeoisie had failed to discharge its "historic responsibilities," and (2) that a "mature proletariat" was absent on the peninsula. The bourgeoisie had not industrialized the nation and, as a consequence, the proletariat had not matured to its revolutionary tasks.[72]

As a consequence, Corridoni argued, revolutionary syndicalists were compelled, by their "historic responsibilities," to commit themselves to the rapid industrialization of the nation. If necessary, they were to "collaborate" with any "dynamic" faction of the bourgeoisie in order to create the preconditions specified by classical Marxism.[73]

The reality was that the circumstances in which the people of Italy found themselves recommended not "class warfare," but class collaboration, in the demanding enterprise of rapid industrial development and economic growth. Success would require that an "heroic spirit, a religious sense of capability, and a willingness to sacrifice in the service of a complete and clear conviction of its proper historic mission" animate Italians.[74]

For Corridoni, the tasks would be onerous. Italy lacked all the natural resources required for rapid industrial development. It was opposed by all the advanced industrial nations that had established, through international trade and financial arrangements, preemptive privileges in the modern world. Italy was a "late developer" in a world already peopled by early industrializers like Great Britain, France and the United States, and, as a consequence, suffered all the entailed disabilities.[75]

By 1915, Corridoni, like many, if not all, revolutionary syndicalists in Italy, had recognized that any thought of Marxist revolution would require antecedent industrialization. To imagine that the realization of the "classless society" might be achieved in an industrially backward economy was irresponsible.

Like many, if not all, revolutionary syndicalists, Corridoni recommended intense collaboration of all elements of Italian society in the industrialization of the peninsula. To those ends, Corridoni, like Panunzio at the time, advocated free trade, free enterprise, and a libertarian reduction in state interference in the economy. He advocated a maximization of individual enterprise, the creation of a national militia rather than a professional standing army, and the introduction of referenda, recall of public officials, and legislative initiatives governing public affairs.

It was the Great War that transformed the libertarian elements of revolutionary syndicalism. It was the war that convinced many revolutionary syndicalists that only nations that were united in purpose, effectively governed, and supported by an expanding and efficient economic system could expect to survive and obtain justice in the modern world.[76] A "proletarian people," like the Italians, having emerged from the war with "a thirst for greatness,"[77] would require organization, direction, and purpose.

Leaders, "heroes," and a committed elite would provide purpose, and the state they would animate, would provide the organization and direction. *Production*, a theme central to syndicalist convictions from the first decade of the new century, would be instrumental to the redemptive revolution of the "proletarian nation."[78]

The *nation* would be the vehicle of redemption, *production* would be its instrument, and the *state* would be its articulate political will. Years of "continuous humiliation" had inspired the effort to make of the proletarian nation that which it could be but was not.[79]

National syndicalism was the synthesis of these sentiments. It was the heir of traditional Marxism and the socialism of proletarian nations.[80] By 1919, it was Fascism.[81]

The Futurists

It was to all of this that the Futurism of F. T. Marinetti lent its energy. Formally founded in 1909, Futurism was a movement of literary and artistic protest against the prevailing traditions of the turn of the century.[82] Profoundly influenced by Friedrich Nietzsche, Henri Bergson, Georges Sorel and Gabriele D'Annunzio, whatever else it was, Futurism was profoundly nationalistic.

Marinetti, together with Papini and Prezzolini, lamented the inertness of Italy and Italians. In its first Manifesto, Futurism spoke of "singing the love of danger, energetic habits, and temerity." There was a call to "courage, audacity, [and] rebellion...." The enemy was "immobility" and "somnolence." The ideal was "aggressive movement, a febrile insomnia, competition, mortal leaps, slaps and blows."

The intent was to liberate Italy from "the fetid cancer of professors, archeologists, tour-guides and antiquarians....of museums and cemeteries"—that "eternal and dysfunctional admiration of the past from which Italians emerge fatally enervated, diminished, and crushed." Futurists called upon Italians to destroy the old, the past, the rachitic, and the slow with merciless "violence, cruelty and injustice."[83]

Italy's preoccupation with the past was to be cauterized. The Fatherland, the "fullest extension of the individual," was to be rendered dynamic, progressive, and developmental, by violent revolution, by war, by a commitment to the "multiplication" of self through machinery, through electricity, through activity and challenge.[84] A passive population, rendered comatose by the toxicity of a dead past, weighed down by a political life shackled to an incompetent parliament, would have to be aroused by revolution, armed conflict, tests of courage and commitment that would render docility and servility suicidal.[85]

Marinetti and the Futurists advocated anarchism, feminism, celibacy, libertarianism, the abandonment of Christianity for a new "religion of velocity," as well as the destruction of all the artworks of antiquity, in the desperate effort to awaken Italians from their submissiveness, indolence, and abject servility.

What seems perfectly clear is that Futurism, however hyperbolic, was part of the effort of revolutionaries to reanimate an inert and passive Italy in an international environment of competition and conflict in which it suffered every disadvantage. Whatever else it was, Futurism "faithfully reflected some of the contemporary needs" of Italy as an economically retrograde and internationally inferior nation.[86] Futurism advocated the pursuit of "grandeur" for the nation, a commitment to rapid industrial growth, the creation of a military capable of projecting power, and a foreign policy of assertiveness against those nations that had preempted space, resources and opportunity at its expense.[87]

The Fascist Synthesis

By the time the first Fascists collected themselves in the Piazza San Sepolcro in Milan in March 1919, the basic elements of Fascism had coalesced around the commitment to the redemption of the proletarian nation, its industrial and economic growth, and its accession to a place in the sun in the community of nations. Nationalists, syndicalists, and futurists were to commit themselves to those purposes without significant reservation.

By 1921, for example, Panunzio could insist that "in the struggle between people, those are victorious who are the most well organized and have the most internal cohesion."[88] The First World War had convinced many syndicalists that "oppressed peoples" could only ensure equity and defend their rights against "plutocratic" and oppressor nations by effectively mobilizing their collective energies in a unitary state.[89]

Basic to such a program was a vast undertaking of industrial and economic modernization. That required a rationalization and centralization of the political infrastructure.

Italian life was to be profoundly modified by the expansion of electric and steam power. Communications were to be developed. Financial institutions were to be rendered more efficient, competitive and survivable. The apparatus of government was to be made more competent. Only in such fashion might "hungry and proletarian peoples" survive in a world dominated by "capitalist and aggressive peoples."[90]

By the first years following the end of the First World War, many syndicalists perceived the state, in an environment of laggard industrial development, as the agency of change, capable of infusing both proletarian and bourgeois elements with the revolutionary energy that might transform society. Animated by the nationalism that inspired the revolutionary interventionists of the left, syndicalism was rapidly transformed into a national syndicalism that approximated more and more the developmental nationalism and statism of Enrico Corradini and Alfredo Rocco.[91]

By 1919, revolutionary syndicalism had become a national syndicalism that conceived syndicalism a tool in the regeneration of Italy. It was an ideology of mass mobilization that would unite all classes and factions in a program of national redemption. That program would commence with insurrectionary violence against the passive and unresponsive parliamentary state. The establishment of a developmental regime would initiate a period of revolutionary dictatorship—a period in which the new legal and institutional forms of the emerging society would be gradually fabricated.[92]

By 1919, nationalism, syndicalism and Futurism had come together in a synthesis that made up the political and economic program of the first Fascism. That there were differences that distinguished the components can hardly be gainsaid, but that there was a core of convictions that held the movement together was equally evident. All sought the rapid economic and industrial development of the nation in order to survive in a Darwinian world of competition. All sought the regeneration of the nation and its accession to the rank of a "Great Power" in a universe of "Great Powers."

In the first stages of the enterprise it was not clear whether the state or the "free market" would be charged with the governance of the developmental enterprise. What was clear was that the process would be governed by elites, by collective energy, by arduous enterprise, by sacrifice, obedience, and discipline.

By the early years of the regime that emerged from the Fascist revolution of 1922, it became clear that the state, informed by an antiparliamentarian, antiliberal and hegemonic vanguard party, led by a charismatic leader, would command the renovative and redemptive enterprise. By 1925, it was clear what Fascism was to mean to Italy and the world.

By that time, the ideology of Fascism had already found expression. It was to be found in the works of intellectuals who had already earned international reputations.

Among the syndicalists, Roberto Michels was one of the most important. Among the "liberal" nationalists, Giovanni Gentile was to provide Fascism's philosophical rationale.

What is most important for the purposes of the present exposition is the fact that Fascism demonstrated a "logic" inextricably tied to the conditions that prevailed in an industrially backward nation on the periphery of modern development. All of the movements that contributed to the articulation of Fascism shared in that logic.

To disassemble that logic by making a point of the "chauvinism" of the nationalists, or the elitism of the syndicalists, or Futurism's advocacy of war and violence, is to miss the very essence of Fascism. To imagine that any act of vandalism, or any opposition to immigration, or any piece of "conservative" advocacy is "neofascist" is to fail to understand Fascism.

That will become increasingly apparent in the treatment of the rationale of Fascism provided by Michels, and that advanced by Gentile. The same interconnected themes to be found in early Italian nationalism, revolutionary syndicalism, and Futurism find their expression in the work of two of our century's finest intellects.

More than that, the exposition of the thought of Michels and Gentile supports the contention, now accepted by the better informed scholars of Fascism, that the regime that dominated the Italian peninsula for the better part of a generation, was informed by a "coherent, logical and well-structured" intellectual synthesis of nationalism and a revision of Marxism "that Georges Sorel and the Sorelians of France and Italy proposed at the turn of the century."[93]

Mussolini's Fascism had intellectual credentials no less impressive than those of liberalism or Marxism-Leninism. That it has been dealt with as though it were empty of thought has left Western intellectuals confused. That Western academics imagine that contemporary "soccer thugs," skinheads, "heavy-metal rocker nazis," and anti-Semites represent contemporary "fascism" leaves us bereft of understanding. As a consequence, we are left confused about much of the modern political world.

The recognition that Fascism possessed impressive intellectual components, and was informed by a sustaining logic, can only influence judgments concerning its contemporary relevance. Those components, and that logic, have surfaced and resurfaced in the immediate present, and unless the present arguments are entirely incorrect, they will make their reappearance at least throughout the first half of the twenty-first century.

Notes

1. See A. James Gregor, *Interpretations of Fascism* (New Brunswick, N.J.: Transaction Publishers, 1997).
2. H. Arthur Steiner, *Government in Fascist Italy* (New York: McGraw-Hill, 1938), pp. 25–26.
3. Ivone Kirkpatrick, *Mussolini A Study in Power* (New York: Hawthorne, 1964), p. 11, quoting Croce's judgments immediately after the termination of the Second World War.
4. Dennis Mack Smith, *Mussolini: A Biography* (New York: Vintage, 1982), p. 35.
5. Zeev Sternhell, *The Birth of Fascist Ideology* (Princeton, NJ: Princeton University Press, 1994), p. 4.
6. See A. James Gregor, *Young Mussolini and the Intellectual Origins of Fascism* (Berkeley: University of California, 1979).
7. See the discussion in Zeev Sternhell, *The Birth of Fascist Ideology* (Princeton, N.J.: Princeton University Press, 1994).
8. The history of the Fascist revolution has been written in exhaustive detail from almost every point of view. The most substantial treatment has been that of Renzo De Felice, *Mussolini il fascista: La conquista del potere 1921–1925* (Turin: Einaudi, 1966).
9. Sternhell, *op. cit.*, p. 6.
10. Giuseppe Mazzini, "To the Italians," in *The Duties of Man and Other Essays* (New York: E. P. Dutton, 1907), pp. 222–234, 240.
11. Mazzini, "The Duties of Man," in *ibid.*, pp. 30, 53, 54, 58; "People and government must proceed united, like thought and action in individuals, towards the accomplishment of that mission," and Mazzini, "To the Italians," *ibid.*, p. 241, and consult pp. 235 and 244–245.
12. Mazzini, "To the Italians," *ibid.*, p. 245.
13. See Gioacchino Volpe, *Pagine risorgimentali* (Rome: Volpe, 1967), 1, pp. 220–221.
14. See Homer Lea, *The Valor of Ignorance* (New York: Harper, 1910).
15. See Anthony Rhodes, *D'Annunzio: The Poet as Superman* (New York: McDowell, Oblensky, 1959), chap. 7.
16. Alfredo Oriani, *La rivolta ideale* (Bologna: Cappelli, 1943), pp. 118–119, 123, 136, 168. Oriani argued that the "single individual could not exist without the collectivity...." See also p. 107.
17. Some saw the necessities of regeneration in the external threats to the integrity of the fatherland, i.e., the expansion of Austria-Hungary into the Balkans. See Scipio Sighele, "Le origini del nazionalismo italiano," in *Nazionalismo e i partiti politici* (Milan: Treves, 1911). Others saw the necessity in the outmigration of millions of Italians because the nation could provide them neither sustenance nor hope.

Still others saw the necessity borne of a lack of "national consciousness" that left Italy exposed to every indignity and imposture by the "great powers." See the discussion in Luigi Valli, "Che cosa è e che cosa vuole il nazionalismo," in Francesco Perfetti (ed.), *Il nazionalismo italiano* (Rome: Il Borghese, 1969), pp. 37–58.

18. Papini as cited in Paola Maria Arcari, *Le elaborazioni della dottrina politica nazionale fra l'unità e l'intervento (1870–1914)* (Florence: Marzocco, 1932–1934), 1, p. 12; see p. 16. The essay of 1903, from which the quote was taken, was reformulated for inclusion in Giovanni Papini and Giuseppe Prezzolini, *Vecchio e nuovo nazionalismo* (Rome: Volpe, 1967) that was first published in 1914.

19. Papini followed Vilfredo Pareto in expecting a rotation of elites in any functional political system. See Arcari, *op. cit.*, 2, pp. 404–407.

20. Papini acknowledged the mobilizing function of myths—even those myths that were "hyperbolic." See Arcari, *op. cit.*, 2, p. 398

21. See Arcari, *op. cit.*, 2, p. 421. See in this context, the discussion of Prezzolini, "Le due Italie," in Papini and Prezzolini, *op. cit.*, pp. 67–73.

22. Papini and Prezzolini, *op. cit.*, pp. 8, 13–15, 24. See Arcari, *op. cit.*, 2, p. 413.

23. As early as 1897, Domenico Gnoli complained that the conviction of their own inferiority has become "chronic" among Italians. See Domenico Gnoli, "Nazionalità ed arte," *Nuova anthologia* (1897) as cited in Arcari, 1, p. 215. The sense of national humiliation was pervasive among the revolutionary nationalist elite. See Arcari, *op. cit.*, 2, pp. 378, 417. In 1909, Corradini reminded Italians that they suffered humiliation throughout the world because the nation had no prestige among modern nations. See "L'emigrazione italiana nell'America del Sud" (1909) in Corradini, *Discorsi politici* (Florence: Vallecchi, 1923), p. 74. Corradini spoke of Italy as having "a disposition to servitude," p. 87. See "Nazionalismo e socialismo," (1914), *Discorsi politici*, pp. 216–217.

24. See Corradini, "Nazionalismo e socialismo," (1914), *Discorsi politici*, pp. 219–222.

25. For Corradini, the "daily creation of more industries" was never conceived as an end in itself. "The material bases of prosperity constitute the foundation for the works and the monuments of national greatness. Out of the obscure labor of humble citizens arises the triumph of the nation...." Corradini as cited in Arcari, *op. cit.*, 2, pp. 388–389. "...For the people and for the nation it is production, the production of energy and spiritual energy with which Italy will enter into its period of full activity and its accelerated enrichment." Corradini, "Per la guerra d'Italia," (1915), *Discorsi politici*, pp. 302.

26. Corradini, *L'unità e la potenza delle nazioni* (Florence: Vallecchi, 1922), pp. 37–40.

27. See Corradini, "Le opinioni degli uomini e i fatti dell'uomo," (1902), republished in Enrico Corradini, *Discorsi politici* (Florence: Vallecchi, 1923), p. 24; "La vita nazionale," (1905), *ibid*, p. 44, and "La morale della guerra," 1912, *ibid*, pp. 142–143.

28. Corradini, *L'ombra della vita* (Naples: Ricciardi, 1908), pp. 285–287.

29. Corradini, "Nazionalismo e democrazia," (1913), *Discorsi politici*, p. 159.

30. See Livio Marchetti's "Order of the Day," at the Nationalist Congress in Florence in 1910, as cited in Arcari, *op. cit.*, 3, p. 7, and the "Order of the Day" of G. Altimasi Menna at the Nationalist Congress in Rome in 1912, *ibid.*, 3, p. 17. See Arcari, *Le elaborazioni della dottrina*, 2, p. 387. See Corradini's invocation of a "mission" in the service of collective accomplishment. See Corradini, "La vita nazionale," *Discorsi politici*, pp. 44–46.

31. Corradini, "Principii di nazionalismo," (1910), *Discorsi politici*, p. 101, and "Le nuove dottrine nazionali e il rinnovamento spirituale," (1913), *ibid.*, pp. 203, 205–206.
32. Corradini, "Nazionalismo e democrazia," (1913), *Discorsi politici*, p. 161. Corradini spoke of the dependency created by the advanced industrial nations in dealing with those less-developed. See "Nazionalismo e socialismo," (1914), *ibid.*, pp. 226–229.
33. Corradini, "Le nazioni proletarie e il nazionalismo," (1911), *Discorsi politici*, pp. 114–116.
34. See the discussion in Corradini, "Stato liberale e stato nazionale," (1914), *Discorsi politici*, pp. 233–247.
35. Corradini, *Il volere d'Italia* (Naples: Perrella, 1911), pp. 205–207.
36. Corradini, "Le nazioni proletarie e il nazionalismo," (1911), *Discorsi politici*, pp. 104–118.
37. See Paolo Ungari, *Alfredo Rocco e l'ideologia del fascismo* (Brescia: Morcelliana, 1963).
38. Alfredo Rocco, "Economia liberale, economia socialista ed economia nazionale," *Rivista delle Società Commerciali*, in *Scritti e discorsi politici* (Milan: Giuffre, 1938), 1, p. 57. See *ibid.*, 1, section 1, for the discussion in Rocco, "Il problema economico italiano."
39. Rocco specifically cites List's work, *Das nationale System der politischen Oekonomie*, as a source in "Economia liberale...," *op. cit.*, 1, pp. 40,47.
40. Friedrich List, *The National System of Political Economy* (New York: Augustus M. Kelley, 1966, a reprint of the 1885 edition). List was a contemporary of Karl Marx. Marx dismissed List's work as "Bourgeois apologetics." See the discussion in Roman Szporluk, *Communism and Nationalism: Karl Marx versus Friedrich List* (New York: Oxford University Press, 1988).
41. Rocco, "Il problema economico italiano," *op. cit.*, 1, p. 18.
42. See the discussion in Rocco, "In piena pratica rivoluzionaria," in *op. cit.*, 1, pp. 117–118.
43. See the discussion in Rocco, "Cause remote e prossime della crisi dei partiti politici italiani," in *op. cit.*, pp. 6–9, and "Il problema economico italiano," in *op. cit.*, pp. 13–19.
44. Rocco, "Economia liberale...," *op. cit.*, 1, p. 57.
45. See the discussion in Rocco, "Che cosa e il nazionalismo e che cosa vogliono i nazionalisti," in Rocco, *op. cit.*, 1, pp. 78–79.
46. J. A. Hobson, *Imperialism: A Study* (Ann Arbor: University of Michigan Press, 1965, a reprint of the 1902 edition).
47. See Rocco's general comments on the "liberal government" of Italy in "L'amnestia, il disgregamento dello stato e gli stranieri d'Italia," *op. cit.*, 1, pp. 235–238.
48. See the account in Rocco, "Economia liberale...," *op. cit.*. 1. pp. 40–45.
49. See the discussion in Alfredo Rocco and Maurizio Maraviglia, "Il programma nazionalista," in Francesco Perfetti (ed.), *Il nazionalismo italiano* (Rome: Il Borghese, 1969), p. 127.
50. Giovanni Papini, "L'Italia rinasce," in Papini and Prezzolini, *op. cit.*, pp. 128–130.
51. See Prezzolini, "Preface," and Papini, "Un programma nazionalista," in Papini and Prezzolini, *op. cit.*, pp. iii, and 27.
52. See Enrico Corradini, *La marcia dei produttori* (Rome: "L'Italiana," 1916), pp. x–xi.
53. An entire literature grew up around the contention that "Latin peoples" were, in fact, "inferior" to Anglo-Saxons. Years later, Roberto Michels was to write a

treatise dealing with such claims. See his *Lavoro e razza* (Milan: Vallardi, 1924). Laments concerning the disabling characteristics of Italians, and how to offset them, are found in all the nationalist literature from Mazzini through the Futurists of F. T. Marinetti. See the comments of Rocco, "Buon anno," *op. cit.*, 1, 233, as an example.

54. Rocco, "L'indomani della neutralità," *op. cit.*, 1, p. 244.
55. Rocco, "L'impero d'Italia," *op. cit.*, 1, p. 257.
56. An expanded form of Masaryk's critique appeared as *Philosophischen und sociologischen Grundlagen des Marxismus* (Vienna: Konegen, 1899).
57. See, for example, Georges Sorel, *Les polemiques pur l'interpretation du Marxisme: Bernstein & Kautsky* (Paris: Girard & Briere, 1900).
58. See the more ample discussion in A. James Gregor, *A Survey of Marxism: Problems in Philosophy and the Theory of History* (New York: Random House, 1965), chap. 5.
59. A. O. Olivetti, "Il problema della folla," *Nuova antologia* 38, 761 (1 September 1903), pp. 281–291; Paolo Orano, *Psicologia sociale* (Bari: Laterza, 1902).
60. In this regard, see Roberto Michels, *Storia critica del movimento socialista italiano* (Florence: La Voce, 1926), chap. 8.
61. Sergio Panunzio, *La persistenza del diritto (Discutendo di sindacalismo e di anarchia)* (Pescara: Abbruzzese, 1910), p. 175.
62. For Mosca, "political myths" were characterized as "political formulae."
63. *Ibid.*, pp. 223, 255.
64. See Sergio Panunzio, *Sindacalismo e medioevo (Politica contemporanea)* (Naples: Partenopea, 1911), pp. 101–103; cf. *ibid.*, pp. 11 and 136.
65. *Ibid.*, pp. 27–28.
66. See the discussion in Sergio Panunzio, *Il sindacalismo nel passato* (Lugano: Pagine libere, 1907) and *Lotta per l'esistenza e associazione per la lotta* (Bologna: Liberta economica, 1910).
67. Panunzio, *Sindacalismo e medioevo*, pp. 130–132. At that stage of his intellectual development, Panunzio was clearly an economic liberal, rejecting government interference in economic matters. *Ibid.*, pp. 125, 138.
68. See Giolitti's account of his decision to embark on the war in Giovanni Giolitti, *Memorie della mia vita* (Milan: Treves, 1922), 2, pp. 287–288.
69. Italy's "proletarian war" was to be fought against "the intrigue, the threats, the cupidity, the capital and the weaponry of the plutocratic nations...." Arturo Labriola, *La scintilla*, 11 October 1911, p. 1.
70. See Sergio Panunzio, preface to *Il concetto della querra giusta* (Campobasso: Colitti, 1917).
71. Filippo Corridoni, *Sindacalismo e repubblica* (Milano: SAREP, 1945. Republication of the 1915 edition.), pp. 19, 23, 75, 82.
72. *Ibid.*, pp. 34, 38, 41, 55, 70.
73. *Ibid.*, pp. 25–26, 48–49.
74. *Ibid.*, p. 39.
75. *Ibid.*, pp. 32–33.
76. Sergio Panunzio, *Stato nazionale e sindacati* (Milan: Imperia, 1924), pp. 30–40. See Francesco Carnelutti, introduction to Leonardo Paloscia, *La concezione sindacalista di Sergio Panunzio* (Rome: Gismondi, 1949), p. 7. In this context, the assessment of Curzio Malaparte, who was later to serve as a major ideologue of Fascism, is instructive. He argued that the war had taught revolutionaries that the Italian people had not achieved a consciousness adequate to the tasks of the new century. The post-war period would see the systematic efforts to create such a national consciousness. See Curzio Malaparte, "La rivolta dei santi maledetti,"

L'Europa vivente e altri saggi politici (1921–1931) (Florence: Vallecchi, 1961), especially pp. 75–81.

77. Malaparte, *op. cit.*, p. 127.
78. As early as the first years of the century, Enrico Leone, among the syndicalists, had argued that *production* was a central commitment of the proletarian revolution. See Enrico Leone, *Il Sindacalismo* (Milan: Remo Sandron, 1910), pp. 20, 82.
79. Malaparte, "L'Europa vivente: teoria storica del sindacalismo nazionale," *op. cit.*, pp. 333, 337–338.
80. *Ibid.*, pp. 350–351, 353.
81. See the discussion in A. James Gregor, *Young Mussolini and the Intellectual Origins of Fascism* (Berkeley: University of California, 1979), chap. 10.
82. See the introduction to Luciano De Maria (ed.), *Marinetti e il futurismo* (Verona: Mondadori, 1973), pp. xiii–xxxviii.
83. Marinetti, "Manifesto del Futurismo," in *ibid.*, pp. 5–8.
84. See Marinetti, "L'Uomo moltiplicato e il Regno della Macchina," "Al di la del Comunismo," in *ibid.*, pp. 38–42, 228.
85. Marinetti, "La guerra, sola igiene del mondo," in *ibid.*, pp. 218–219.
86. See the discussion in Giuseppe Prezzolini, "Fascismo e futurismo," in Luciano De Maria (ed.), *Marinetti e il futurismo* (Verona: Mondadori, 1973), pp. 286–287.
87. F. T. Marinetti, *Futurismo e fascismo* (Foligno: Franco Campitelli, 1924), p. 20.
88. Panunzio, *Stato nazionale e sindacati*, pp. 82, 85–89.
89. *Ibid.*, pp. 88–89. Panunzio's essay, "Contro il regionalismo," cited above, was written in mid-1921.
90. See Sergio Panunzio, *Diritto, forza e violenza* (Bolognia: Cappelli, 1921), pp. xxiv–xxv.
91. See the discussion in Vincenzo Amoruso, *Il sindacalismo di Enrico Corradini* (Palermo: Orazio Fiorenza, 1929).
92. See Sergio Panunzio, *Stato nazionale e sindacati* (Milan: Imperia, 1924) and its fullest expression in *Teoria generale dello stato fascista* (Padua: CEDAM, 1939), part 1, chap. 1; part 5, chap. 1.
93. Zeev Sternhell, *The Birth of Fascist Ideology* (Princeton, N.J.: Princeton University Press, 1994), p. 8.

3

Roberto Michels and the "Logic" of Fascism

Roberto Michels was perhaps the most accomplished of the revolutionary syndicalists. He was to become one of the major social scientists of the twentieth century. It was he who drew together many of the propositions that made up the intellectual substance of syndicalism to produce what was to be the ideology of Fascism, as coherent a body of thought as any political belief system in the twentieth century.

Until very recently, the suggestion that Italian Fascism had any ideological substance was counted a sure sign of intellectual indigence, or an instance of political apology.

Every other political movement in our century, including the most mindless and bizarre, has been credited with the possession of an ideological rationale. Only Mussolini's Fascism has been traditionally characterized, more often than not, as a kind of unthinking reaction, an irrationalism that burst upon Italy as a kind of moral disorder.[1] Without political scruple, ethical concern, or theoretical conviction, Fascism is supposed to have dominated the Italian peninsula for a generation through the exercise of terror and political oppression.

The fact is that there was a rationale of Fascism, a studied system of thought advanced to legitimize the mass-mobilizing, developmental dictatorship that represented Italy for more than two decades in the twentieth century. Whatever the ultimate assessment of the Fascist experiment, contemporary scholarship has been compelled to recognize the existence of a body of thought, produced by a distinguished collection of scholars, articulated to defend the political, moral, and intellectual integrity of Mussolini's regime.

It serves very little cognitive purpose to argue that the Fascist regime did not, in practice, embody the empirical, logical and/or normative convictions of its intellectual spokesmen any more than it serves any purpose to point to the failures of liberal democratic regimes that fail to meet the requirements of equality, or liberty, or fairness, embodied in the works of their intellectual spokesmen. The rationale for any political system provides the parameters within which any regime acts out its overt behaviors and against which it is to be judged. No less can be said of Fascism.

Whatever else it was, the rationale of Fascism existed first of all as a systematic body of thought. Whether, in fact, that body of thought governed the behaviors of Benito Mussolini and his entourage is a question that cannot be addressed or resolved here—any more than the question of whether the behaviors of Josef Stalin or Mao Zedong were *really* informed by the ideological convictions of Karl Marx or Friedrich Engels.

Whatever the ultimate judgment of the political regime, the rationale produced in its support merits separate and responsible consideration for a number of reasons, not the least of which is to provide the opportunity for identifying its reemergence in different national, economic, and intellectual environments. Only then can anyone responsibly decide whether tax protestors, patriots, survivalists, soccer thugs, or skinheads are really "fascists."

More than that, a case can be made that there are entailments to the persuasive logic of Fascism not fully anticipated by its most well-intentioned advocates—and which carry implications for our own time whenever one or another variant of fascism makes its appearance. For at least those reasons, Fascist ideology merits dispassionate review.

Beyond that, the suggestion that the Italian people lent their consent to mindless rule for a quarter century looks very much like simple prejudice. The intelligent and responsible people of Italy must have been afforded some rationale for Fascist rule. They may well have been deceived—but one is at least compelled to grant that they were deceived by a seeming coherence.

Roberto Michels and the Revolutionary Tradition

Roberto Michels was not only one of the most important political sociologists of the first half of the twentieth century, he was also among the most important of the ideologues of Fascism. Not only has his volume, *Zur Soziologie des Parteiwesens (Political Parties)*, become a classic in our time, the point of departure for much of the contemporary work in the sociology of political parties,[2] but Michels was also a distinguished and committed Fascist intellectual. He not only contributed to that current of opinion now characterized as "antiparliamentarian" and "ademocratic,"[3] but he was one of the major architects of the ideology of Fascism.

That is true not only because of Michels' overt commitment to Fascism by formal entry into the *Partito nazionale fascista*, his personal admiration for Mussolini, or his defense of Fascism in his *Italien von Heute* or his *Corso di sociologia politica*.[4] Nor is it true solely because Mussolini personally selected him to instruct Fascist intellectuals in the "ideas of the new theory of the state, its evolution and potential for development."[5] Michels was more than an apologist for, or a convert to, Fascism. In a significant sense Michels, like Sergio Panunzio and A.O. Olivetti, materially assisted in the formulation of Fascist doctrine before there was a Fascist movement—much less, a Fascist regime.

Michels' work embodied every syndicalist theme we have reviewed. His published works advance arguments for every major claim bruited by the most radical left-wing thought in pre-World War One Italy. Fascist thought was not the product of the idiosyncratic reflections of single individuals. Michels spoke for an entire generation of radical Marxist revolutionaries, many of whom were to become Fascists.

While it is now generally recognized that Michels' Fascist convictions were neither opportunistic nor casual,[6] his personal contribution to the maturation of Mussolini's political thought and the ideological development of Fascism is not similarly acknowledged.[7] The fact of the matter was that not only was Michels' work well known to the young Mussolini,[8] but similarity in the thoughts of both suggests that Michels may have had decisive influence on Mussolini's ultimate convictions. Primarily for these reasons, Michels, on the occasion of his death in 1936, was identified by the leadership of the Fascist party as "one of our own."[9]

Roberto Michels was, in a significant sense, one of the principal ideologues of Fascism. Much of the intellectual substance of Fascism was a product of his multifaceted intelligence, research acumen, and scholarly diligence.

Michels, Revolutionary Syndicalism, and the Leadership of the Masses

Roberto Michels was born in Cologne on the ninth of January in 1876 to a well-to-do merchant family of mixed German and French origin. With first maturity, he concerned himself with what qualified, at the time, as the "social question"—the perceived injustices that char-

acterized industrialized society. By the turn of the century, he identified himself as a socialist.[10] By the middle of the first decade of the new
century, he was active in the syndicalist faction of the Marxist left.[11]

In 1907, Michels attended a revolutionary convention in Stockholm,
as a delegate of the syndicalist wing of Italian socialism. In that same
year, he assumed academic responsibilities at the University of Turin.
From that point on, he became inextricably involved in Italian affairs—
to ultimately opt for Italian citizenship.

In 1908, Michels published his first major work, *Il proletariato e la
borghesia nel movimento socialista italiano*.[12] It was an important work
for a number of reasons. In the first instance, in the preface to the volume, Michels announced his intention to devote his energies to an "analytic study of political parties"—a preoccupation which was to later
mature into his classic *Zur Soziologie des Parteiwesens*. Moreover, in
the text of *Il proletariato e la borghesia*, one can find Michels making
allusion to those influences, technical and psychological, that were to
constitute the foundation of his subsequent, and now classic, "law of
oligarchies."

In *Il proletariato e la borghesia*, for example, Michels referred to
the irrepressible need on the part of contemporary political organizations for competent organizers and effective managers—both in limited supply. He also alluded to the apparent generic disposition on the
part of the "mass" to seek out and submit to leaders—preferably intellectuals possessed of oratorical abilities, prophetic demeanor and evan-
gelical enthusiasm. He even addressed himself to the chronic "suggestibility" of the "masses"—all factors that were conceived, in his *Zur
Soziologie des Parteiwesens*, as causes of the oligarchical tendencies
that characterize modern organizational life.[13]

All of these themes were part of the intellectual armarium of the
revolutionary syndicalists. In the work of Michels, they received academic accreditation. The final sections of his *Il proletariato e la
borghesia* contain an exposition of syndicalist conceptions at once both
competent and sympathetic. For Michels, the syndicalist current of his
time represented the most modern, responsive, dynamic, and idealistic
component of the modern socialist movement.

Michels held syndicalists like Arturo Labriola, Enrico Leone, Walter
Mocchi, Costantino Lazzari, Ottavio Dinale, and A. O. Olivetti to be
among the most important revolutionary leaders on the Italian peninsula. They represented, for Michels, the defenders of the purity of the
socialist idea—against what he perceived to be the corruption of petty-

bourgeois influences, the conservatism of the Socialist Party organization, as well as the velleity, incompetence, and suggestibility of the proletarian masses themselves.[14]

Michels construed syndicalism an intransigent revolutionary and idealist current within the socialist movement, whose intended effect was to "lift the consciousness of the masses to the height of their mission as a class."[15] In effect, as opposed to the socialist orthodoxy that imagined that the class consciousness of the proletariat would be the "automatic" product of economic processes, Michels understood the political and moral maturation of the working class to be a function of the educative enterprise of a minority of revolutionary intellectuals.[16] He spoke of the "mass" as the "generality of *humanitas*" with which gifted individuals must interact to effect "extraordinary" purpose.[17] The "mass," for Michels, was the material with which creative minorities fashioned extraordinary historic events. Gifted individuals and creative minorities required receptive masses to accomplish their purposes.[18] The claims were those of Italy's foremost syndicalists.[19]

The conviction that "masses" were intrinsically "passive" until caught up in a "grand vision," or an "historic ideal," formulated and bruited by a "vanguard minority,"[20] became central to Michels' views. The interaction of a "revolutionary aristocracy" and the "masses" was governed by the "laws" of collective, or "crowd," life—the core of Michels' "law of oligarchy."

As early as 1903, it was obvious that the Marxism of Michels was a Marxism of a special sort. It was more "idealist" than "materialist" in the sense that Michels was prepared to attribute more historic importance to psychological, intellectual, and moral variables than had been traditionally the case with Marxist "orthodoxy."[21] Furthermore, Michels' Marxism was more "individualistic" in the sense that he was prepared to identify extraordinary individuals as critical to historic development.

While he was convinced, as were most radical syndicalists, that economic and historic trends prepared the substructure of social change, he, once again as most syndicalists, held ideal factors, individual "will," "commitment," and "inspiration," to be essential causal determinants in the complex succession of historic, economic, and political events.[22] For Michels the "mass" constituted the necessary, but not sufficient, foundation for social renovation. The "mass" remained "incompetent" and "passive" without the intercession of "extraordinary" leadership animated by "great ideas."

In this sense, Michels was not only a syndicalist, he also gave expression to that collection of ideas easily isolated in the writings of the young Mussolini (who was seven years his junior). It was during these years, particularly between 1905 and 1909, that the young Mussolini identified himself with syndicalist views. Every idea that distinguished the syndicalists from the more "orthodox" Marxists—every idea Michels had made his own—is to be found in the published writings of the youthful Benito Mussolini.[23]

Mussolini's insistence that the task of socialist intellectuals was to elevate the "torpid consciousness of the working masses" to the ideals of the revolution—his appeal to a dedicated and "vanguard elite"—his recognition that masses were moved by sentiment, ideas and moral purpose—all identify him with syndicalism and with the early theoretical work of Roberto Michels.[24] The measure of influence is unmistakable.

Whether the young Mussolini was directly familiar with the writings of Michels prior to 1909 is a matter of little consequence. Most of Michels ideas were, in part, reflections and, in part, elaborations of those syndicalist convictions he shared with a number of Italian intellectuals. Both Mussolini and Michels were part of the selfsame left-wing intellectual and ideological tradition that predated the First World War.

The recognition that Michels and Mussolini shared the same syndicalist convictions is critical to an understanding of Michels' contribution to Fascist ideology. More than that, it documents the origins of Fascist thought in the heretical Marxism of the period.

Michels and Parliamentary Democracy

Michels, as a syndicalist, gave the fullest expression to the syndicalist opposition to parliamentary democracy, an opposition that resonated throughout Fascist doctrine for the next three decades. To understand Michels' argument is to understand a good deal about Fascist political convictions.

Because of a failure on the part of many Anglo-American political theorists to recognize Michels as a syndicalist we have often failed to recognize the principal political thrust of his arguments. The author of *Zur Soziologie des Parteiwesens* is, for example, sometimes spoken of as a "disappointed democrat"—as someone who deplored organization because it undermined genuinely democratic possibilities. Sometimes, he is spoken of as "ademocratic"—as someone possessed of a scrupulously and exclusively scientific concern with the real possibilities of parliamentary democracy. In point of fact, it seems clear that Michels shared with Italian syndicalists a profoundly anti-parliamentary disposition.

Michels always conceived parliamentary democracy animated, in fact, by a "cult of incompetence."[25] As early as 1903, for example, he insisted that the popular "mass" could only be a "passive" element in social change.[26] In 1908, he repeated the same judgment: the majority of mankind remains either passive before political issues or is incompetent to resolve them.[27] In assuming such a position Michels reaffirmed prevailing syndicalist judgments—judgments that were to become those of Fascism.

Arturo Labriola made the case very simply: "Democracy lacks the faculty of influencing the specific processes of social life. Its principal characteristic is incompetence." More than that, Labriola, like Michels, argued that the personal disabilities of the average man—corruption and prejudice, together with a susceptibility to parochial and special interests, as well as a concern for personal advantage—all precluded the possibility that representative democracy might usher in the vast social changes anticipated by European revolutionaries.[28]

Most of these judgments found their original source in the various writings of Georges Sorel who distainfully spoke of the "democratic bog," of the "inert masses," and of "servile politicians," when referring to representative democratic arrangements.[29] Like the Italian syndicalists who were to follow him, Sorel conceived revolution to be a function of the intercession of a rigorously selected minority, capable of firing the enthusiasm and dedication of "masses," in order to overthrow a corrupt and incompetent system.[30]

Once again, these were revolutionary conceptions shared by the young Mussolini.[31] Michels, Sorel, and Mussolini shared them all. About the same time Mussolini wrote an approving review of Michels' monograph on "*Cooperazione*," he wrote a long, incisive and laudatory review of Sorel's essay on revolutionary violence.[32]

Michels' classic *Zur Soziologie des Parteiwesens* was, in a real sense, an exposition of syndicalist opinion. As such, the book was not animated by a disappointment with parliamentary democracy. It was infused with a conviction that saw parliamentary and representative democracy as "servile, corrupt, bourgeois, conservative and incompetent" in the face of real issues. This was not because organizations, per se, were corrupt and conservative, but because the "masses" were naturally disposed to ape the manners and political postures of those who happen to rule.[33]

Since most political leaders were bourgeois, it was clear that for Michels the hierarchical and oligarchical tendencies inherent in organization furthered the compromising, corrupt, and conservative behaviors characteristic of the masses. The natural disposition of the average man was, in Michels' judgment, to remain inert, mimetic, and conservative. Only a select leadership, charged with revolutionary elan and a commitment to "principle" and "comprehensive theory," was capable of furthering revolutionary purpose by mobilizing those otherwise indifferent and incompetent.[34]

Michels concluded his major work with the judgment that "the objective immaturity of the mass is not...a transitory phenomenon eliminable through socialist democratization. It is, instead, intrinsic to the very nature of the mass as such, which is amorphous and requires a division of labor, a specialization and a direction which even if organized is incapable of resolving all the problems that afflict it....Individuals are destined to be guided, and that need for guidance will increase, because the activities of modern life become continuously more specific. The group, which consists of single individuals, feels the need of guidance incomparably more."[35]

It is clear that in Michels' judgment the "guidance" required by the masses—if that guidance were to serve revolutionary purpose—could only be provided by declassed bourgeois intellectuals equipped with revolutionary "science" and inspired by the vision of an alternative future. Michels insisted, for example, that "socialist theory originated out of the thought of philosophers, economists, sociologists, and historians. There is not a single word in the socialist programs of all the different lands that is not the product of scholars. The progenitors of modern socialism have been, with only few exceptions, intellectuals. It was the union of science and moral sentiment that created socialism out of the protean proletarian movement. Out of an instinctual, unconscious movement without goals, created one possessed of conscious, relatively clear and well defined aspirations."[36]

Michels did not deplore organization because it made representative democracy impossible. He deplored organization because it provided the opportunity for corruption and a departure from revolutionary theory. For example, in various places, Michels alluded to the fact that the leadership of socialist organizations *did* respond to what they conceived to be the "will" and the special interest and the immediate welfare demands of their heterogeneous constituency.[37] Michels did not applaud such response, for in so doing, the leaders of socialism, desirous of "popular" and electoral support, sacrificed "the unity and purity of the ends of the movement...."[38] Under such circumstances, "with the growth of organization, the struggle for grand ideals becomes impossible."[39]

It is not that organizations, and the leaders that inhabit leadership roles, were not responsive to the "popular will" that provoked Michels' objections. It was rather that organization tends to foster passivity, incompetence, conservatism, and moral corruption. "Demagogues" become abundant. They become "adulators of the popular will and, instead of elevating the masses, they prostrate themselves before them...."[40] Divested of revolutionary and "ideal" purpose, the "party" becomes simple "organization" and becomes an end-in-itself.[41] The discharge of "great tasks" becomes impossible.

It was not organization, per se, that Michels deplored. Organization was, for Michels, the most effective means for fostering collective purpose.[42] Furthermore, it is clear that the failure of leadership to "represent" the will of the membership did not in itself, distress him.

Michels recognized that the masses must be led. They were, in his judgment, diffident, inept, incompetent, and driven by personal and narrow interests. They were, in fact, afflicted with an "atavistic need...to be guided by someone...."[43]

Michels was convinced that there were dispositional properties "common to all of humankind" that made minority rule inevitable. Not only were the "masses" incompetent, indifferent, and inert without guidance, but "among the masses there is a real and profound impulse to venerate those above them."[44] He understood the "masses" to be "suggestible," to be eminently susceptible to "political fictions," "myths," and "ideal purpose."

Such mobilizing myths could range from the meanest dissemblings to the highest and most responsible goals.[45] In general, the technical requirements of organization—the necessary division of labor, the need for long tenure in office, the demand for special competence—made rule by elites all but inevitable, and myth essential to their purpose and success.

Unfortunately, the desire of leadership to remain in positions of authority and privilege, as well as the competition between established and aspiring organizational leadership, tended to produce elite dominance that was more often than not "demagogic," "accommodative," and "conservative." The very nature of organization, the disposition of established or aspiring leadership, to appeal to the immediate interests of its constituencies, reduced revolutionary ideals to the level of the lowest common denominators.

The fact is that, as a syndicalist, Michels' conception of ideal revolutionary leadership and subsequent rule was embodied in a notion of governance by an aristocracy of men of revolutionary will who also possessed the technical capabilities requisite to the complexity of modern life. Michels recognized that such leaders were rare and could not accede to leadership other than under the most unusual circumstances.

As a consequence, Michels was prepared to grant that under ordinary circumstances, parliamentary democracy, whatever its intrinsic shortcomings, was, in most times and under most circumstances, the least of evils.[46] Only with the appearance of a true leader of men—a "duce" capable of infusing masses with enthusiasm for a "great mission"—a "hero" possessed of an irrepressible conviction in his own destiny—would Michels opt for "charismatic leadership" and an "elite party."[47] He recognized the option as fraught with peril, but it was an option alive with great promise and the possibility of guiding a people through a revolutionary period under the aegis of "comprehensive theory" infused with "ideal purpose."

Michels' vision was, thus, sorellian in character. He sought a world in which popular masses could be reborn to live life more intensively, and with more profound commitment. In this sense, Michels forever remained true to the syndicalism of his youth. And in this explicit sense, Michels was a Mussolinian revolutionary.

Michels recognized in Mussolini the charismatic "duce" he had anticipated in his youth. And Mussolini recognized in Michels the theoretic spokesman for elitist "charismatic consensus government."[48]

Michels' transit from revolutionary syndicalism to Fascism followed an itinerary that can now be reconstructed with some clarity. It began with his critical assessment of the shortcomings of the orthodox Marxism of his time. His syndicalism was the leavening out of which his Fascism was destined to grow.

Michels and the Critique of Marxism

Michels' transit from revolutionary syndicalism to Fascism was fostered, in large part, by his critique of theoretical Marxism, the "scientific" rationale of the modern working class movement. Even in his earliest writings Michels displayed a number of critical reservations concerning the scientific pretensions of the orthodox Marxism of his time.

Among his first published works, as a case in point, Michels expressed a conviction that the substance of socialism's revolutionary potential was to be found not in its specific scientific pretensions, but in its *ethical* convictions.[49] He was, like all syndicalists, an "ethical" and "idealist" intransigent. Throughout his life he remained convinced that a revolutionary movement, properly scientific, could not fail to understand the role of moral imperatives in providing incentives to action.[50]

What this meant for the analysis of social dynamics is clearly expressed in Michels' work. As we have suggested, even in his *Il proletariato e il borghesia*, he argued that the organization of the revolutionary proletariat required the intercession of ethically motivated and intellectually gifted representatives of the bourgeoisie to serve as leaders of the working class movement. Only they could render the movement effective.

To recognize the role of ethical considerations in moving human beings to action would not be "irrational." The recognition would reflect the results of the scientific appraisal of human conduct. It was essentially the same kind of account one finds in V. I. Lenin's turn-of-the-century analysis of revolution.[51]

In substance, Michels argued that social change requires that men, under specific circumstances, opt for a course of revolutionary action. The pursuit of revolutionary action, in turn, could only be immediately motivated by ethical and ideal impulses.[52] Whatever the remote, or ultimate, cause of individual or collective action, it was clear to Michels that ethical and moral sentiment constituted its proximate cause.

For Michels, orthodox Marxists seemed to argue that the economy, "in the last analysis," was in some real and exclusive sense, the ultimate determinant of historic development and social change. Michels agreed that economic factors were of critical importance in understanding historic, social, and political events, but he denied that there could be any scientific sense in insisting that, in some obscure "final analysis," economic factors were the ultimate determinants of those events.[53]

Michels argued that Engels, years after Marx's death, had radically modified the "materialist conception of history" by allowing that in history "there are...innumerable dynamic tendencies, which cross each other reciprocally, an infinite series of parallelograms of the forces out of which, as a result, the historic happening springs."[54] As a consequence, Michels maintained, Engels had, in substance, denied the "ultimate" importance of economic variables in historical development. Economic variables were but one set among an indeterminate number of other causal variables.

In his analysis of revolution, Michels continued to maintain, throughout his active life, that economic circumstances provided the preconditions for massive social change, but he went on to indicate that an indeterminate number of other factors contributed to the success of the outcome. Michels insisted that "man is not an economic counter. His life is a continuous struggle among economic necessities, a social stratum to which he belongs, and a conceded traditional sphere of interests and duties on one side. On the other side, impulses which stand, so to speak, above and perhaps beyond his material and social position may arouse in his heart passions likely to divert him from his natural economic course and to give his activity another direction, sometimes even utopian in nature."[55] In effect, Michels denied that class provenance determined moral conscience, or that the commitment of human beings as the automatic consequence of material interests.

In point of fact, much of Michel's subsequent work constituted an attempt to identify, isolate, and analyze those factors, neglected by orthodox Marxists, that influence the outcome of revolutionary events. His major works, essentially his *Zur Soziologie des Parteiwesens* and his "Psychologie der antikapitalistischen Massenbewegungen," are extended analyses of the factors influencing the origin, growth, and political efficacy of the European, working-class, revolutionary movement.

Michels not only significantly modified the orthodox Marxist interpretation of history, he argued that the orthodox Marxist had neither a clear conception of the psychology of masses nor an understanding of the basic principles of revolutionary organization. Michels maintained that the Marxists of his time failed to understand that the immediate impulse to action among men originated in ethical or ideal sentiment—without which men lapse back into a form of apolitical torpor.[56]

Orthodox Marxists, he argued, had made the mistake of attempting to eliminate the influence of ethical considerations among men by pretending to make their socialism exclusively "scientific." Karl Kautsky's *Ethik und materialistische Geschichtsauffassung*, for example, had succeeded in making ethics and moral sentiment by-products, epiphenomena, of economic factors—and had thereby reduced their efficacy as a mass-mobilizing force.

The young V. I. Lenin, while still an orthodox Marxist, could argue that Marxism "did not contain a grain of ethics from beginning to end"[57]—a conviction that cast itself athwart the behaviors of an untold number of Marxists throughout the twentieth century, who insisted that they were guided by moral concerns and ethical principle. It would be hard to find a single Marxist leader in the twentieth century who did not insist that his behaviors were governed by moral considerations.

Michels insisted that to read an amoral determinism into history was, in fact, to divest human agents of the will to action. He maintained that the entire notion of economic determinism was not only scientifically inadequate, but was counterproductive in terms of the revolutionary mobilization of masses.[58]

The masses, without the animation provided by a missionary ideal, would succumb to the influence of their most immediate, factional, and debased interests. Leaders, incapable of energizing the masses with uplifting ideals, would themselves lapse to the level of the insensitivity and amorality of the masses. Revolutionary organizations would become increasingly compromissary and "conservative," serving whatever material and parochial interest promised organizational survival and tenure for the organization's bureaucracy.

Michels conceived his revolutionary syndicalism as both a scientific adjunct to Marxist theory and a corrective to Marxist organizational pretenses. Like many of the most prominent of the syndicalists of the period before the First World War, Michels maintained that orthodox Marxism had not developed a competent theory of individual or collective psychology.[59] The absence of such theory constituted not only a theoretical embarrassment, it left the revolutionary movement without guidance with respect to mass-mobilization and mass organization. Michels argued that classical Marxism was incapable of accounting for individual or collective human behaviors—and any social theory deficient in that respect could neither by considered competent for explanatory nor predictive purposes, or serve as a guide for revolutionaries organizing large numbers of men for revolution.

Michels' assessment, like that of the syndicalists of his time, was influenced by the work of such notables as Gabriel Tarde, Gustave Le Bon, Scipio Sighele as well as Vilfredo Pareto. All had argued that men could only be set into motion by appeals to "ideal," as distinct from simple material, interests.

The syndicalists, Michels among them, further maintained that any pursuit of simple material interest must necessarily be divisive. The proletariat in the armaments factories seek to defend their jobs and their standard of living; those in non-armaments-related industries want a reduction of government expenditure on military hardware; those in the textile mills insist on tariff protection against free-trade competition; those involved in the export trade want a reduction in tariffs in the effort to reduce the probability of retaliation by their export counter-parts. On the other hand, a "grand mission," a commitment to an "he-roic enterprise," provides the sentimental ligaments that securely bind a collection of persons together in common purpose. Shared struggle, inspired by a collective vision of a possible future, together with in-volvement in a common belief-system, can unite the most disparate collection of men.

"Sentiment," "ideals" and "faith" must be understood to be critical components in any scientific effort to understand society, politics, revo-lution and their mutual interaction. Moreover, revolutionary organiza-tion and tactics require a clear understanding of the fact that persons are moved to common political struggle through the medium of collec-tively felt sentiment and ideals.

Throughout his active intellectual life Michels argued these theses. As early as 1903, he was defending these arguments against the "re-formists" in the German Social Democratic ranks—and long after his entry into the ranks of Fascism, in his "Psychologie der antikapital-istischen Massenbewegungen," he made a spirited defense of them. Nor is all this in the least surprising. Mussolini, a contemporary of Michels, followed essentially the same intellectual trajectory, carried the same convictions into Fascism, and persisted in their defense throughout his active revolutionary and intellectual life.

As early as 1905, as we have seen, the young Mussolini identified himself with the current of ideas associated with French and Italian syndicalism. Like Michels, the young Mussolini conceived syndical-ism to be a saving supplement to the orthodox Marxism of his time. With Sorel and Michels, the young Mussolini lamented the disposition on the part of Socialist Party theoreticians to read a kind of fatalistic automaticity into the revolutionary processes they anticipated.[60] Mussolini maintained that there could be no simple "formulae" gov-erning the process of revolution. The commitment to revolution, in fact, was predicated not on the scientific study of revolution, but on the "moral reality" that inspired human beings to pursue it as an "alternative."[61] Mussolini, as a consequence, identified himself as a revolutionary "ro-mantic" and a "sentimentalist"—because he insisted that "psychology has demonstrated that sentiments constitute the dynamic motives of human action."[62] Since such was the case, he argued, the success of socialist ideas could only be assured if socialist leadership could effec-tively influence "the torpid consciousness of the working masses" by inspiring in them an irrepressible revolutionary sentiment. By 1908, he identified revolutionary potential with the availability of a "proletarian elite" possessed of a suitable collection of mass-mobilizing political ideas—notions of revolutionary mobilization he expressly identified with the convictions of Vilfredo Pareto.

Pareto, in his *I sistemi socialisti*, had argued that revolution is the function of the availability of a contending elite possessed of a mass-mobilizing "faith." History was, in fact, "nothing more than a succession of just such elites."[63]

The young Mussolini, like Michels, had made recourse not only to Pareto, but to the works of Gustave Le Bon,[64] and sought to supplement orthodox Marxism with the insights gleaned from the contemporary social psychology and the social science of his time. Again like Michels and the revolutionary syndicalists, the young Mussolini had little confidence that parliamentary maneuvering and the pursuit of votes could further the revolutionary process. In his review of Werner Sombart's *Sozialismus und soziale Bewegung im neunzehnten Jahrhundert*, Mussolini identified the tutelary task of the "vigilant vanguard" of the proletariat as that of "preparing the consciousness" of the masses for revolution.

The proposed revolutionary vanguard elite, the advance guard of the "new men" of the twentieth century, must foster the real, rather than the immediate, interests of the revolutionary masses. Only in such fashion could the elemental energy of number, quantity, be transformed into a qualitatively significant revolutionary force. What the masses needed was an animating "myth," a missionary "faith." "...Mankind," Mussolini asserted, "has need of a faith. It is faith that moves mountains...."[65]

Predicated on prevailing economic and political reality, faith captures the sentiment of broad segments of the revolutionary mass. The mass must find militants, apostles, and evangelists to lead them.[66] Such a vanguard elite would effectively marshall and organize the meager energies of isolated individuals into an integrated collective force, united around "moral incentives," and grounded in a felt solidarity of interests. Such a conception of the organizational, mass-mobilizing, and moral prerequisites of successful revolutionary tactics the youthful Mussolini identified as "a new socialist conception which was profoundly 'aristocratic.'"[67] Fascism grew out of the left-wing convictions of Michels and the radical revolutionary syndicalists.

These convictions concerning the role of elites, mass-mobilization, and mass organization, which Mussolini shared with, and in part learned from, Michels, remained constant throughout his life. In 1932, for example, in his conversations with Emil Ludwig, Mussolini, then the "Duce" of Italy, repeated those same convictions.[68] He spoke of the masses as a source of the elemental energy that must needs be fashioned into revolutionary force through the employment of myth, and choreographed through the use of ritual, symbol, and uniform—all the techniques, in fact, now regularly invoked by mass-mobilizing revolutionaries of both left and right.

The ready recourse to the "grand anti-imperialist, and anti-capitalist mission," the employment of flags, slogans, and symbolic speech, the inculcation of "moral incentives" through slogans and political catechisms, the prevalence of uniforms and military models, are all more than reminiscent of Michels' tactical suggestions, and exemplify the mobilizing techniques of Mussolini's Fascism. Those suggestions and those techniques grew out of Michels' syndicalist critique of classical Marxism.

It was Michels, as a Fascist ideologue, who provided the rationale for all such employments. While modern revolutionaries, the most left-wing among them, are often loathe to acknowledge, in fact, what they do in practice, Michels attempted an explicit defense of what was then standard practice among Fascists.

More than that, Michels' criticism of the Marxism of his time marked the first phase of a progressive ideological development that was not to conclude with the recognition of the impact of sentiment and "myth" in the mobilization and organization of revolutionary masses. His analysis, like that of Mussolini, was to ultimately address itself to alternative mythic constituents—to sentiments other than those of class—that could be tapped in the effort to conjure up and organize the revolutionary energies necessary for the vast social changes of our time.

Very early in his intellectual career, in a process remarkably similar to that which shaped the political convictions of Benito Mussolini, Michels identified *nationalism* as one of the most potent sentiments that might well animate the masses of the twentieth century. As a consequence, his, and Mussolini's, original Marxist persuasions were to undergo still further change—to ultimately produce not only the belief system of Fascism, but the rationale for revolution in our time.

Notes

1. Dennis Mack Smith has insisted that Fascism had no doctrine. Fascism was nothing else but a "technique for winning power...." It was a "force to be reckoned with in politics, but not as a body of beliefs to be taken seriously." Dennis Mack Smith, *Mussolini: A Biography* (New York: Vintage, 1983), pp. 138, 139.

2. Frederick G. Engelmann identifies Michels' volume on political parties as one of the two foremost works on the sociology of political parties written in the first half of the century. See F. G. Engelmann, "A Critique of Recent Writings on Political Parties," in H. Eckstein and David Apter (eds.), *Comparative Politics: A Reader* (New York: The Free Press, 1963), p. 378.

3. See the introduction to the Italian edition of *La sociologia del partito politico* (Bologna: Il Mulino, 1966) by Juan Linz, "Michels e il suo contributo alla sociologia politica," pp. vii–cxix. See also the general treatment of Michels as a "theoretician of the elite" in G. Parry, *Political Elites* (New York: Praeger, 1969), chaps. 1 and 2.

4. Roberto Michels, *Italien von Heute* (Leipzig: Orell Fuessli, 1930), particularly part III, and *Corso di sociologia politica* (Milan: Istituto Editoriale Scientifico, 1927).

5. See W. Roehrich, *Robert Michels: Vom sozialistisch-syndikalistischen zum faschistischen Credo* (Berlin: Duncker & Humblot, 1972), pp. 10f.

6. See F. Pfetsch, *Die Entwicklung zum faschistischen Fuehrerstaat in der politischen Philosophie von Robert Michels* (Heidelberg: Philosophischen Fakultaet der Ruprecht-Karl Universitaet, 1964).

7. H. Stuart Hughes went so far as to suggest that Mussolini "may simply not have heard of [Michels]." H. S. Hughes, *Consciousness and Society* (New York: Collier, 1958), p. 272.

8. Mussolini wrote a contemporary review of Michels' 1909 work on *Cooperazione*. See B. Mussolini, "Fra libri e riviste," *Opera omnia* (Florence: La fenice, 1951–1963. Hereafter referred to as *Opera*.), 2, pp. 248–249.

9. Paolo Orano, "Roberto Michels: l'amico, il maestro, il camerata," in *Studi in memoria di Roberto Michels* (Padua: CEDAM, 1937), pp. 9–14.

10. Cf. R. Michels, "Werner Sombart," *Bedeutende Maenner* (Leipzig: Quelle & Meyer, 1927), pp. 9–14.

11. Cf. R. Michels, "Eine syndikalistisch gerichtete Unterstroemung im deutschen Sozialismus (1903–1907)," in *Festschrift fuer Carl Gruenberg zum 70 Geburtstag* (Leipzig: Hirschfeld, 1932), pp. 343–364, and "Le Syndicalisme et le Socialisme en Allemagne," in *Syndicalisme & Socialisme* (Paris: Riviere, 1908).

12. R. Michels, *Il proletariato e la borghesia nel movimento socialista italiano* (Turin: Bocca, 1908).

13. *Ibid.* pp. 369, 372.

14. Cf. *Ibid.*, p. 392.

15. Michels, "Le Syndicalisme et le Socialisme en Allemagne," *op. cit.*, p. 23.

16. Michels, *Il proletariato...*, p. 395.

17. Michels, "Begriff und Aufgabe der 'Masse,'" in *Das freie Wort*, 2 (1903), pp. 408f.17.

18. *Ibid.*, p. 410, cf. *Il proletariato...*, pp. 28f.

19. Cf. A. O. Olivetti, *Questioni contemporanee* (Naples: Partenopea, 1913), p. 11; A. Labriola, "Da Sindacalismo e riformismo," in R. Melis, *Sindacalisti italiani* (Rome: Volpe, 1964), pp. 46f.

20. A. O. Olivetti, "I sindacalisti e la elite," *Pagine libere*, July 1, 1909.

21. Michels, *Il proletariato...*, p. 33. A similar case can be made of the Marxism of Lenin. By the time he wrote *What Is To Be Done?* Lenin understood revolution to be a function of a professional vanguard leadership. See A. James Gregor, *A Survey of Marxism* (New York: Random House, 1965), chap. 6.

22. Michels, "Eine syndikalistisch gerichtete Unterstroemung im deutschen Sozialismus," pp. 350f; cf. G. Volpe, *Italia in cammino* (Rome: Volpe, 1973), pp. 120ff.

23. Cf. A. J. Gregor, "The Ideology of Fascism," in G. Weinberg (ed.), *The Transformation of a Continent* (Minneapolis: Burgess, 1975), pp. 257–267, and *L'ideologia del fascismo* (Rome: Il Borghese, 1974), chap. 3.

24. Cf. for example, Mussolini, "La gente nuova," "Ne l'attesa," "Pagine rivoluzionarie: 'Le parole d'un rivoltoso'," "Intorno alla notte del 4 Agosto," "L'attuale momento politico," "Intermezzo polemico," *Opera*, 1, pp. 19f., 40f., 50–53, 62, 120, 128. Cf. Mussolini, "Fra libri e riviste," *Opera*, 2, 248–249. Michels' essay, "L'uomo economico e la cooperazione," was republished as chapter 2 of his *Saggi economico-statistici sulle classi popolari* (Milan: Sandron, 1919).

25. Michels, "Eine syndikalistisch gerichtete Unterstroemung im deutschen Sozialismus," p. 350.

26. Michels, "Begriff und Aufgabe der 'Masse,'" p. 410.

27. Michels, "L'oligarchia organica costituzionale," reprinted in *Studi sulla democrazia e sull'autorità* (Florence: La nuova Italia, 1933), pp. 8f.

28. A. Labriola, *Riforme e rivoluzione sociale* (Naples: Partenopea), pp. 8 and 9.

29. G. Sorel, *Reflections on Violence* (Glencoe: The Free Press, 1956), pp. 87f., 106, 201, 247, 253. Cf. P. Pastori, *G. Sorel: Le illusioni della democrazia* (Rome: Volpe, 1973).

30. Sorel, "Unity and Multiplicity," in *Reflections on Violence*, p. 298.

31. Mussolini, "Lo sciopero generale e la violenza," *Opera*, 2, 163–168.

32. Cf. Mussolini, "Fra libri e riviste," *Opera*, 2, 248–249.

33. Cf. Linz, *op. cit.*, p. xvii; cf. J. D. May, "Democracy, Organization, Michels," *American Political Science Review*, 59, 2(June, 1965), pp. 417f.

34. Michels, *La Sociologia*, p. 413.

35. *ibid.*, p. 528.

36. *Ibid.*, p. 321.

37. Cf. Michels, *Il proletariato...*, p. 365, *La sociologia...*, pp. 486f.

38. Michels, *Il proletariato...*, p. 390.

39. Michels, *La sociologia...*, p. 486.

40. *Ibid.*, p. 497f.

41. *Ibid.*, pp. 497f.

42. Michels, "L'uomo economico...," pp. 45f., *La sociologia...*, pp. 55f., "La democrazia e la legge ferrea delle elites," *Studie sulla democrazia e sull'autorità*, p. 31.

43. Michels, *Il proletariato...*, p. 372.

44. Michels, "La democrazia e la legge ferrea delle elites," p. 41.

45. Michels, *Corso di sociologia...*, pp. 45ff.

46. *Ibid.*, p. 532.

47. Michels, "Some Reflections on the Sociological Character of Political Parties," *American Political Science Review*, 21, 4 (November 1927), 753–772.

48. Cf. E. Gentile, *Le origini dell'ideologia fascista* (Bari: Laterza, 1975), p. 402.

49. Cf. Michels, "Zur Ethik des Klassenkampfes," *Ethische Kultur*, 12, 3 (1904).

50. Cf. Michels discussion in "Eine syndikalistisch gerichtete Unterstroemung im deutschen Sozialismus (1903–1907)," and "Psychologie der antikapitalistischen Massenbewegungen," in *Grundriss der Sozialoekonomie* (Tübingen: Mohr, 1926).

51. See the discussion in Gregor, *A Survey of Marxism*, pp. 210–226.

52. Michels, *Il proletariato...*, pp. 22, 33f., 369, 374.

53. Cf. Michels, "Zum Problem: Wirtschaft und Politik," in *Probleme der Sozialphilosophie* (Leipzig: Teubner, 1914), reproduced as "Intorno al problema dei rapporti tra economia e politica," in *Problemi di sociologia applicata* (Turin: Bocca, 1919), and as "The Relation of Economic Events to Personality and Politics," in *First Lectures in Political Sociology* (New York: Harper & Row, 1965).

54. Engels, letter to J. Bloch, September 21–22, 1890. Cf. Michels, *First Lectures...*, p. 18; *Probleme...*, pp. 189f.

55. Michels, *First Lectures...*, p. 27.

56. *Ibid.*, pp. 301f.

57. V. I. Lenin, "The Economic Content of Narodism and the Criticism of It in Mr. Struve's Book," *Collected Works*, 1, pp. 420f.

58. Michels, "Die Deutsche Sozialdemokratie im Internationalen Verbande," *Archiv*, 25, 1 (1907), p. 230.

59. The intellectual crisis that settled down on orthodox Marxism between the death of Engels and the advent of the First World War is discussed in some detail in A. J. Gregor, *The Fascist Persuasion in Radical Politics* (Princeton, N.J.: Princeton University Press, 1974), chap. 4.

60. Cf. Werner Sombart's comments in a book familiar to Mussolini, *Sozialismus und soziale Bewegung im neunzehnten Jahrhundert* (Jena: Fischer, 1897), chap. iv.

61. Cf. Mussolini, "La necessità della politica socialista in Italia," and "La gente nuova," in *Opera*, 1, pp. 15, 19.

62. Mussolini, "Ne l'attesa," *ibid.*, pp. 40f.

63. Mussolini, "La crisi resolutiva," and his later "Karl Marx," *ibid.*, pp. 70, 103. Cf. also Mussolini, "Dopo l'eccidio di Roma," "L'attuale momento politico," and "Intermezzo polemico," *ibid.*, 1, pp. 115, 120, 128.

64. Years later Mussolini was to indicate that as a student at Forlimpopoli he had entertained an "intense interest in the psychology of human masses—the crowd," and that "one of the books that interested me most was the *Psychology of the Crowd* by Gustave Le Bon." Mussolini, *My Autobiography* (London: Paternoster, 1936), pp. 25, 36.

65. Mussolini, "Da Guicciardini a... Sorel," *Opera*, 4, 174.

66. Mussolini, "L'attuale momento politico," *ibid.*, I, pp. 119–122.

67. Cf. Mussolini, "Socialismo e movimento sociale nel secolo XIX," "Pagine rivoluzionarie, 'Le parole d'un rivoltoso,'" "'Monnetier,' (La culla dei Savoia)," "Intorno alla notte del 4 Agosto," "Per Ferdinando Lassalle," "Opinioni e documenti: la crisi risolutiva," *ibid.*, pp. 44f., 51f., 57, 62, 65, 70.

68. E. Ludwig, *Colloqui con Mussolini* (Milan: Mondadori, 1932), pp. 119ff.

4

Roberto Michels, Nationalism and Corporativism

Michels' reform of Marxist theory proceeded throughout his young manhood. Critical to that reform was his assessment of the motivating role of revolutionary ideals and their predication on felt sentiment on the part of masses.

Initially, Michels conceived that the felt sentiment that would fuel revolutionary activity in his time was the product of life and struggle shared by workers in "proletarian associations." Proletarian associations were "communities of destiny," in which workers shaped their lives and anticipated their future.

As has been suggested, in the years between the commencement of the twentieth century and the First World War, all that was to change. Events seemed to overwhelm the revolutionary proletarian organizations so carefully put together by syndicalist leaders. Michels understood the entire process. He had lived through it and had attempted its analysis.

By the end of the First World War, Michels provided an analysis of the abiding sentiments that had apparently animated many Italians— and those sentiments were far from "proletarian" in any meaningful sense. If the sentiments were non-proletarian, the revolutionary ideas intended to inspire masses could hardly be proletarian. Michels was compelled by the logic of his own analysis to significantly modify or abandon proletarianism.

What emerged from Michels' analysis was a recognition that the sentiment of nationality—nationalism—was the psychological foundation not only for moral ideals, but the basis for the articulation of a practical guide to the resolution of urgent contemporary problems. Michels' analysis of nationalism as the animating myth of the revolution of the twentieth century remains arresting, far better than anything found in traditional Marxism.

Classical Marxism never delivered itself of a competent analysis of nationalism. Michels attempted just that. It was to serve as the center-piece of Fascist ideology.

Michels and Nationalism

Like the Marxists of his time, Michels originally assumed that the identification of workers with their "proletarian" organizations provided the basis for systemic revolution. It was the nature of those revolutionary organizations, and the critical role of leadership, that constituted the core of Michels' preoccupations in his most important works. Nonetheless, he early touched on an issue that was to transform his analysis.

He very early gave evidence of an interest in the nature and function of nationalism as a mobilizing sentiment. As early as 1903, for example, Michels attempted a treatment of nationalism and national sentiment that would make both compatible with the proletarian internationalism that presumably animated the syndicalism of his time.[1]

Michels recognized that human beings, in general, were disposed to organize themselves in communities of restricted size, to identify with others with whom they shared geographic, cultural, economic, and sentimental interests. He recognized, with Pareto, that men were animated by group-building impulses—that human groups tended to organize themselves in self-regarding communities, and that the nature and extent of those communities were determined by historic circumstances.

In the modern world, one of the communities in which men were in fact organized, was the historic nation-state. One form in which group-building dispositions, in such circumstances, manifest themselves is as an exclusive and tendentially xenophobic national sentiment. Michels recognized the contemporary intensity such a sentiment might assume, and sought some way in which that sentiment might be effectively integrated into the "internationalism" that animated the Marxist revolutionaries of the turn of the century.

Because national allegiance was so forceful a sentiment, Michels argued that an effective internationalism would have to make suitable accommodation for it. To fail to do so might cause necessary revolutionary energies to be channeled into nationalism at the cost of proletarianism.

Thus, as early as 1903, Michels recognized the mobilizing character of nationalism and national sentiment. He conceived nationalism as a force that would have to be both acknowledged and accommodated if internationalism was to constitute a viable option for the future.

At that time and in that respect, Michels shared with the young Mussolini the same convictions concerning the relationship of national sentiment and theoretical internationalism. As early as 1905, the young Mussolini had spoken, without embarrassment, of his own national sentiments.

In that year, in a letter to Captain Achille Simonetti, Mussolini had spoken with pride of Italian heroes who had "with their blood, cemented the unity of the fatherland"—and he went on to maintain that Italians must be prepared to defend their homeland against anyone who might attempt to reduce Italy, once again, to a "geographic expression."[2] As we have seen, the young Mussolini early recognized that men were moved to political action not only by economic factors, but by "moral sentiments." Some of those sentiments arose out of a sense of community born of "blood, geography... and intellectual interests...."[3]

Later, when Mussolini found himself in the Trentino, he was compelled to attempt to integrate his convictions concerning *national* sentiment with his *internationalist* convictions—and the resolution he sought was in terms similar to those found in the early work of Michels. Thus, Mussolini spoke of recreating an Italian "national spirit" adequate to the demands of a new age.[4] He spoke of an Italian national sentiment that would be "encompassed" in an internationalist "grand dream of brotherhood."[5] Within that internationalism, he advocated the maintenance of the "ideal integrity of the nation," recognizing its "historic and moral rights...."[6]

Thus, while internationalist in intention, both Michels and Mussolini argued, while still convinced Marxists, that a viable internationalism must provide a place for the natural group sentiment that found expression in nationalism. Such convictions were predicated on a recognition that men are naturally disposed to organize themselves in selected communities with which they share common cultural and historic traits. When the young Mussolini reviewed Michels' treatise on *Cooperazione* in 1909, for example, he specifically alluded to the general disposition among men to identify with a community of restricted size—to share with that community sentiments of belonging, and to display diffidence with respect to out-groups or members of alien communities.[7]

It is clear that the group building disposition to which both the young Mussolini and Michels alluded was a *general* disposition. The groups into which individuals tend to organize themselves vary —they might be familial, tribal, or national—or they might be groups drawn together by immediate economic and material interests. Whatever the case, all such groups were understood to be animated by group sentiments, an affection for group members, a diffidence toward out-group members, a readiness to sacrifice for the community, as well as a commitment to intragroup discipline and unity.

Michels addressed himself to the group-building properties of men in many places, and it seems reasonably clear that he was prepared to treat the human disposition to organize into self-regarding and exclusive communities of mutual support as a "residue," a natural inclination generic to all human beings.[8] Michels employed the concept of "residue" in much the same fashion as had Pareto.

A "residue" was a disposition or predisposition to behave in a certain fashion. Human beings, in Pareto's judgment, had many such dispositions—among them group-building dispositions that included those that found overt expression in solidarity and cooperation. It seems clear that Michels treated in-group amity and cooperation, and out-group hostility and diffidence, as expressions of generic human dispositions. Such dispositions variously manifested themselves as family-feeling, religious and class sentiment, as well as national consciousness.

While it is evident that class-consciousness was a critical concern for Michels (as it was for the young Mussolini), it is equally evident that national-consciousness ultimately became of no less importance. In the introduction to *Zur Soziologie des Parteiwesens*, Michels indicated that the "principle of nationality" was of "undeniable" importance in understanding our epoch—and that the problems surrounding "nationality" have always been "inherent" in human psychology.[9] In his essay on *L'imperialismo italiano*, Michels reminded his readers that he had occupied himself with the problems of the "fatherland" and "nationality" for "many years."[10] In fact, the same human properties that fostered *class* consciousness among the proletariat, produced among members of the national community a national consciousness that found expression in nationalism.

By 1914, Michels was prepared to argue that national sentiment was an independent determinant among the complex of factors that influenced human political behavior.[11] Ultimately, Michels (like Mussolini) was to insist that the resolution of contemporary social problems could not be accomplished with the neglect of the potent sentiment of nationality. He insisted that modern populations, however much they were moved by class sentiments and class-solidarity, responded to national sentiments and national consciousness as well.[12] In fact, under certain conditions, the masses, moved by suitable political invocation, responding to collective suggestion, make national sentiment the principal historic determinant.[13]

At a time when socialists had made a fetish of their anti-nationalism and their "proletarian internationalism," Michels reminded them that socialism bore within itself a long tradition of nationalism. He reminded them of the "patriotic socialism" of the martyred Carlo Pisacane. He reminded them of the patriotism of the Paris communards. Although the socialists of Italy had made a political point of renouncing national sentiment, he urged them to remember that Pisacane and the early Italian revolutionaries had forever linked nationalism and socialism in the sentiment of Italians.[14]

Michels saw in Pisacane's revolutionary convictions a prefiguration of an emerging "national socialism." Pisacane had recognized the significance of economic variables in the mobilization of men, but he also recognized the undeniable significance of ideals—among which national ideals played a critical role.

Pisacane had argued that the resolution of material problems required the mobilization of men whose immediate material interests were not always compatible. Only by appealing to some broader and more inclusive interests, could all potentially revolutionary forces be mobilized. Those interests were to be found in the nation, the infrangible and irreducible common substratum of collective contemporary interest.

In the modern world, Italy, as a nation, was disadvantaged in the international competition for place and succorance. It constituted a "great proletariat" in a contest with advantaged and wealthy opponents.[15] Only a *national* socialism could unite all the forces for social change available on the peninsula.

The theme of a national, as distinct from an intransigently international, socialism became a recurrent item in the works of Michels after Italy's war in Tripoli in 1911. Michels' volume, *L'imperialismo italiano*—written on the occasion of that war— constitutes a catalog of the reasons moving Italy to take up arms in that conflict. The book was, in fact, treated by contemporaries as an argued defense of "Italy's proletarian nationalism."[16]

True to his convictions, Michels argued that Italy's entry into the war of 1911 had been the consequence of a constellation of material interests—demographic, strategic, economic, and cultural—but the final determinant had been an all-pervasive sense of nationalist urgency shared by vast strata of the population, including the "international" working class. In Michels' judgment, Italy's war in Tripoli found its origins in the sentiments shared by Italians that their nation had been denied a proper and equitable place in the sun. Italy's war was the consequence of a reactive national sense of inadequacy and inferiority in the face of advantaged and privileged nations. Italy, a nation only recently politically united, weak in terms of industrial capability and resources, at last demanded the pride of place its civilization and culture had long since earned for it.

The war in Tripoli had awakened many Italians to the fact that their future was inextricably bound up in the future of their nation. The nation had become the ultimate repository of their loyalty. In its service the most radical revolutionaries, the syndicalists, had abandoned the factitious internationalism that had divided them from their conationals.[17]

For Michels the conjunction of economic and demographic needs and the manifestation of a pervasive sense of outrage suffered by a community of men long treated as inferiors by the privileged nationalities of Europe, had kindled an irrepressible national sentiment among Italians.[18] National sentiment had become the common denominator for the collective life-interests of men who might otherwise pursue more immediate and sometimes incompatible concerns.[19] Group pride, born of group struggle, had animated the population of an entire political community.

After the war in Tripoli, the First World War further convinced Michels of the correctness of his analysis. In the future, Michels argued, nationalism, and the sentiment which accompanied it, would have to figure in any revolutionary calculation.[20] Only men incapable of learning from the most self-evident experience could fail to understand that fact.[21]

To drive home these points Michels devoted a considerable part of his research efforts to the analysis of patriotism as a contemporary political, revolutionary, and psychological reality. His *Der Patriotismus: Prologomena zu einer soziologischen Analyse* constitutes a major effort at sociological analysis. In that volume Michels undertook an extended exposition of the genesis, character and ultimate impact of national sentiment on the mobilization of men. Michels argued, in an exposition that is at once extremely relevant, almost prescient, that national sentiment serves to overcome the sense of inferiority and incompetence that afflicts entire communities of men in the hard competition that characterizes the modern world.[22] Nationalism, as a mobilizing sentiment, steels the population of a politically defined aggregate to defend its integrity and assure its survival. It is a sentiment often invoked in "wars of liberation" against "oppressor nations" that impede the development and integrity of a community.

Nationalism unites a people in a grand and mythic mission. Every people mobilized by nationalist appeals conceives itself in the service of a "mission"—invested by history with a secular obligation. Quickened by such a conviction, masses are moved to selfless sacrifice and admirable discipline. The nation becomes a "charismatic object of loyalty" in which the individual is merged with a collectivity.[23] Great and demanding tasks can be thus undertaken, for they enlist the services of a united and inspired population. By the termination of the First World War Michels was convinced that national sentiment—patriotism—constituted a critically important revolutionary force.

Michels had early recognized that men were predisposed to identify themselves with associations of limited membership, drawn together by affinities in speech, opinion, physical appearance, culture, and geographic location. He also recognized that such group-building affinities were strengthened by competition with out-groups.

For a people circumstanced as the Italians were during the first two decades of the twentieth century, generic appeals to the nation's interests were intrinsically attractive. Italy was a poor and despised "proletarian" nation among its rich and powerful neighbors. Italian immigrant workers found themselves mistreated throughout Europe and the Western hemisphere, not because they were workers, but because they were Italians. Italy, devoid of industry and resources, was excluded from the serious political and diplomatic maneuverings of the "Great Powers" of the Continent. Every Italian, of whatever class and category, found himself disadvantaged, not because he was a worker, or an artisan, or an intellectual, but because he was an Italian.

In effect, nationalist appeals could address themselves to the most basic interests of all Italians irrespective of class provenance. Michels, like many of his syndicalist confreres, had already begun to understand that before the advent of the First World War. It was the advent of that war which brought the full reality of all these considerations home not only to Michels, but to the young Mussolini as well.

Thereafter all the arguments already articulated by Michels made their regular appearance in Mussolini's writings and speeches. The war had revealed the revolutionary character of national appeal. Men could be, and were, mobilized in the service of a "grand mission"—a mission that would ultimately involve the creation of a "new" and "greater" homeland. On the twenty-eighth of December, 1914, the young Mussolini reminded socialists that they had neglected the evident facts of mass psychology. In the same speech in which he referred to Michels by name, Mussolini told socialists that

> ...the nation has not disappeared. We used to think that it had been extinguished. Instead, we see it arise as a living thing, palpitating before us! One is compelled to understand...that class cannot obliterate the nation. Class is a collectivity predicated on common interest, but the nation is a history of sentiments, of traditions, of language, of culture, of consanguinity. One can graft class on the nation, but the one does not eclipse the other....One must examine [all questions] from both a socialist as well as a national point of view.[24]

In the ensuing months and years Mussolini spoke of employing the "myth" of the nation to conjure up the commitment and the sense of sacrifice that would transform backward Italy into a modern and powerful nation. He spoke of a "vanguard elite" capable of employing symbolic speech and mythic language to engage the elemental energies of the "multitudinous masses" of Italy, in the service of national redemption. He spoke of class, regional and special interests merging into the larger and more fundamental interests of the disadvantaged nation. And in the subsequent mobilization and orchestration of the Italian people Mussolini employed every tactic catalogued in the work of Roberto Michels.

The mass-mobilizing elites of Fascism were intransigent and struck those "heroic" poses that were to serve as mimetic models for the "masses." Symbols, ritual, and ceremony were employed to create the sense of unity and commitment. Uniforms, moral suasion, and ultimately the threat of violence, were used to generate a sense of involvement and collective identity.

In substance, during the period between the advent of the First World War and the organization of the Fascist movement in March 1919, the ideology of Fascism was put together out of constituents prefigured in the work of Roberto Michels. Fascism, in effect, made its revolution animated by as coherent and compelling an ideology as any modern revolutionary movement. In fact, nascent Fascism possessed an articulate and explicit ideology that involved both a specific political strategy and specific political tactics. While many revolutionary movements in the twentieth century have pretended to invoke the "proletariat" to make their revolution—in environments where there were no "proletarians"—and employed nationalist appeals while insisting on their "internationalism"—Fascism undertook its revolution with a clear comprehension and a public defense of both its tactics and intentions.

Almost every modern revolutionary movement in the twentieth century has employed analogues of Fascist tactics for the mobilization and organization of masses behind "vanguard elites" and "charismatic leaders." Almost all employ national symbols and slogans in their "wars of national liberation." Almost all insist that the interests of their "disadvantaged" and "anti-imperialist" nation absorbs the special interests of essentially all classes of their populations. Almost all conceive their revolution as "regenerating" a nation long underdeveloped or denied equity in competition with advantaged states. The "socialism" of modern revolutionary movements is essentially a "socialism" that advocates a collective commitment to national regeneration and economic development. In effect, and irrespective of what they are disposed to say, contemporary revolutionary movements are national in character and predicate mass-mobilization on national sentiment.

While many modern commentators recognize the function of "the nation" as a "charismatic object of loyalty," the source of allegiance and commitment, among the revolutionary populations of the contemporary world,[25] there are few treatments of "patriotism" as competent as that left us by Michels and employed by Fascism as part of its ideological rationale.

Ultimately, "patriotism," the sentiment of nationality, was to become central to Michels' analysis of contemporary revolution. Those workers' organizations that he had early seen as the seedbed of a new society were to be absorbed by institutions understood to represent not the proletariat, but the nation in its entirety. As a consequence, Michels came to conceive the "syndicates" of workers, in which he early had invested so much confidence, as cells of a more inclusive organic structure: the nation. That subordination found expression in Fascist "corporativism."

Corporativism in the Thought of Michels

Immediately before his death, the Istituto Nazionale Fascista di Cultura published Michels' modest *Cenni storici sui sistemi sindacali corporativi*. The monograph had few pretensions. Michels recognized the work as an "introductory effort," essentially historic in character and didactic in intention.[26] In point of fact, almost all of Michels' published work devoted to "corporativism" could be so characterized. This is true at least in part, because Michels' discussions concerning economics are, themselves, almost all exclusively descriptive and historical in character. In them, there is no sustained effort to formulate any specifically *theoretic* propositions. In fact, Michels seemed disposed to treat economic "theory" not as a catalog of scientific "truths," but rather as a function of the economic conditions and the economic requirements of any specific time.

In his *Introduzione alla storia delle dottrine economiche e politiche*, for example, Michels argued that economic theory takes its point of departure from prevailing economic conditions, but does not simply reflect those conditions. Economic theories of any given time necessarily take their point of departure from prevailing reality, but they also embody the aspirations of men as well.[27] Men formulate economic theory not only to summarize and anticipate experience but also to shape that experience to prescriptive ideals, in what Michels called the "triumph of the idea over matter."[28]

Given this interpretation of economic theory, it becomes understandable that Michels' treatment of corporativism was historic and prescriptive, rather than analytic and substantive, in character. Thus he divided economic theories into categories like "optimistic" and "pessimistic," into those that conceive a "positive" role for the state and those that treat the conception of the state "negatively."[29] Since at least some of the critical constituents of any economic theory are understood to be necessarily *normative* or *prescriptive*, Michels could hardly argue that any given economic theory is either simply "true" or "false."

Each economic theory might well contain true or false constituents, but the essential service of economic theory is to mobilize men to normative purpose. A theory that successfully accomplishes such purpose is more effective, more "functional." An economic theory must be as true as economic theory can be—but more than that, it must be effective.

By the time of his entry into the *Partito nazionale fascista*, Michels understood political behavior to be governed by a number of identifiable constants. As has been indicated, he was prepared to argue, for instance, that the effective governance of masses requires the leadership of an aggressive, competent and articulate elite. That elite could organize the masses behind a collection of political formulae—mobilizing myths—that would multiply energies and direct collective effort. Myths so employed evoke a sense of missionary zeal among the masses; they inspire citizens to the fulfillment of a grand design. Such myths, national in character, steel the resolve of hitherto apathetic masses, and instill confidence among those burdened by a sense of inadequacy and inferiority. Such myths, moreover and as a consequence, become the legitimizing "charter myths" that vindicate allegiance, obedience, and sacrifice.[30] They are most effective in those nations we now identify as "underdeveloped" or "less-developed"—relative to the more advanced nations of the earth.

It is clear that, for Michels, Italy was the "Great Proletariat," in fateful competition with the "plutocratic nations" of the world. What is equally clear was the fact that, for Michels, Italy had found its myth in the renovative and regenerative nationalist intentions of Fascism. Fascism had arisen out of that collective frustration that found Italy's potential impaired not only by its industrial backwardness and its lack of raw materials, but by the impostures of the "Great Powers."[31]

In order to begin to resolve its most pressing economic disabilities, postwar Italy required, in Michels' judgment, an abatement of the "class struggle"—a resolution of the conflict between entrepreneurs and workers—between capital and labor. What Italy required was the class collaboration that would produce an accelerating increment in overall productivity.[32] Given such a construal, the Fascist program of "class collaboration" was a functional requirement in view of the objective disabilities of the economy of the peninsula.

The nation had suffered a protracted incapacity to provide even a minimum subsistence for large numbers of its inhabitants. Italians had been forced to emigrate by the hundreds of thousands for decades.

After the First World War, inflation and business failures had further exacerbated the disabilities of the peninsula. Not only had the socialists failed to understand that Italy's most fundamental problems were problems surrounding the inadequacy of production, rather that those that attend maldistribution, they had further impaired production by fostering domestic class conflict.

As distinct from the "proletarianism" of the more orthodox socialists, Fascism not only understood the requirements of mass-mobilization, and political organization, but under the influence of the injunctions of Vilfredo Pareto and Maffeo Pantaleoni,[33] one of the "fundamental principles" of the movement became "productivism," a studied emphasis on industrial production.

Both Pareto and Pantaleoni had argued that socialism, with its emphasis on redistribution, had failed to appreciate the fact that the problems that beset most of the peoples of the world were not problems of distribution, but problems of production. As has been indicated, by the time of the founding meeting of the Fascist movement, in 1919, Mussolini had made the protection and fostering of industrial production one of the cardinal objectives of Fascist policy.[34] What inevitably followed was an emphasis on the collaboration of classes in the enterprise.

Like Mussolini, Michels conceived the abatement of class strife a necessary condition for Italian economic expansion and modernization. Only the collaborative integration of all the essential factors involved in production could meet the challenge of Italy's postwar renovation and expansion. All those involved in the productive process—manual, technical, clerical, and professional workers, as well as entrepreneurial personnel, financiers and those capable of providing the requisite investment capital—had to be effectively integrated under the auspices of the state.[35]

For Michels the liberal state, predicated on a concept of social atomism that conceived that government best which, in principle, governed least, was a state that could not meet the challenge of assuring Italy a place in the modern world. Michels insisted on the positive role of the "strong state" in the effort to overcome Italy's economic disabilities.[36]

The state would have to serve as the capstone in a hierarchically structured corporative organization of all the factors of production. The state would be the guarantor of social peace and class collaboration. It would authoritatively arbitrate disputes, allocate resources, stimulate selective industries, and expand and refurbish the economic infrastructure of the peninsula. In his *Italien von Heute*, Michels explicitly celebrated all that in the industrial expansion and the articulation of the air, road, rail, telegraphic and telephonic communications infrastructure of the Italian peninsula.[37]

In substance, Michels treated corporativism as a means to an end. Fascism was, for Michels, a "missionary movement," animated by a "grand myth"—the creation of a "Greater Italy." To the fulfillment of that purpose, the domestication and organization of all the factors of production were instrumental. For Michels, "corporativism" served that explicit function.

It is true that Michels spoke of corporativism as satisfying the demand for equity and social justice, but it seems clear that corporativism, for him, served instrumental purpose rather than intrinsic ends. In that sense corporativism remained, for Michels, "experimental"—a work in progress—characterized by its pragmatic and functional employments. Its features were not fixed.

Corporativism, in his judgment was, and for all intents and purposes would remain, "elastic" and "tentative."[38] Its principal function was to ensure the hegemonic dominance of the political state.

Michels, like many of Italy's syndicalists, recognized that orthodox socialism had failed to accord itself with the problems that beset industrially retarded nations in the modern world. Marx and Engels had spoken of socialist revolution as a function of advanced industrialization and the "withering away of the state."

For Marx and Engels, revolution was on the agenda for the advanced nations of Europe and North America. The syndicalists of Italy early recognized that if that were true, an industrially retrograde Italy would be left in the backwaters of contemporary history. Italy was an underdeveloped nation. Its population a "proletarian people."

The fact was that Italy's circumstances made traditional Marxism irrelevant. The "class enemies" of "proletarian Italy" were not its domestic industrial entrepreneurs, but the "plutocratic nations" that had denied Italy its place in the sun. By the time of the advent of the First World War, the Italian syndicalists had begun to make common cause with the nationalists of the peninsula who anticipated a revolutionary doctrine based on the rapid modernization and industrialization as the first requirement of any revolution in the twentieth century.[39] The effort involved in such an enterprise would provide the lineaments of the "grand mission" that Michels had anticipated as the mass-mobilizing myth of Italy's revolutionary elite. Corporativism provided its instrumental institutional structure.

Michels' nationalism transformed the syndicalist convictions of his youth. Like many other revolutionary syndicalists, Michels saw in Fascism the realization of his revolutionary aspirations. Like many other syndicalists, Michels had made the transit from syndicalism to Fascism without effort.

More often than not, the transfer of allegiance from proletarian syndicalism to statist corporativism has been considered a shift from the political left to the political right —a betrayal of the Enlightenment traditions of Europe's "revolutionary" nineteenth century. It is not at all clear that such a notion is entirely accurate.

Michels and the Nineteenth Century "Left-Wing" Tradition

In the past, the suggestion that Fascism shared any affinity whatsoever with the revolutionary traditions of the left succeeded in scandalizing almost everyone. Any argument suggesting such an affinity was greeted with derision.

The outrage and scandal notwithstanding, there is an unequivocal sense in which Fascism was, indeed, an heir of the revolutionary traditions of the left. In point of fact, the work of Michels very clearly traces the itinerary followed by many syndicalists from the radical left-wing to Fascism.

Almost half a century ago, J. L. Talmon published his *The Origins of Totalitarian Democracy* in which he made a persuasive case for the thesis that radicals both of the right and left (however one conceives the distinction) share affinities with the radical left-wing traditions of eighteenth- and nineteenth-century Europe. Beginning as early as the political thought of Jean-Jacques Rousseau, European revolutionaries entertained convictions that clearly made up not only some of the intellectual substructure of the political thought of Roberto Michels, but of Fascism's ideological rationale as well.[40]

Even the most casual reading of Rousseau's *Emile* and his *La Nouvelle Heloise* reveals that he was prepared to argue that the circumstances of the "civil state," in which men find themselves, requires a form of "behavioral engineering" in order to adapt citizens to a politically organized social existence. Rousseau conceived human beings, as human beings, as necessarily denizens of politically organized communities.

Rousseau conceived men, "by nature," disposed to pursue their immediate and self-centered passions in the "state of nature." The conditions governing the civil state require careful reeducation so that they might satisfy their natural needs in a manner compatible with a humanity without which they would remain something less than human.

For Rousseau, organized social life, the condition for true humanity, was understood to be animated by a "general will" that represented not the immediate interests of individuals or parochial interest groups, which were often divergent, but the "true" and "ultimate" interests of the politically organized community. In that community, the "*moi commun*," or "collective self," finds expression in the state which is the agent of the informing "general will." That will, as distinct from the factious and divisive immediate will of individuals and groups, is an expression of the collective will. The state expresses the general will—a will that is not befuddled by passion or moved by local or personal interest.

In order to assure the operation of the general, as distinct from the immediate, will, Rousseau argued that the state must necessarily assume *pedagogical* and *tutelary obligations* with regard to its citizens. For Rousseau, the state educates its citizens to their "true liberty," for liberty means freedom to act in accordance with one's ultimate and fully rational will—that is to say, to act in accordance with the general will. It is only the state that can assure an environment in which true liberty can obtain, for the state is the ultimate defense against the individual of collective pursuit of personal, class, or category interests to the detriment of the general will.

For Rousseau, the state was obliged to educate citizens to the recognition of their total involvement and identification with the political community in which they discover their true selves. Without the intercession of the pedagogical, tutelary, and fundamentally ethical state, individuals and groups would lapse back into the hostility of the "state of nature." The social engineering of the individualistic and self-centered personality of men requires a retraining of their competitive instincts in order to harness them to collective purpose. Education and law are the two principal tools available to the state for the making of the "civil man."

For Rousseau, the term "education" involved a host of public strategies that included the invocation of collective festivals, organized demonstrations, and the suppression of divisive and factional opinion, in order to foster collective sentiment, pride of citizenship, and a sense of collaborative unanimity. Statesmen, Rousseau warned the readers of the *Social Contract*, have regularly neglected the function of education, broadly understood, as a means of fostering the sense of collective communion. The task of political education was the creation of citizens who would will only that willed by the general will. Once properly educated, the individual, hitherto torn by selfish interests and personal concerns, would immerse himself in the full sentiment of participation in the corporative collective body politic. That collective body, and its general will, gave expression, for Rousseau, to man's "higher, or real self."

The purpose of political life is to recreate the individual. To make of him something "better," to produce a "higher self."

In effect, Rousseau's convictions can be read as not only totalitarian in intention, but infused with an intense moral urgency that lent them the properties of a secular religion. Rousseau's "civil religion" was no less than a recognition of that fact. Rousseau's state had pedagogical and tutelary obligations because that state was supremely moral or ethical. In order to fulfill its obligations, the state must necessarily represent that general will which is understood to be the ultimate ground of all individual and subsidiary group interests. Political parties that represented immediate and parochial interests could be, at best, obstructions to the realization of the general will—at their worst, they were malevolent forces of disruption.

These elements, antiliberal, antiparliamentarian, messianic, and to-talitarian, surfaced and resurfaced in the works of all the French revo-lutionaries throughout the eighteenth and nineteenth centuries. They are clearly discernible in the works of Morelly and Mably, in those of the Jacobins, and Babeuf. Among them all, there were appeals to the "unitary will," to plebiscitary rather than parliamentary democracy, to "vanguard elites" possessed of the true vision of society, and to the domestication of individual and class selfishness. There was, in effect, a remarkable continuity between the European revolutionary "left-wing" tradition and Fascism.

Such elements were only muted in the works of Marx and Engels. Both Marx and Engels, for example, conceived of a revolutionary soci-ety in which the interests of individuals would be *identical* with those of the collectivity. As early as 1845 Engels insisted that in the future "communist society...the interests of individuals do not conflict, but are identical....Public interests no longer differ from the interests of each individual."[41]

For Marx and Engels, the "general will," on which such an identity of interests would rest, was understood to be a function of basic eco-nomic processes. The "proletariat," for instance, as a consequence of economic development, would become the "vast majority" of the popu-lation, and with the abolition of private property, all men would share the same fundamental interests. The "inevitable" processes governing social and economic development would produce the collectivistic so-ciety in which "egoism" and "selfishness" would no longer divide men. The "proletariat" would have one common, sustaining interest. Society would be informed by a "general will." There would be no divisions in society; everyone acting in his own interest would act in the interest of all. There would be an effortless freedom, for all interests would be collective interests.

With the disintegration of classical Marxism upon the death of Engels in 1895, a number of alternative interpretations of "Marxist revolu-tion" settled down on the working class movement.[42] The "reformists" insisted that the "proletariat" failed to display the unanimity of "class consciousness" that Marx and Engels had conceived the byproduct of economic processes. As a consequence they argued that Marxists were committed to a policy of reform based on the variety of interests ex-pressed by the variety of classes and fragments of classes that pursued their parochial concerns in modern society. The "radical" and "revolu-tionary" Marxists, on the other hand, insisted that the "unanimity of class consciousness" that Marx had expected to be the automatic consequence of economic processes must be understood, rather, as a product of the intercession of a revolutionary "vanguard elite."

If the proletariat failed to share an integral collective spirit, in which the interests of each was the interest of all, it was because revolutionary leadership had failed to instill the requisite consciousness in the "proletariat." Ultimately, that task was to be the task of the revolutionary elite—and, ultimately, the task of the revolutionary state.

By the advent of the First World War, syndicalists had supplemented the argument with the recognition that in industrially less-developed communities, one could hardly expect a spontaneous commonality of purpose. In backward economic circumstances, material interests were diffuse, parochial and narrow. Agrarians had local and divers concerns and they were fundamentally different from the interests of entrepreneurs establishing infant industries and maintaining those that had already been established. The only way all those interests could be synthesized was through the agency of a revolutionary elite, committed to rapid economic and industrial growth, capable of mobilizing masses to collective purpose through myth, ceremony and ritual.

While V. I. Lenin had early rejected the notion that a uniform revolutionary spirit might grow spontaneously from the circumstances in which the "proletariat" found itself, it was the Fascist theoreticians that rounded out the argument with an acknowledgment of the role economic backwardness played in the process. It was Mussolini who was to become spokesman for the latter argument.

Like Lenin, Mussolini argued that a collective spirit of sacrifice and dedication could only by generated by a vanguard elite, employing every modern strategy of mass mobilization and indoctrination. Such leadership must "uplift" the consciousness that Marx had understood would be a simple "reflection" of economic conditions. Both Mussolini and Lenin, at approximately the same time, insisted that the masses, left to their own devices, would lapse into a pursuit of selfish and immediate interest—at the expense of more fundamental revolutionary interests. It was Mussolini, however, who linked the entire enterprise to economic and industrial development to the service of the nation's redemption.

Both Lenin's Bolsheviks and the Italian syndicalists argued that revolution required the effective mobilization, careful organization, and systematic education of the masses. Neither believed that the masses would spontaneously transcend local and selfish interest in the austere service of that unitary and collective interest understood to provide the foundation of the new society. That unitary and collective consciousness must necessarily be a product of the careful cultivation by a vanguard elite possessed of a clear insight into the course of human history. It was Fascism that tied all this together with late economic and industrial development—a connection made only much later by Marxist-Leninists in general.

Within that context, and out of a tradition that numbered Rousseau among its founders, Roberto Michels articulated a revolutionary strategy, and anticipated a revolutionary society, that was ultimately to provide the substance of the ideology of Fascism. It was within the reality of that revolutionary and developmental society that Michels conceived corporativism as instrument.

Michels was prepared to grant that the new society would be one predicated upon a consciousness of a community of interest in which individual self-interest would identify with the interests of the totality. Michels recognized that such a consciousness could only be the consequence of careful cultivation. Revolutionaries must necessarily appeal to the most general and diffuse interests of the mass. They must conjoin "ideal" and "sentimental" interests with the more specific "material" and "immediate" interests of the masses in order to generate the collective unanimity and mass ardor required by nationalist and developmental revolution.

By the end of the first world conflict, Michels was convinced that a sense of collective purpose could be fostered among the masses largely through the invocation of nationalist appeal. National interest was the most pervasive collective concern of the modern masses. A "secular religion," a dedication to the interests of the nation in its struggle for equity and justice in a modern competitive world, would provide the "ideal" ingredients of revolutionary mass-mobilization. Ideally, that purpose, the pursuit of justice and equity, should find its embodiment in a tribune, a "charismatic leader," who would articulate the "ultimate interests" of the collectivity—who could orchestrate the energy of the masses. Corporativism served as an instrumentality within that orchestration.

For Michels, modern mass-mobilizing revolutionary parties were those still animated by "grand ideals," by a "theoretical purity," capable of articulating a nation's most profound collective sentiments.[43] It was, for Michels, a missionary "ideal" that distinguished revolutionary mass-mobilizing movements from the liberal and parliamentary parties. The former represented the most profound and most exalted interests of men; the latter gave expression to the local, parochial, immediate and selfish interests of individuals and groups. The former re-shape and discipline the energies of men; the latter reflects their basest impulses. The former has a "grand purpose"—the uplift of the oppressed nation, the moral regeneration of its citizens—while the latter allows individuals to succumb to their most immediate and transitory impulses.

For Michels, corporativism was part of the entire panoply of institutional adjuncts to the education of masses to collective purpose. Corporativism, through its agencies, would "educate" both workers and entrepreneurs to their responsibilities to the state—a state that represented the ultimate "real" interests of all.

None of this was seen as anything other than the fulfillment of the most relevant expectations of the revolutionary nineteenth century. For Michels, Fascism—with its reactive nationalism, elitism, charismatic leadership, developmentalism, anti-parliamentarianism, and corporativism—was the only form that revolution might coherently assume in the twentieth century.

Notes

1. Michels, "Nationalismus, Nationalgefuehl, Internationalismus," *Das freie Wort* (Edited by M. Hennig. Frankfurter Verlag, 1903), pp.107–111; cf. "Der Internationalismus der Arbeiterschaft," *Ethische Kultur*, 12, 15 (August 1904), pp.113f.
2. Mussolini, letter dated February 26, 1905, *Opera omnia* (Milan: La fenice, (1951–1963. Hereafter referred to as *Opera.*), 1, 216.
3. Mussolini, "Per Ferdinand Lassalle," *ibid.*, 66.
4. Mussolini, "La voce," *Opera*, 2, p. 55.
5. Mussolini, "Lo sciopero dei cantonieri," *ibid.*, 196.
6. Mussolini, "Cicaiuolo," *ibid.*, 203.
7. Mussolini, "Fra libri e riviste," *ibid.*, 248f.
8. Cf. Michels, "Intorno ai problemi della solidarietà e della formazione delle caste," in *Problemi di sociologia applicata* (Turin: Bocca, 1919), pp. 15–37. In the "Vorwort" to *Der Patriotismus: Prologomena zu einer soziologischen Analyse* (Munich: Dunker & Homblot, 1929), p. vii, Michels speaks of "residues" as dispositional motives for human action.
9. Michels, *La sociologia...*, p. 4.
10. Michels, *L'imperialismo italiano* (Milan: Libreria, 1914), p.v.
11. Michels, *Problemi...*, pp. 193f.
12. Michels, "Nation und Klasse," *Die Arbeit 3*, 2 (February 1926), 158–166, 227–237; "Psychologie der antikapitalistischen Massenbewegungen," in Michels, *Grundriss des Sozialoekonomie* (Tuebingen: Mohr, 1926), pp. 275–276.
13. Cf. Michels, "Patriotism," *First Lectures in Political Sociology* (New York: Harper & Row, 1949), pp. 156–166.
14. Michels, "Der patriotische Sozialismus oder sozialistische Patriotismus bei Carlo Pisacane," *Archiv fuer die Geschichte des Sozialismus und der Arbeiterbewegung* (Carl Gruenberg, Ed. Leipzig: Hirschfeld, 1914), pp. 222f.

15. *Ibid.*, p. 242.
16. See the discussion in F. Naumann, "Proletarischer Imperialismus," *Hilfe*, May 12, 1912.
17. Michels, *L'imperialismo italiano*, pp. 178f.
18. Michels, *L'imperialismo italiano*, p. 180; cf. *Italien von Heute* (Leipzig: Orell Fuessli, 1930), pp. 208–212.
19. Michels, "Nation und Klasse," p. 227.
20. *Ibid.*, p. 233; cf. *Italien von Heute*, p. 216.
21. Michels, "Nation und Klasse," p. 236.
22. Michels, *Der Patriotismus*, p. 1.
23. *Ibid.*, pp. 30f., 39f.
24. Mussolini, "Il dovere dell'Italia," *Opera*, 7, pp. 99, 101.
25. Cf. E. Shils, The Concentration and Dispersion of Charisma," *World Politics* 22 (October 1958), p. 4; W. C. Runciman, "Charismatic Legitimacy and One-Party Rule in Ghana," *European Journal of Sociology* 4 (1963), p. 154; I. L. Horowitz, "Party Charisma: Political Practices and Principles in the Third World Nations," *Indian Sociological Bulletin* 3 (October 1965), pp. 75–78.
26. Michels, *Cenni storici sui sistemi sindacali corporativi* (Rome: Cremonese, 1936), p. 5, note.
27. Michels, *Introduzione all storia delle dottrine economiche e politiche* (Bologna: Zanichelli, 1932), pp. 79–81.
28. *Ibid.*, p. 81.
29. *Ibid.*, chap. 1. Essentially the same essay appeared as "Il concetto di Stato nella storia delle dottrine economiche," *Rivista di Politica Economica* 19, 6 (1929), 543–551.
30. Cf. Michels comments in *Der Patriotismus*, pp. 1f., *Italien von Heute*, pp. 209–211, 225, and *Studi sulla democrazia e sull'autorità* (Florence: La Nuova Italia, n.d.), chap. 2.
31. Michels, *Italien von Heute*, pp. 212f., 226f.
32. *Ibid.*, pp. 226f., 232, 237.
33. Cf. M. Pantaleoni, *Bolscevismo italiano* (Bari: Laterza, 1922).
34. See the discussion in A. James Gregor, *Young Mussolini and the Intellectual Origins of Fascism* (Berkeley: University of California, 1979), chaps. 9 and 10.
35. Michels, *Introduzione...*, pp. 107f.
36. Michels, "Lo stato forte e la politica economica," *Critica fascista* 10, 22 (November 15, 1932), 433f.
37. Michels, *Italien von Heute*, pp. 240–245.
38. *Ibid.*, p. 239.
39. Even the young Filippo Corridoni, before his death in action on the Austrian front in 1915, argued in his "political testament," that what Italy required as a precondition of revolution was "accelerated industrial development...." F. Corridoni, in *Sindacalismo e repubblica* (Rome: SAREP, 1945), p. 111.
40. Cf. J. L. Talmon, *The Origins of Totalitarian Democracy* (New York: Praeger, 1960), chap. 3, and L. G. Crocker's introduction to J. J. Rousseau, *The Social Contract and Discourses on the Origin of Inequality* (New York: Washington Square Press, 1967).
41. F. Engels, "Zwei Reden in Elberfeld: I," in K. Marx and F. Engels, *Werke* (Berlin: Dietz, 1957), 2, 539, 642.
42. Cf. the discussion in A. J. Gregor, *The Fascist Persuasion in Radical Politics* (Princeton, N.J.: Princeton University Press, 1974), chap. 4.
43. Michels expressed his summary judgments in various places, but the most important were written during the Fascist period. Cf. Michels, *First Lectures...*, chaps. 5–8; and *Studi sulla democrazia e sull'autorità*, Chap. 1, parts 3 and 4, chap. 2.

5

Giovanni Gentile and the Philosophy of Fascism

If there was anything distinctive of Fascism, that marked it apart from most of revolutionary Marxism—as revolutionary Marxism came to be understood in the twentieth century—it was the appeal to moral sentiments in the mobilization of political actors. If general material interests subtended political behaviors, human behavior could only be energized by ethical motives.

While Fascist enjoinments to mobilization were generally cast in terms of sentiment and a kind of political liturgy, there was an entire ethical rationale to which Fascists appealed in serious exchanges. If Roberto Michels provided the empirical and social science arguments in support of Fascism, Giovanni Gentile articulated its specifically philosophical and ethical rationale.

Gentile's rationale was neo-Hegelian in origin,[1] the same source out of which Marxism and Marxism-Leninism were to emerge. In fact, Gentile understood Marxism so well that his essay on the thought of the young Marx has not only withstood the test of time,[2] but was, on the occasion of its publication, recommended as particularly insightful by V. I. Lenin.[3]

More than that, there is persuasive evidence that the thought of Karl Marx exercised considerable influence over all Gentile's subsequent philosophical development.[4] It can be said, in a qualified sense, that Gentile entertained considerable sympathy for the neo-Hegelian Marxist intellectual tradition.[5]

Born on May 30, 1875, in Castelvetrano, Gentile was to involve himself deeply in the intellectual and political life of Italy until his assassination on April 15, 1944, while serving the Fascist government of the Italian Social Republic.[6] From the time that he was called to serve as Minister of Education in the first Fascist cabinet in October 1922, until his death, Gentile identified himself with Fascism.[7] In that course of time, he was selected by Mussolini, over the protests of the Roman Catholic Church itself, to write the definitive philosophical portion, "Idee fondamentali," of the official *Dottrina del fascismo* that appeared in the *Enciclopedia italiana* in 1932.[8]

That Mussolini chose Gentile to author the philosophical portion of Fascism's official doctrine provides evidence of the confidence Fascists entertained with respect to Gentile's thought.[9] Perhaps more important still, is the fact that Gentile's thought—although uncommonly philosophical and abstract—follows the same trajectory as that which we have traced in the Fascist thought of Roberto Michels.

The Political Philosophy of Giovanni Gentile[10]

Gentile identified the cardinal difficulty afflicting the modern political theorist as that which arises out of the felt conviction that the state, in some essential sense, is antagonistic to the "self" or true individuality of human beings.[11] Acknowledging that the majority of social and political thinkers in the West entertain such a notion, Gentile reminded his audience that contemporary theorists, nonetheless, have generally held that a certain minimum of state "interference" in the life of individuals is essential to the full development of personhood.[12]

Thus, while Jeremy Bentham could argue that every law was an evil and government was a choice of evils,[13] it was maintained, at the same time, that without the prevalence of law there could be no significant liberty for the individual. Thus, individual liberty was somehow thought to be enhanced by its subtraction at the hands of the state—which suggests that "liberty" is not all of a piece, like a bolt of cloth, but rather something like a plant that flourishes only with judicious pruning.

Gentile argued that if that were so, the pruning could hardly be conceived as destructive of liberty. Those "restraints" in law that foster the increased freedom of the individual—by affording certain elementary securities—cannot seriously be deprecated as antagonistic to liberty.

The source of the difficulty, Gentile suggested, seems to lie in the conception that the claims of "others" upon the "self" is destructive of liberty—in the notion that "others" somehow obstruct our freedom to do what we will. It is counterintuitive to unsophisticated thinkers, Gentile maintained, that in surrendering our individual willfulness and our thoughtless pursuit of our "independence" to law, we might actually be enhancing that true liberty that contributes to the realization of personhood. The apparent "surrender" of our presumptive independence, provides for the general recognition of social and juridical rights that enlarges, through reciprocity, the capacity for life and development in the individual.

Gentile argued that the concept of the individual existing in "liberty," anterior or exterior to a law-governed society, could only be a fiction.[14] He maintained that the notion that the individual, living in a "state of nature," might enjoy meaningful freedom—withdrawn from the law-governed organization of society with its state system of reciprocal obligation—was totally unconvincing.

Outside society man finds himself the subject of nature, not one who is to assert dominion over it. In such a state of nature, the individual is the enemy of all and friend of none. He is threatened by persons and things alike. He finds himself in a state of abject dependence. There is no freedom, no security, with each man exposed to the open wrongs of everyone and anyone. In such circumstances, there is no assurance of life, much less of liberty. The freedom which man is supposed to barter away in part, upon entering society, in order to secure the remainder, has no reality anterior to that very society. It is, according to Gentile, an imaginary possession which is then, by an imaginary transfer, conveyed to society.

Gentile maintained, with Marx, that the "essence" of man is not individual—but social. The human person is a function of a complex pattern of interactions with both nature and other persons in a law- and rule-governed environment. The human being is essentially a social creature (a *Gemeinwesen*)—and outside society, loses humanity.[15]

Gentile argued that only if the individual is conceived in an entirely abstract manner could he be imagined to possess "liberty" outside the network of human exchange.[16] Individuals, by nature, are social animals, and achieve humanity and liberty only in association. In reality, the maximization of the self and individuality becomes possible and substantial only through life lived in community—in which one conforms in his or her behavior to that "real" and "universal" will, that fosters spiritual growth. A thoughtless obedience to one's momentary, unthinking, and "empirical" will could only be dehumanizing.

Political theorists, Gentile reminded us, have long recognized the legitimacy of constraint when applied to the momentary zeal of individuals—when, as a matter of fact, their eagerness might involve injury to themselves or to others. The right to impose constraints on individuals derives its legitimation from the fact that the restraining agencies act to effect what is understood to be the *real* will of the individuals involved.[17] Those agencies constrain the individual to act as he or she would act were his or her will not temporarily clouded by enthusiasm or passion.[18] The "real" or "universal" will is understood to be, at those times, at variance with, if not diametrically opposed to, the individual's immediate, unthinking desire—but for all that, conformity to such a will cannot be considered, in any meaningful sense, a surrender of freedom.

For Gentile, the agencies of the state have the right to act, in law, in the name of the "real" will of individuals in restraining those whose "empirical" will is clouded or distracted. Given this account, it is only in a law-governed society—shaped by history, tradition, and thought— that the individual can realize the "real" freedom that renders him or her a personality.

In obeying the laws of the state—which are always in the process of dialectical renewal—human beings obey the intrinsic laws of their own evolving selves.[19] Only in such fashion does the individual attain positive freedom.

Positive law is the willed will of the community; it is the product of collective moral commitment in time-conditioned circumstances; it sustains the ordered interpersonal relations of those in the political community throughout the exigencies of historic development; it protects the individual before he achieves the moral maturity that renders him a self-conscious member of society; it fosters and guarantees the possibility of social life and transmits the spiritual heritage that constitutes the most substantial components of any and every human being, if that human being is to be a person.[20] Gentile recognized such a conception of the law as an inheritance from Greco-Roman antiquity.

More interesting for our purposes is the fact that Gentile shared much of the substance of these views with the tradition of the Enlightenment and the revolutionism of the nineteenth century. As has been suggested, in the *Social Contract*, in his discussion "Of the Civil Condition," Rousseau contends that the individual enjoys moral freedom only in the state, where freedom from the slavery of necessity and appetite is alone possible, and one can be master of oneself by obeying the "general will" which he or she, as member of a law-governed community, prescribes for himself or herself.

The fictive individual "natural liberty," outside and prior to society, so much prized by liberal theorists, implied for both Rousseau and

Gentile little more than "animal isolation." The individual becomes truly human only within the state, in civil society—where law creates an ordered environment in which he or she can fulfill his or her human potential.[21] In such circumstances, the state, and law, enjoy moral priority.[22] Gentile, like Aristotle, accorded presumptive priority to the state and the political community vis-a-vis the empirical individual self.[23]

Gentile argued that Rousseau recognized a law and a will, the general will, with which the empirical self may be at odds, but which represents the truer and fuller self—a will imperative as against the momentary, trivial, and confused will of the empirical self.[24] It is that will that constitutes, as Rousseau argued, the true will of the individual, embodying, concretizing his or her desire to be that which he or she can, and should, be—his or her highest self. Submission to the general will, as law and the state, is that which liberates the individual from the momentary desires and endemic limitations of the empirical and transient self—and dedicates him or her to the enterpise that augurs the full development of his or her essential humanity.[25]

Thus, Gentile held that such an analysis turns on a conception of the general, real, or universal will not unfamiliar to theoreticians on the left. Karl Marx and Friedrich Engels, for example, both conceived true individual liberty to be a function of a life lived in effortless association and in compliance with the "universal will" of "history," the inevitable and ineluctible outcome of materialistic processes.[26] For Marxists, by implication, any individual who attempted to resist the inevitable march of the proletariat was to remain unfulfilled, destined for the dustbin of history.

However much Gentile objected to the materialism of Marxism and many of the left-wing positivists of the nineteenth century, he acknowledged his affinities with them through the "dialectic" of Hegel. For Gentile, liberty was—as it was for Hegel and Rousseau —"liberty in law, and therefore liberty within a strong state conceived as an ethical reality."[27]

Marxism, the Masses and Elites

Gentile's objections to Marxism were rooted in his epistemological and ontological idealism. As such, his objections were, at their source, critically different from those raised by syndicalists and/or social scientists like Michels. Nonetheless, however different their respective thought was in terms of their particular domains of cognitive discourse, they shared some remarkable similarities in overt expression.

Gentile was familiar with the standard criticism of Marx's "historical materialism." He acknowledged the implausibility of human actors, under any conceivable circumstances, being moved to action on
the basis of "economic factors" alone without the interposition of "ethical
and sentimental motives, moral judgments and faith."[28] His criticism,
however, as his judgment, was much more fundamental.

Gentile argued that Marx's "materialism" was anything but materialistic. For Gentile, the notion that "matter" might serve as the presup-
position of any philosophical system was totally implausible. Unless
that "matter," of which Marx and Engels were to speak, was invested
with all the properties of "spirit," it would be impossible to explain the
progressive complexity of the world—the appearance, for example, of
sense and *intelligence* in it, not to speak of social and economic change
over time.[29]

For Gentile, the notion that "matter" should give rise to sense and
intelligence implied that matter, *ab initio*, possessed the potential for
both, meaning that such an ontological "matter" could only be a very
strange substance. Gentile's argument was that Marx understood all
that, and, as a consequence, in Marx's early writings, one finds clear
evidence of an half-articulated ontological idealism.[30]

For Gentile, the entire notion of *praxis*, as it finds expression in the
early writings of Marx, reveals the non-materialistic foundations of classical Marxism. The very fact that the young Marx refused to consider
the external "real" world as a simple object of contemplation, but rather
the consequence of interactive revolutionary "practice," suggested to
Gentile that "materialism" was an inappropriate characterization of
Marx's philosophical posture.

Gentile argued that the "practice" that Marx conceived as arising
from the interaction between "subject" and "object" in the real world,
irresistibly conveyed the impression that the real world could not proceed through historic change without a recognition of a "dialectical"
reciprocity between conscious human subjects and the prevailing material reality to which those subjects presumably made response.[31] Gentile saw the relationship as reciprocal in the sense that an explanation
for the one could not be forthcoming without an assessment of the other.
Empirical human behavior was inexplicable without taking into account
the context in which it occurred, but change, itself, was opaque unless
human moral choice was introduced as a functional variable.[32]

In that sense, Gentile's criticism of Marxism as a "left-wing degen-
eration" of Hegelianism,[33]shares features with that of revolutionary

syndicalism and Michels. Both rejected a simple form of "economic determinism" that excluded the conscious moral choice of participants in developmental historic *praxis*. Both recognized that if humans were enjoined to "change the world," they were equally charged, in any given context, with the responsibility of making moral choices. There was nothing mechanical about the world nor the changes in it.[34]

For Gentile, the essence of the human condition was choice. Human beings were compelled to deal, through choice—however thoughtless—with inherited reality. That reality inextricably involved historically determined social relations.

The virtue of Marxism, as it found expression in the youthful writings of Karl Marx, was, according to Gentile, the recognition that individuals were not "social atoms"—entities that lived in "natural freedom" before bartering away that freedom for some measure of security—but social creatures who found their concrete fulfillment through moral choice in complex relations.[35] Marx's commitment to human "practice" in social settings, however much to be recommended, revealed the fundamental, and fatal, contradiction of a materialistic "revolutionary socialism."[36] Revolution, however construed, inevitably involved human deliberation, human will, and human choice. "Economic determinism" could only be a fiction.

If socialism were to be revolutionary, it would have to invoke the moral and intellectual commitment of those who would transform society. Neither immediate material interests, nor prevailing economic, social, or political realities could accomplish that. What was required was a moral and intellectual conviction on the part of "significant" actors that society required systemic change.

It was in that context that Gentile, long before he identified himself with Mussolini's Fascism, spoke of individual human beings who, in themselves, "represented tendencies" that had matured in specific populations. Such "intuitive leaders" were destined to significantly influence, "as real and operant forces," change and development in society.[37] Such individuals were political "geniuses," "heroes," "privileged and providential spirits," who, in themselves, "incarnated"[38] the real will of their times. They were capable of correctly assessing the problems of the real, empirical world, as well as intuiting the collective psychology of masses,[39] and thereby become instrumental in transforming prevailing reality.

Gentile argued that systemic social change was often, if not always, the product of the activities of a "guiding minority" leading a "guided majority."[40] That vanguard minority was not only capable of making calculated judgments concerning prevailing realities, but was effective only when its convictions "incarnated" the "real will" of the inarticulate majority. Under special circumstances, a *single person* might give expression to political ideas that made overt the implicit will of an entire population.[41]

Even before the advent of Fascism, Gentile argued that such a leader, capable of assessing reality, and cognizant of the prevailing psychology of his people, becomes their voice.[42] He becomes the spokesman "of the free, intrinsic, forces of the people themselves."[43] The logic of Gentile's argument is perfectly clear and finds its familiar counterpart in V. I. Lenin's elitist and minoritarian notions of revolution.

For his part, Lenin made very clear that revolutions were made by exiguous minorities. For Lenin, only declassed bourgeois intellectuals were capable of solving "all the theoretical, political, tactical, and organizational questions" that afflict "masses" in motion. The "'ideologist'…worthy of the name *precedes* the spontaneous movement."[44]

For Lenin the true revolutionary recognizes the imperative of history; he expresses the "true will" of the masses—because that will was consonant with that historical evolution that would render human beings free and fulfilled.[45] Out of that persuasion was to arise the Marxist-Leninist variant of the "charismatic leader" so familiar in the twentieth century.

What distinguished Gentile's Fascist rationale from that which came to characterize the legitimating rationale of Marxism-Leninism was Gentile's identification of the nation—rather than the "proletariat"—as the community of destiny that would shape our time. For Gentile, proletarians represented only component elements of a larger organic community: the nation. In the modern world, only the nation could provide the material, intellectual, political, and moral environment in which the individual might find fulfillment.

Unlike Marxists and Marxist-Leninists, Gentile saw the contemporary world governed by urgent realities. Only the nation provided the individual the vehicle that might successfully negotiate those realities. There could be no alternative for our time, confined as it was by history and circumstance.

For Gentile, Italy, only recently unified as a nation in 1861, was the "easy prey of foreigners," a "negligible force in a world dominated by the great powers." It was an Italy without influence in the course of modern civilization.

Like Michels, Gentile spoke of the necessity of a sacrificial commitment on the part of all to "produce more and consume less," in order to construct the material base necessary for a "great nation," animated by an historic "mission."[46] Italy, Gentile argued, required a commitment, on the part of its citizens, to undertake a "mission" devoted to making that new nation, through their "efforts and sacrifice...a manifest and living reality," that might carry "weight in the modern world...." Italy could no longer "remain in the shadow of nations" who dominated the modern world[47]—to the humiliation of Italy and Italians.[48]

Neither faction nor class could transform the international reality that faced the combat troops who had served in the First World War. Emerging from the greatest war in the history of humankind, disappointed by the treatment Italy had received at the hands of the Great Powers, the survivors of the trenches sought a new Italy in a new world.[49]

There were those who responded to those sentiments that had gradually matured over the long years of Italy's somnolence—its failure to realize the promise of its Risorgimento. They were the Fascist revolutionaries who had fought for the fulfillment of that promise through Italy's long war against Austria-Hungary. They were the Fascist revolutionaries who had fought against the Marxist revolutionaries who chose to deny a future for the nation. They were the Fascist revolutionaries committed to the creation of a Great Power out of the potential of the nation that arose out of the Risorgimento in the nineteenth century.[50]

Nationalism, Morality, and the State

In the modern world, only the nation, for Gentile, provided the environment necessary to sustain and foster the full moral realization of personhood—which, for Gentile, constituted the ultimate moral imperative that governed the life of the individual.[51] In that sense, Gentile's conception of nationalism—among the other forms of nationalism that had made their appearance in Italy before the First World War—was theoretically distinctive.

For Gentile, the nation was not an end in itself; it was of instrumental value in the progressive moral fulfillment of self.[52] Unlike the standard Italian nationalists of the turn of the twentieth century, Gentile's nationalism was exclusively *moral* in emphasis—and the nation, in and of itself, possessed instrumental and not intrinsic value. Unlike some of the nationalists that inhabited turn-of-the-century Italy, Gentile insisted that the nation was not a simple artifact of territory, history, or culture.[53] It was the moral ground for the fulfillment of ethical ends.

The nation was not a simple function of a *material* reality. It was not the product of history, the use of a common language, or the possession of a peculiar culture. All those things contributed to the reality in which the individual human being was born, but that preexistent reality did not engage the individual until that individual chose to morally commit himself or herself to the nation as a moral "community of destiny."

For Gentile, "a nation is not to be defined in terms of common soil or common life, and the consequent community of traditions and customs, language or religion, etc. All this is only the matter of the nation, not its form; for the nation can only exist where men are conscious of this matter, and accept it in their hearts as the substantial content of the national personality and the proper object of the national will...."[54] A nation is a moral and political reality only when it is accepted as such by the conscious decision of its members. It is fully engaged only when individuals recognize in its empirical reality the opportunity of moral fulfillment.

Once a population accedes to that recognition, it creates a "virtual state," and it is the state, the product of conscious, moral choice, that gives the nation its concrete expression.[55] By virtue of the collective decision to declare its unity and independence, a people gives full expression to its political will and thereby establishes itself through a real or virtual state.[56]

The state is an expression of a determined, historic, collective will.[57] It is a people morally conscious of its historicity—of its place within a community of nations and in the history of nations.

It is within that state that the individual pursues moral purpose, and it is that law-governed reality that provides the arena in which the individual attains personhood.[58] For Gentile, the state is a "spiritual" or moral substance that constitutes the "form" in which a truly human life unfolds.[59] It proscribes and prescribes the acceptable or unacceptable ranges of human behavior; it preserves the legacy of the past within which the individual functions; it communicates the traditional concepts of good and evil; and it educates the community to historic purpose.

In an ultimate sense, the state not only provides the context of a moral life, but, Gentile argued, it also creates the nation. It is the state that furnishes a population not only with moral form, but with effective political existence as well.

Given Gentile's understanding of the conditions of empirical life in the twentieth century, he conceived the state, the informing principle of the nation, as charged with the responsibility of creating a moral environment in which the individual, surrounded by distraction and afflicted by self-serving passions, might be able to imbue the narrowness of self with the fullness of humanity.[60] For Gentile, it was the state's ethical responsibility to provide that moral environment.[61]

For Gentile, the entirety of political life was like a schoolroom.[62] Himself a pedagogue of international reputation, he forever conceived politics, and its expression in the state, as having singularly pedagogical, disciplinary,[63] and tutelary responsibilities. It is the state that creates the conditions that make the moral realization of self possible for each human being—and, as a consequence, the state has the moral right to demand, at minimum, disciplined obedience,[64] compliance, and conformity from the individual. At the maximum, Gentile argued that the state has every right to expect the individual to accept the obligation, if necessary, of protecting the community with whom he or she has identified with his or her life.[65]

In the historic conditions of the nineteenth and twentieth centuries, Gentile reminded his audience, Italy was not "something in nature, but a great spiritual reality.... [It was] a mission, a purpose, something that [had] to be realized—an action."[66]

Invoking the enjoinments of Giuseppe Mazzini, the spiritual mentor of the unification of Italy, Gentile argued that the nation was the vehicle for the realization of "that sovereign and ultimate good for which all sacrifices are gladly borne, without which man cannot live, outside of which he finds nothing that satisfies him, nothing that is conducive to life's labors." That understood, he went on to insist that "a people cannot timidly insist upon recognition from others, but must themselves assume the responsibility for their existence, make it manifest by their willingness to fight and die for their independence in and through their nation."[67]

A people becomes a nation through a state that gives expression to its "active faith, and its will to accomplishment."[68] Participation through acts of faith, willed commitment, and personal sacrifice is that which shapes the moral character and the personal worth of individuals.

In the course of those accomplishments—national unity and the creation of statehood—faith, commitment, and sacrifice on the part of individuals are necessary constituents.[69] It is in and through the accomplishments of statehood that a community achieves "its moral personality and its own collective consciousness," and it is in that realization, and its entailed collective capacity, that a people becomes capable of defeating "enemies and liberating itself from its oppressors."[70]

In the defeat of enemies, and in liberation from oppressors, the individual finds the occasion for the greatest sacrifice and the ultimate moral choice. In the struggle, he or she creates the circumstances for moral development. In those eventualities, war provides the ambience for the human being's final and ultimate discharge of moral duty.

It is the nation that provides the network of created circumstances within which the individual may achieve moral personhood—and the nation is realized only in the state that is itself the result of willed sacrifice and unstinted effort. It is within the network of social relationships, governed in law by the state, together with the challenges that accompany the activities of the state, that the individual enters into the realm of the moral universal and faces the decisive choices that make up a life lived in morality.[71]

As has been suggested, in even the most liberal states, the rudiments of such an analysis are understood. Even in "demoliberal" communities, the state is charged with the responsibility of acting to obstruct the behaviors of individuals if those behaviors are understood to involve consequences that the individual would not have chosen were he or she lucid. In such instances, compliance with the laws of the state is not conceived a diminution of liberty. Obedience to law is understood to be the enhancement of liberty.[72]

In fact, in even the most liberal of states, there is an expectation not only that each individual obey the law, but that each individual be prepared to sacrifice his or her life in the defense of the community—and their obedience and sacrifice are celebrated, not deplored. Irrespective of the conviction that individuals have an "unalienable right to life," and possess the liberty to "pursue happiness" as they see fit, the sacrifice of individual life, and the surrender of personal happiness, is heralded as an unparalleled moral achievement.

Gentile argued, in fact, that the "agnosticism" of the liberal state, with all its "freedoms" to do what one chooses, was largely a delusion.[73] All governments, no matter how liberal, enact laws that proscribe wrongdoing and seek to promote, sustain, and foster those behaviors held to be ethical. The pretense that one cannot distinguish between good and evil, Gentile insisted, leads only to ethical confusion, moral torpor, and the prevalence of evil.[74]

Gentile's entire conception of politics argues that any collection of human beings that conceives itself a nation is obliged to give itself over to a relatively specific, and "national," conception of life.[75] In the case of a Fascist nation, informed by a Fascist state, that specific conception of life sees individuals intrinsically and morally united in a community, informed by an historic tradition, and disciplined by an arduous mission.[76]

For Gentile, Italians were charged, at the commencement of the twentieth century, with the moral responsibility of lifting their motherland to the level of a "Great Nation," no longer subject to the infamies and impostures of the "advanced powers." The mission imposed on Italians was that of cancelling the shame of having allowed the nation to have fallen so low in itself and in the esteem of others.[77]

Those were, for Gentile, the historic circumstances in which Italians found themselves at the commencement of the second quarter of the twentieth century. It was within those circumstances that individuals were to elevate themselves to the moral fullness of self by uplifting their community to that station that its history, its creativity, its talents, and its prospects warranted. It was, in Gentile's judgment, the responsibility of the Fascist state to establish the disciplined moral environment in which that elevation of both the individual and the nation would take place.

As we have seen, in Gentile's judgment, individuals who obey the moral imperative to seek the fullness of personhood, must become denizens of organized and law-governed communities.[78] Not to seek moral fulfillment is to opt for selfishness in such communities and that, at best, is anarchistic, and, at worst, criminal.[79] In such instances, the state has the obligation not only to impose discipline[80] or sanction, but, in specific instances, to coerce.[81]

Individuals submit their will, otherwise capricious, uninformed, irrational, and egoistical,[82] to discipline either when they are convinced that such submission contributes to the ultimate realization of self, or when they are guided by enlightened mentors. It is clearly possible to have individuals submit to discipline when it is to their evident advantage. Even infants implicitly acknowledge the creative role of discipline by submitting to the rules of language use.[83]

There are, however, Gentile argued, occasions when coercion becomes necessary. For Gentile, in those instances when individuals, either as a consequence of ignorance or moral failure, refuse to acknowledge the rules that govern social conduct, or fail to participate in the moral mission of the community, coercion to exact compliance should be understood to function as a "moral force."[84]

However it is considered, it is clear that even some of the most liberal societies use coercion, and even capital punishment, in the attempt to control deviance and elicit compliance behavior—but the issue joined by Gentile deals, more than anything else, with the question of the employment of violence to control *political* dissidence. In a century in which the rulers of nations have destroyed countless lives on political pretexts, the issue of political violence has become a concern of fundamental moral importance.

For Gentile, political violence is morally justified primarily in revolutionary crises—when radically different moral conceptions of life struggle for political dominance.[85] In the absence of an overarching state control of behaviors, revolutionaries, in the defense of an alternative conception of the moral life, are, under certain conditions, compelled to defend their commitment with violence.

Thus, for Gentile, the Fascist use of violence during the revolutionary crisis before the March on Rome was no different, morally, than the use of violence during liberal revolutions—nor was it less morally justified than the political violence used in the Bolshevik "Marxist" revolution of 1917. Political violence characteristically attends revolution.

What is undeniably clear is that, for Gentile, violence—particularly the use of deadly force—was to be used only with the utmost gravity and only after the most careful deliberation. For Gentile "human life [was] sacred," and was to be taken only in the rarest of circumstances. For Gentile, human life was sacred because "the human being [*l'uomo*] is spirit, and as such has an absolute value." "Things," Gentile went on, "are instruments, human beings are ends."[86]

That commentators have found this kind of circumspection with respect to the taking of human life difficult to accommodate to the commonplace understanding of Fascism is probably the consequence of the pervasive conviction that Fascists, in general and with little qualification, were committed to the wholesale, instrumental, demonstrative, and pathological employment of violence.

To imagine that to be unqualifiedly true would be to imagine that millions of Italians, for a quarter of a century, were prepared to accept governance by such a system. More plausible, in fact, would be the view that many, if not most Italians, recognized the necessity for the employment of violence under reasonably specific circumstances—and that Gentile's account reflected, in large part, their convictions. Few Italians, and few Fascists, seemed committed to the wholesale taking of lives in any conceivable set of ordinary political circumstances.[87]

In fact, Fascist ideologues were careful to provide a rather elaborate rationale for their employment of violence. Sergio Panunzio, for example, wrote an entire treatise on the use of violence in political crises.[88] It was characterized by rules predicated on the value of individual and collective human life.

Like all revolutionaries, Fascists had every reason to provide moral principles that might govern the use of violence—if only to allay the misgivings of the "good burghers" that made up some of their potential constituency. Fascist literature regularly affirmed "Gentilean" principles concerning the value of human life.

Balbino Giuliano, who served as Minister of Education under the regime, regularly expressed the conviction that "all human beings merit respect if for no other reason than that they are human and are the products of divine creation....We must never forget our obligations...with respect to our ideal of human dignity."[89]

In the standard books devoted to popular education, Fascist authors intoned that "One of the principal duties [of Fascists] toward human beings is to do good for the sake of doing good....One must be unqualifiedly good with everyone and to particularly help those who are weak and disadvantaged. One must see in others a brother...whatever his social condition, whatever his Fatherland, and whatever his faith."[90]

To imagine that Fascists did not articulate such notions is to entertain some very curious notions about human sensibilities. To imagine that Fascists mobilized popular support by appealing to "irrational violence" and "anti-humane hatred," rather than an invocation to general moral principles, is a notion so bizarre as to merit dismissal without inspection.[91]

The fact that Fascist rule, like authoritarian, dictatorial, and totalitarian rule everywhere, might lead to violence against individuals and groups of individuals is an entirely different issue and must be inspected on its merits. The point to be made is that Fascist intellectuals did recognize the generic distinction between moral and immoral acts and made every attempt to provide a normative account of the behaviors of the Fascist regime.

The fact is that Fascist thinkers did provide a moral rationale for Fascist rule. Among them, Gentile was perhaps the most sophisticated. If a serious attempt is to be mounted in the effort to explain Fascism's appeal, one must accept the realization that Fascists, no less than Marxist-Leninists, and no less than liberal democrats, advanced a philosophical and moral rationale, as well as an empirical justification for their peculiar form of political rule.

That Gentile's moral position influenced his personal behavior is clear from the evidence. Many Fascists, Gentile not the least among them, became increasingly uncomfortable when, after 1936, Fascist Italy inextricably tied its destiny to that of National Socialist Germany. Gentile, like many Fascists, explicitly abjured biological racism, even after Mussolini had drawn Italy into the "Pact of Steel" with Nazi Germany.[92] When the Fascist government, in its effort to placate Hitler, proceeded to anti-Semitic posturing, Gentile continued to befriend and protect Jewish scholars at considerable personal risk.[93]

Throughout his life, Gentile consistently held that there was a Fascist conception of the state that understood the state to represent the philosophical and ethical universality of persons. Individuals were the state writ small, just as the state was the individual writ large.[94] The one was suffused, "sublated," in the other. Gentile's moral philosophy conceived that in a "transcendental and totalitarian" sense, the interests of the one were ultimately identical with the interests of the other.[95]

In all of this, Gentile recognized, throughout his life, that there were those who were identified, or identified themselves, as Fascists, who were unworthy of moral responsibility.[96] Gentile acknowledged that there were those who called themselves Fascists who, for their own personal advantage, violated every moral principle and every Fascist ideal.[97]

That acknowledgment notwithstanding, Gentile maintained that the conception of a "Fascist ideal society" had sufficient merit to warrant the sacrifices demanded for its realization. He insisted that a revolution, intended to consummate systemic change, altering the entire pattern of collective and individual life, could only gradually achieve its purpose. Along its trajectory of growth one would inevitably find moral failure and criminal departures—just as one found similar failures and departures in each and every other revolution.

For Gentile, while "heroic and providential" leaders might initiate revolutionary processes, the processes would be invariably long, time-consuming, and tortured by moral infraction. Fascists were never slow to remind liberals that democratic society was fathered by slave holders, imperialists, and the oppressors of workers and peasants.[98] They never tired in rehearsing all the horrors of Bolshevik rule.

What distinguishes Gentile's thought from that of those who have provided, and now provide, the rationale for Marxist-Leninist or liberal democratic rule, is his unrelieved emphasis on the deliberate moral character of politics.[99] For Gentile, life itself is inextricably a moral enterprise. The state, itself, is an ethical entity, charged with moral responsibilities. The individual who lives within its confines, and either conforms, or fails to conform, his or her will to its laws necessarily acknowledges its ethical substance.

To conform, or not to conform, to public law is to make a moral choice.[100] Political life, as a critical element of living life in common, is critical to the realization of self.

The state, according to Gentile, must allow the citizen maximum independence in making choices. But in no case does the state abandon its moral obligations. Gentile insists that is as true in "liberal," as it is in "authoritarian" states.

In the Fascist state, individuals deliberate in all the formal and informal associations that make up the fabric of political society, and respect is shown to dissent,[101] but once a course has been chosen all dissent must cease, and each must assume his or her responsibilities[102]—in what Mussolini identified as an "authoritarian democratic" arrangement, and in what we all recognize as a form of Lenin's "democratic centralism." The political and moral character of the one is essentially that of the other.

Gentile was convinced that every philosophical and empirical argument confirmed the reality that communities were suffused with a collective sense of right and wrong—and that under specific historic conditions, whole populations palpitated with a "mythic" and sentimental commitment to "missions" that defined a life lived in common. Out of that "faith," and that collective "sentiment," a revolutionary leadership, even a single "hero," could articulate a doctrine that would inspire and guide masses to historic moral purpose.[103]

Totalitarianism and Corporativism

For Gentile, discharging the moral purposes imposed on the Italian people at the turn of the twentieth century necessarily entailed their mobilization into unqualified unity. So demanding were the obligations laid upon them by time and circumstances, that all moral energy was to be marshalled to the service of the nation. The disciplined marshalling of the nation's potential was the necessary condition for the creation of an environment in which the individual could achieve fulfillment.[104]

In such circumstances, and in order to achieve such ends, "there is nothing really private...and there are no limits to state action....The state is the will of the individual himself in its universal and absolute aspect...."[105] It is the will of the individual shorn of its immediate time- and circumstance-conditioned frailties. It is the will of the individual enlarged to encompass the enduring interests of the historic commu- nity as well as its time-specific secular concerns. Finally, and in its universal moral sense, it is the will of the individual observed from a timeless, and fully rational, perspective.[106]

"Totalitarianism," for Gentile, meant precisely the identification of the individual, and the individual in associations of special interest, with the state as the manifest political expression of the nation.[107] To- talitarianism, for Gentile, meant the immediate or gradual assimilation of individuals and special interests into the state, so that the interests of the one might be, with only the most minor qualification, the interests of the other.

For Gentile, the tutelary state would gradually educate the sentiment and "faith" of the masses—until those masses, as individuals and asso- ciations of individuals, would come to appreciate the profound realities of the world and their responsibilities in it.[108] They would be educated, in effect, to the conviction that there was nothing outside the state, nor anything against the state, if Italy were to attain its place in the sun. They would be "new men." All interests would be united in a single and all-encompassing mission.

In that sense, just as the state is the individual "conscious of this own real complex individuality," so the state is the real will of special interest associations.[109] For Gentile, the totalitarian state was the express and gen- eral will of all the individuals and associations of which it was organi- cally composed,[110] and it was to that general will that the constituent parts of the organism would "harmonize" and "discipline" themselves.[111]

For Gentile, the "corporative state" was an expression of totalitari- anism as totalitarianism dealt with economic categories. Within the dis- cipline of the state, the associations of labor and of enterprise "harmo- nized" themselves.[112] Like most Fascist thinkers, the entire notion of "corporativism," for Gentile, was a component part of the concept of the "totalitarian state."

For Fascists, the totalitarian state sought the synthesis and integra- tion of the energies of individuals, and individuals in association, in the service of the nation.[113] The particular institutional form that political and social synthesis, and that integration of productive forces assumed in the course of Fascism's history, was not particularly important. What was essential was the achievement of the ends of the state—the creation of a nation—the equal of any other, and master of its own destiny—capable of providing the material and spiritual environment in which individuals singly, or in association, could mature to the moral fullness of self.

Conclusions

What is perhaps most instructive in all of this is the fact that however expressed, in the locutions of empirical social science, or the abstract language of normative assessment, many of the immediately recognizable features of historical Fascism unequivocally emerge. In both Michels and Gentile, the nation is the center of deliberations, and the state provides the institutional center of the entire totalitarian enterprise.

The nation is formed of geographic, economic and cultural elements, welded together in the ideological convictions of a catalyzing, vanguard few, who, through their invocations, marshall the existing sentiments, and nascent faith, of masses, to revolutionary purpose. A revolutionary party, under the charismatic leadership of an intuitive leader, assumes hegemonic control of an entire population, and through the employments of all the state's institutions—directive, administrative, hortatory, punitive, tutelary, ceremonial, and educational—creates in that population a plebiscitary consensus.

That population is mobilized, persuaded, cajoled, conscripted, and coerced to political purpose—to create a "Great Nation"—a nation equipped with the economic and military potential to stand against any opponent. It was to provide that political "logic" with its rationale that Roberto Michels and Giovanni Gentile lent their talents.

What is clear is that there was a "logic" to Fascism, however much its spokesmen differed in articulating its rationale. As ontological idealists, metaphysical realists, or epistemological pragmatists, Fascist thinkers all shared a critical collection of ideas that all together made up the totalitarian ideology of Mussolini's Fascism. The Fascism that played its role on the world stage between the two world wars gave fulsome expression to that ideology—an expression that provides some insight into how "fascism" might be defined and understood.

Notes

1. See the discussion in A. James Gregor, *Contemporary Radical Ideologies* (New York: Random House, 1968), chap. 5, and H. S. Harris, *The Social Philosophy of Giovanni Gentile* (Urbana: University of Illinois, 1960), chap. 3.

2. See A. James Gregor, "Giovanni Gentile and the Philosophy of the Young Karl Marx," *Journal of the History of Ideas* 24, 2 (April-June 1963), pp. 213–230.

3. Giovanni Gentile, "La filosofia di Marx," in *I fondamenti della filosofia del diritto* (Florence: Sansoni, 1955), p. 147.

4. See, in this regard, Ugo Spirito, "Gentile e Marx," in *Giovanni Gentile: La vita e il pensiero* (Florence: Sansoni, 1948), 1, pp. 313–334.

5. This is particularly true of Gentile's subsequent treatment of the concept, "*praxis*," which many have held derives, in substantial part, from the youthful study of Marx's works. See Marialuisa Cicalese, *La formazione del pensiero politico di Giovanni Gentile (1896–1919)* (Milan: Marzorati, 1972), pp. 20–60. Gentile, in that regard, shared the intellectual sentiments of Mussolini, himself. In December 1921, at the height of the conflict with the Marxists of Italy, Mussolini could affirm that "between us and the communists there are no political affinities, but there are affinities that are intellectual." Mussolini, "Per la vera pacificazione," *Opera omnia* (Florence: La fenice, 1955–1963. Hereafter *Opera*), 17, p. 295.

6. "I speak to you as a Fascist, which I am proud to be...," Giovanni Gentile, "Discorso agli italiani," in Benedetto Gentile (ed.), *Giovanni Gentile dal discorso agli italiani alla morte* (Florence: Sansoni, 1951), p. 67.

7. *Ibid.*; see Primo Siena, *Gentile* (Rome: Volpe, 1966), pp. 9–18.

8. The "Idee fondamentali" is contained in Mussolini, *La dottrina del fascismo* (Milan: Hoepli, 1935), pp. 3–39; see Nino Tripodi, *Il fascismo secondo Mussolini* (Rome: Borghese, 1971), p. 9.

9. This is not to suggest that every thinker who identified himself as a "Fascist" during the tenure of the regime, was in full agreement with the complex philosophical thought of Gentile. In this context, those who had been minor figures during the Fascist regime and survived to be "neofascists" after the Second World War, rejected Gentile as "their" philosopher. By that time, in fact, it was clear that some of the figures of which this was true had never qualified as "Fascists." After the war, as a case in point, Julius Evola, perhaps one of the most important of these persons, simply resumed the same non-fascist mystical and anti-humane postures he had always held during the regime. See Julius Evola, "Gentile non è il nostro filosofo," *Minoranza* 2, nos. 5–7 (20 October 1959), pp. 22–27. The argument here is simply that Gentile was a major Fascist thinker and that his thought, like that of Michels, and unlike that of Evola, proved to be fully compatible with official Fascist ideology.

10. The social and political thought of Gentile was complex and profound. In the summary account offered here, only the essentials will be attempted. One of the better books devoted to Gentile's social and political thought available in English is Harris, *op. cit.* Gentile's epistemological and ontological idealism will be touched on briefly in chapter six of the present text.

11. Gentile, *Genesi e struttura della società* (Florence: Sansoni, 1946), p. 14; *I fondamenti...*, p. 103.

12. Gentile, *I fondamenti...*, pp. 104f.

13. Thus "To do as one pleases," T. Smith argues, "this alone is liberty," and "...Liberty means no less than doing as one pleases." *The Democratic Way of Life* (New York: Mentor, 1960), pp. 53, 55.

14. A. D. Lindsay, for example, in his objections to Mill, maintains: "Real liberty is possible, not in a world where we have no relations with other people, but where our relations with them are the expression or reason. In so far, therefore, as the state substitutes ordered and reasonable interference for the arbitrary interference of individuals, it increases freedom." Introduction to John Stuart Mill, *Utilitarianism, Liberty and Representative Goverment* (New York: Dutton, 1950), p. xxv.

15. Gentile, *I fondamenti...*, pp. 163–164.
16. Gentile, *Riforma dell'educazione* (Florence: Sansoni, 1955), pp. 20f.; *Genesi...*, pp. 60, 66f., 109f., 115.
17. Gentile, *I fondamenti...*, p. 129.
18. Gentile, *Discorsi di religione* (Florence: Sansoni, 1955), p. 88.
19. Gentile, *Che cosa è il fascismo* (Florence: Vallecchi, 1925), pp. 120f. Gentile recognized that laws may often be unreasonable, even tyrannical, but he held that any cavalier violation of law brought with it the threat of anarchy and the disintegration of community, without which the individual could neither attain moral stature nor fulfillment. See the discussion in Harris, *op. cit.*, pp. 121–122.
20. Gentile, *Riforma dell'educazione*, p. 25 and *I fondamenti...*, p. 102.
21. See Gentile, "La filosofia della prassi," *I fondamenti...*, pp. 228–229.
22. Gentile, *Genesi...*, p. 67.
23. "...the state is by nature clearly prior to the family and to the individual....And he who by nature and not by mere accident is without a state, is either a bad man or above humanity....If all communities aim at some good, the state or political community, which is the highest of all...aims at good in a greater degree than any other, and at the highest good." Aristotle, *Politica*, book 1, 1252a, 3–6, 1253a, 3–4, 19–21.
24. Gentile, *Genesi...*, p. 2 and *I fondamenti...*, p. 85.
25. The issue here, of course, is how one might determine if a law or rule is unjust and does not satisfy the ultimate, real interests of the individual. For Gentile, and Fascists, in general, the conviction was that law would be filtered through an array of hierarchically arranged public institutions, ranging from youth, through professional and legislative bodies until reviewed by the Grand Council of Fascism and the Head of the Government, himself.

    All of the intermediate deliberations should be free of constraint and should involve everyone touched by the law or rule. See Gentile, *Fascismo e cultura*, pp. 130–131; Harris, *op. cit.*, pp. 120–121.
26. See Gentile, *I fondamenti...*, pp. 187–190; Harris, *op. cit.*, pp. 49–51.
27. Gentile, *Che cosa è il fascismo*, p. 129.
28. See Gentile, *I fondamenti...*, p. 183. Gentile's youthful essays on the work of Karl Marx, "Una critica del materialismo storico," and "La filosofia della prassi," appear as appendices of *I fondamenti...*.
29. Thus Friedrich Engels, in attempting to address this issue, insisted that both "matter" and "motion" had existed from all eternity, and could neither be "created" nor "destroyed." Lenin, in attempting to deal with the issue, insisted that "matter" possessed within itself the "potential for sensation." The *metaphysical* character of these assumptions is evident. See A. James Gregor, *A Survey of Marxism* (New York: Random House, 1965), pp. 47–48, 82–83. Compare Gentile, *I fondamenti...*, pp. 294–295.
30. See the discussion in Gentile, "La filosofia della prassi," *I fondamenti...*, pp. 214–215, 220; Spirito, "Gentile e Marx," *Giovanni Gentile*, 1, pp. 321–329.
31. See, for example, Gentile, "La filosofia della prassi," *I fondamenti...*, p. 298. Because Gentile was an epistemological, as well as an ontological idealist, his arguments are much more complicated than this summary exposition allows. See Gentile, *Teoria generale dello spirito come atto puro* (Bari: Laterza, 1924).
32. Gentile, *I fondamenti...*, p. 301.
33. *Ibid.*, p. 156.
34. See Cicalese, *La formazione...*, pp. 25–34.
35. Gentile, *I fondamenti...*, p. 298; see the comments of Gentile to Benedetto Croce with respect to the activities of human beings as determining their realization of

self in a letter dated June 30, 1899, *Giovanni Gentile lettere a Benedetto Croce* (Florence: Sansoni, 1972), pp. 188–189, and the relevant comments in Ferruccio Pardo, *La filosofia di Giovanni Gentile* (Florence: Sansoni, 1972), p. 320.

36. Gentile, *I fondamenti...*, p. 303.
37. Gentile, *Dopo la vittoria* (Rome: "La Voce," 1920), p. 5.
38. Gentile, *Fascismo e cultura* (Milan: Treves, 1928), p. 47.
39. Gentile, *Origini e dottrina del fascismo* (Rome: Libreria del littorio, 1929), p. 23.
40. Gentile, *Origini...*, p. 5.
41. Gentile, in Mussolini, *La dottrina del fascismo*, p. 15.
42. In his discussion of Fascism, Gentile maintained that Mussolini possessed "a secure intuition of collective psychology." See Gentile, *Origini...*, p. 23.
43. Gentile's argument, formulated before the very founding of Fascism in 1919, was that only in such a relationship between the "leaders" and the "led," might "true democracy" emerge. Gentile, *Dopo la vittoria*, p. 6.
44. V. I. Lenin, "A Talk with the Defenders of Economism," *Collected Works* (Moscow: Foreign Languages, 1960–), 5, p. 316.
45. See the discussion in Gregor, *A Survey of Marxism*, chap. 5.
46. See, for example, Gentile, "L'esempio del governo," and "La crisi morale," in *Dopo la vittoria* (Rome: "La Voce," 1920), pp. 65, 84–86.
47. Gentile, *Origini...*, p. 7.
48. Gentile, *Che cos è il fascismo*, p. 27.
49. Gentile, *Origini...*, pp. 28–30.
50. *Ibid.*, chaps. 1–8.
51. Gentile, *Genesi...*, pp. 7–9.
52. Gentile affirmed that "the Fatherland is sainted, but it is not an end in itself." Cited in Armando Carlini, "Il pensiero politico di G. Gentile," *Studi gentiliani* (Florence: Sansoni, 1958), p. 104. That conviction characterized the position of Michels and most serious Fascist thinkers.
53. Gentile, *Origini...*, pp. 44, 47; Cicalese, *op. cit.*, chap. 4.
54. Gentile, *Genesi...*, p. 57.
55. Gentile, in Mussolini, *La dottrina del fascismo*, p. 15.
56. *Ibid.*
57. Gentile, *Origini...*, p. 52.
58. Gentile, *Introduzione alla filosofia* (Rome: Treves-Treccani-Tumminelli, 1933), p. 180; see pp. 174–188.
59. Gentile, *Origini...*, p. 47; see p. 46, and *Che cosa è il fascismo*, p. 120.
60. Gentile's philosophy was clearly a form of "existential" humanism. See Ugo Spirito, *Giovanni Gentile* (Florence: Sansoni, 1969), chap. 6; Vito A. Bellezza, *L'esistenzialismo positivo di Giovanni Gentile* (Florence: Sansoni, 1954). It is instructive, in this context, that even those Fascist theoreticians who were non-Gentileans, accepted all the implications of Gentile's analysis, that is to say, Gentile's ideas were not only compatible with, but informed, Fascist moral thought. See Carlo Costamagna, *Dottrina del fascismo* (Turin: UTET, 1940), pp. 324, 333–334, 337–338.
61. See Gentile, *Genesi...*, pp. 6–9 where he characterizes the ethical imperative governing the life of the spirit, and Carlini, *op. cit.*, pp. 103–112.
62. "We Fascists do not want an agnostic state;...we desire a state that is both educator and teacher." Gentile, *Che cosa è il fascismo*, p. 100.
63. Gentile spoke candidly of the specifically disciplinary function of the state. See Gentile, "Discorso agli italiani," *Giovanni Gentile dal discorso agli italiani alla morte*, p. 69. Compare Costamagna, *op. cit.*, p. 330. Mussolini had early em-

phasized the role of discipline in rendering the nation capable of entering into competition with other states. See the account in Mussolini, "L'azione e la dottrina fascista dinanzi alle necessità storiche della nazione," *Opera*, 18, p. 413. See Mussolini, "Disciplina," *Opera*, 17, p. 67.

64. See in this context, Gentile, *Scritti pedagogici* (Rome: Treves-Treccani-Tumminelli, 1932), 3, pp. 5–6, and *Sommario di pedagogia come scienza filosofica* (Florence: Sansoni, 1959), 1, p. 227.

65. Gentile, as we shall see, argued that even liberal states, predicated on the inalienable rights of the individual to life and the pursuit of happiness, recognized the intrinsic value of self-sacrifice in the defense of the community. See Gentile, "Il liberalismo di Cavour," in *Che cosa è il fascismo*, pp. 179–196.

66. Gentile, *Riforma dell'educazione*, p. 12.

67. *Ibid.*

68. *Ibid.*

69. Gentile, *Origini....*, p. 7.

70. *Ibid.* Gentile follows very closely the ideas of Mazzini, expressed in *The Duties of Man* and his *To The Italians* found in their English version in Giuseppe Mazzini, *The Duties of Man and Other Essays* (New York: E. P. Dutton, 1912).

71. Gentile, *Introduzione alla filosofia*, p. 180.

72. "What the philosopher ought always to emphasize is that authority must not destroy liberty, nor should liberty pretend to do without authority." Gentile, *Genesi...*, p. 60.

73. Gentile, *Fascismo e cultura*, p. 100.

74. See the discussion in Gentile, *Riforma dell'educazione*, chaps. 2 and 3.

75. See *ibid.*, chap. 1.

76. Gentile, "Idee fondamentali," in *La dottrina del fascismo*, p. 6; *Introduzione alla filosofia*, pp. 184–187.

77. At the end of his life, Gentile identified the mission that Italians could not renounce was that of making the nation "great." Gentile, "Discorso agli italiani," *Giovani Gentile dal discorso agli italiani alla morte*, pp. 68–69; see also Gentile, *Che cosa è il fascismo*, pp. 14–24, 26–28, *Origini...*, p. 7.

78. See Gentile, "Il mio liberalismo," *Che cosa è il fascismo*, pp. 119–122.

79. "The man who, in his singular personality, feels himself estranged from the [self-consciousness of the nation that is the state] becomes an historic abstraction. He is either a delinquent who violates the law, or an amoral creature who fails to sense the pulse of conscience." Gentile, *Introduzione alla filosofia*, p. 181.

80. Gentile held that he was "firmly convinced" that to accomplish its moral tasks, a "strong state" was required to impose an "iron discipline" on all. Gentile, *Che cosa è il fascismo*, p. 121.

81. Gentile, *Genesi...*, p. 60.

82. Gentile, *Sommario di pedagogia...*, 2, p. 37.

83. Gentile's followers regularly invoked that argument in making the case for general discipline in the population. See Ugo Spirito, *Capitalismo e corporativismo* (Florence: Sansoni, 1933), p. 29.

84. Gentile's statement, made almost immediately after the March on Rome by the Fascist forces, that the truncheon could be a "moral force," scandalized his critics who forever charged him with being an apologist for Fascist violence. Gentile, *Che cosa è il fascismo*, p. 50. In that instance, Gentile was making essentially the same argument made by Mussolini in September 1922, before the Fascist accession to power.

85. Gentile, "La violenza fascista," *ibid.*, pp. 29–32. Gentile's position on political

violence mirrored that of Mussolini. Before the accession of Fascism to power, Mussolini said, "Violence is not immoral. Violence is, on appropriate occasions, moral." He went on to specify some of the conditions that distinguished "moral" from "immoral" violence. Fascist violence, he maintained, would have to be employed against the immoral violence of others if it were to serve moral purpose. It must be employed in a manner that is intelligible to others. Political violence may be employed when it is understood to be "liberating," employed against those that would deny the nation its freedom, and its citizens, their lives. He cited the massacre of hundreds of thousands in Bolshevik Russia as the kind of violence against which Fascist violence would oppose itself. Fascist violence would have to be a violence opposed to that "violence that is immoral and stupid." "Violence," Mussolini insisted, must be calculated and rational and must never be allowed to become "a school, a doctrine, or a sport." Mussolini, "L'azione e la dottrina fascista dinanzi alle necessità storiche della nazione," *Opera*, 18, p. 413. In 1921, Mussolini deplored the fact that there were times when "violence employed by individuals or groups of individuals had taken a character completely antagonistic to the spirit of Fascism"—devoid of discipline and/or serving personal or episodic interest. Mussolini, "Disciplina," *Opera*, 17, p. 67.

86. Gentile, "Stato etico," *Che cosa è il fascismo*, p. 35.
87. While the fact that Fascist Italy was characterized by a relatively mild political system is now generally recognized, the issue clearly requires more substantial treatment reserved for the tentative concluding chapter of this work. See, in this context, Irving Louis Horowitz, *Taking Lives: Genocide and State Power* (New Brunswick, N.J.: Transaction Publishers, 1997), pp. 224–227.
88. Panunzio published his rationale for the employment of violence during the long violent struggle for power between 1919 and 1922. Sergio Panunzio, *Diritto, forza e violenza* (Bologna: Cappelli, 1921). I have provided a short descriptive account of the "Fascist philosophy of violence" in A. James Gregor, "Some Thoughts on State and Rebel Terror," in David C. Rapoport and Yonah Alexander (eds.), *The Rationalization of Terrorism* (Frederick, Md.: Alethia, 1982), pp. 56–79.
89. Balbino Giuliano, *Elementi di cultura fascista* (Bologna: Zanichelli, 1929), p. 120.
90. Lyno Guarnieri, *Fascismo e coscienza* (Ferrara: SA Industrie grafiche, 1927), pp. 239–240.
91. See the discussion in the introduction to A. James Gregor, *Interpretations of Fascism* (New Brunswick, N.J.: Transaction Publishers, 1997), pp. xxiii–xxvi.
92. Gentile, *Memorie italiane e problemi della filosofia e della vita* (Florence: Sansoni, 1936), p. 384.
93. See the discussion in Harris, *op. cit.*, pp. 244–245.
94. See Gentile, *Introduzione alla filosofia*, chap. 9, "Stato etico," *Che cosa è il fascismo*, pp. 34–36, *Genesi..*, chap. 12.
95. Gentile, *Genesi...*, p. 71, "Dottrina fascista dello stato," *Che cosa è il fascismo*, pp. 33–35, "Carattere totalitario della dottrina fascista," *Origini...*, pp. 35–36, "Idee fondamentali," *La dottrina del fascismo*, pp. 12–13.
96. Gentile, *Fascismo e cultura*, pp. 54–55.
97. Gentile, *Che cosa è il fascismo*, p. 31, "Discorso agli italiani," *Giovanni Gentile da discorso agli italiani all morte*, p. 68.
98. There is an abundance of literature of that sort, but see Guido Puccio, *Lotta fra due mondi* (Rome: Edizioni italiane, 1942) as a representative example.
99. Gentile, *Origini...*, p. 57.

100. Gentile, *Genesi...*, pp. 66–70.
101. Gentile, *Che cosa è il fascismo*, p. 90.
102. Gentile, *Fascismo e cultura*, p. 121.
103. See the discussion in Gentile, *Origini...*, chaps. 10 and 13.
104. Gentile argues, for instance, that "an Italian can only be free insofar as the Italian people is free....[The] free individual is the free state...." *Genesi...*, p. 66.
105. *Ibid.*, p. 121.
106. *Ibid.*, chaps. 6, 12. In these circumstances the ideal state is never realized. The state is always in the process of becoming.
107. *Ibid.*, chaps. 2, 4 and 6, as well as "La filosofia del fascismo," in the appendix of *Origini...*, pp. 57–59, *Introduzione alla filosofia*, pp. 180–181.
108. See, for example, Gentile, *Fascismo e cultura*, pp. 42–43, 46–49, 50–51, 65, 73, 88–90.
109. Gentile, *Genesi...*, pp. 64–66.
110. *Ibid.*, pp. 113–114.
111. Gentile, *Origini...*, pp. 49–50.
112. See Gentile's comments in "Discorso agli italiani," *Giovanni Gentile dal discorso agli italiani alla morte*, p. 71.
113. See, for example, Gentile's comments in the concluding report of the Commission of the Eighteen, presented to Mussolini by Gentile on July 5, 1925, in *Che cosa è il fascismo*, pp. 231–241, particularly pp. 234–236 and 238–239. In this context, compare Carlo Costamagna, "Il principio corporativo dello stato fascista," in Luigi Lojacono (ed.), *Le corporazioni fasciste* (Milan: Hoepli, 1935), p.79.

6

Totalitarianism and the Interpretation of Fascism

Giovanni Gentile's political philosophy afforded the general rationale for the Fascist system. At a more profound level, it was Gentile's metaphysics that pretended to provide the normative justification for its totalitarianism. That justification invoked a conception of life and reality that was ontologically, epistemologically, and normatively, "totalistic." Within that conception and in some ultimate Hegelian sense, the individual, society, and the state were conceived as one.

It was that kind of totalitarian conviction that animated Fascism, and the concept, itself, is generally recognized as a Fascist product. It was Gentile who initially gave it political currency.[1] The term "totalitarian" lost its specifically fascist character when it became increasingly popular in academic circles after Fascism's defeat in the Second World War.

With the turn of the 1950s, the introduction of "totalitarianism," to identify an entire class of political systems, transformed the character of the discussion concerning paradigmatic Fascism. The concept was introduced as a taxonomic notion having general application.

Like the descriptive categories provided by Linnaeus to house a systematic arrangement of types of plants and animals, taxonomies in social science are, and have been, descriptive pretheoretical formulations designed for essentially didactic and heuristic convenience. They are employed as preliminary instructional devices, as mnemonic aides for easy storage and recall.

A concept like "totalitarianism" serves not to define any political system in all its particulars, but to locate such a system in a schema of classification at a given level of abstraction. A descriptive, if relatively abstract, concept like "totalitarianism" is not expected to provide idiographic detail of any political system, nor, as pretheoretical, is it expected to explain the factors that give rise to totalitarianism or afford an account of its future.

When not strictly didactic, a concept like "totalitarianism" is intended to categorize a collection of systems for the purposes of empirical inquiry. Empirical inquiry could conceivably, under the best circumstances, provide the occasion for generalization and, ultimately, prediction.[2]

Probably stimulated by the tensions generated by the cold war, social scientists took increasing note of the similarities shared by the generic fascism defeated in the Second World War, and the Marxist-Leninist systems that loomed large after its conclusion. Whatever motives may have inspired the researchers of the period, the concept "totalitarianism" proved to be of considerable cognitive consequence.

At the time of its introduction, many intellectuals opposed the dilation of the term to include Marxist-Leninist systems, so convinced were they that "totalitarianism" could apply only to the inhumane systems on the "right" rather than the well-intentioned, if errant, systems on the left.[3] Others objected that the concept was too "narrow" to serve as a useful category for comparative analysis of contemporary one-party systems or to accommodate the growth of diversity among Marxist-Leninist systems themselves.[4] Once the biases were neutralized, however, and explanations of departures from the "model" in any one, or any set of totalitarianisms, were forthcoming, it became reasonably clear that the concept had, and has, empirical reference.[5]

Such a pretheoretical formulation provides us an incomplete set of attributes that afford *prima facie*, nonrigorous, but intuitively plausible, criteria for admission into the class "totalitarian." We are told that the term "totalitarianism" applies to established political systems that feature a syndrome of traits that include (1) potential single party control over all aspects of life; with (2) a "charismatic leader" typically serving as party leader; employing (3) an eschatological formal ideology to legitimate (4) state control of the economy; (5) as well as a state monopoly of education, communication, and coercion.[6]

The phenomenon so characterized was understood to be sufficiently distinctive from other political forms, ancient or modern, to allow for its identification and to recognize it as peculiar to the twentieth century.[7] In fact, as early as November 2, 1929, the *London Times* seems to have recognized as much. The terms "totalitarian" and "unitary state" were used to refer to both Mussolini's Fascism and Stalin's Communism. Both Fascism and Communism were seen as exemplars of those singularly modern dictatorial regimes intrinsically opposed to representative democracy.

In 1934, George Sabine classified the Soviet Union, National Socialist Germany, and Fascist Italy—governed by "unitary parties"—as "totalitarianisms."[8] Many intellectuals thus recognized the traits of totalitarianism in the years before the Second World War. The concept, in effect, has been in service for more than three quarters of a century, and while it has little true theoretical yield in terms of predictive power, it provides a significant order of interpretive insight.

The Concept "Totalitarianism"

Had it not been for the neo-Hegelian thought of Giovanni Gentile, Fascism would probably not have made recourse to the rich vocabulary of totalitarianism. Without that vocabulary, Fascists —like the ideologues of the Soviet Union—would have used an alternative language common to all those dictatorships that have seen themselves as representing a truer form of "democracy" than any to be found among the "bourgeois democracies" or the "demoplutocracies" elsewhere.[9]

Without Gentile, there probably would have been no talk of totalitarianism. Academic language, in some measure, would have been impoverished, but a great deal of confusion might have been avoided.[10]

Like other totalitarians, Fascists would have extended their control over the economy, education, communication, and social life in general, through appeal to a formal, exclusivistic, and purportedly inerrant doctrine. They would have produced their political army, and their youth corps—and imposed, on all, their prescriptive model of a "new man"— all in the name of "direct" democracy. They would have had their *Duce*, just as the Soviets had their *Vozhd*, and National Socialists their *Fuehrer*. They would have had their "corporative state," just as the Soviets had their "proletarian state," and the National Socialists their "Volksstaat."

With or without the specific language of totalitarianism, of course, the concept, by whatever name, would have empirical reference. Years before the advent of Fascist totalitarianism, as we have seen, Gentile and Michels had argued that an abiding sense of national humiliation, economic backwardness and frustrated collective expectations could be expected to precipitate a reactive, developmental nationalism that would shape the political future of economically retrograde communities under the auspices of a mass-mobilizing, hegemonic party and charismatic leadership.

Now that an increasing number of influential scholars have "seen Stalinism as a modernizing regime called forth by the imperative to overcome Russian backwardness for the sake of national survival," pioneering a path "different from and superior to that of capitalist Europe...[employing] the expansion of centralized state power, mass political participation, and....a sacramental idea of rulership"—with the ruler "the repository of truth"—the real existence of a general class of reactive, developmental and nationalist dictatorships, seeking "totalitarian" domination of all aspects of life, is no longer easily dismissed.

That Soviets, like Fascists, long held that their nation "had a mission that set it apart from other nations" reaffirms the conviction that totalitarian systems, at an appropriate level of abstraction, share many features.[11] By the mid-1990s, the most influential of Western sovietologists recognized that Stalinism shared totalitarian properties with both Fascism and National Socialism.[12]

Giovanni Gentile and the Rationale of Totalitarianism

Gentile served Fascism in many ways. Recognizing that the rapid acceleration of economic growth and industrialization was necessary to the renaissance of the nation, Gentile, like Michels, recognized that an environment of strict political order, at any cost, would be necessary—if the nation were to survive and prevail in order to fulfill that historic mission.[13] All these enjoinments, injunctions, and invocations were to appear and reappear as imperatives in *all* totalitarian states.

All that is now reasonably well known. But Gentile sought to accomplish more in the service of Fascism. What was distinctive about Gentile's position was the epistemological and ontological rationale that sustained Fascism's totalitarianism, and gave the class of modern revolutionary regimes their name.

Years before the advent of Fascism, Gentile had been the spokesman of a particular form of neo-Hegelian idealism out of which the metaphysical concept of political totalitarianism was to grow. It was that neo-Hegelianism that supplied not only the vocabulary of totalitarianism, but its justificatory logic as well.[14]

A full account of Gentile's metaphysical rationale for totalitarianism would exceed the limits of space and patience. It cannot be the purpose here to attempt a synoptic presentation of the complex ontological and epistemological neo-Hegelianism that lay at its roots.[15] Gentile's political philosophy has been given sufficient exposition to suggest its intrinsic totalitarian affinities.

What is important, at least to address the issue of cognitive closure, is a recognition that Gentile, like Hegel, conceived a world in which all things, in some sense, and at a certain level of abstraction, are united. Like Hegel, Gentile held that to imagine that the world is composed of "independent" and "objective things" that we come to know by confronting and observing them, is self-contradictory and intellectually absurd.

Gentile, like all epistemological idealists, maintained that anything that existed "outside" or "independent" of the knowing self—like the *noumena* of Immanuel Kant—would be, by definition, unknown and unknowable. The absurdity is overcome when it can be shown that the opposition between the knower and the known resolves itself in one all-encompassing reality: thinking itself—a "concrete, universal consciousness." "Immanent" in that consciousness are all things and beings.[16]

Gentile's fundamental conviction was that the ultimate reality of the world was "spiritual"—thinking as pure act—and knowledge is comprehension of how all multiplicity is systematically resolved in the unity of thinking. We know things only because they are elements in a consciousness which we all share. Thinking, in its maximum "concreteness," is a kind of universal spirit.[17]

Gentile conceived all humankind united in a transempirical spiritual reality in which "empirical individuals" realize their most fundamental intellectual and moral selves in an "immanent" community of consciousness. We have seen what that means in his general political philosophy, where his ideas receive commonsense expression.

For Gentile, "empirical individuals," the individuals of "common sense," are "abstract moments of mind." In ultimate reality—in that reality required by a coherent conception of the world and the knowledge of the things and beings in it—empirical individuals are "unreal." "True" individuality, the "true" self, is a function of living a fully cognitive, and entirely moral life in which the duality of object and subject are "sublated" in the greater "spiritual" community.

It is in that collective thinking life, in that "indivisible nexus which is the system of consciousness or of thought," that nature is affirmed in all its "infinite wealth of categories"—among which one finds individual "things" and "individual selves." "Objective reality" and "individual selves" are the products of a processional sorting-out in thinking. Outside of thinking, individual things and individual selves possess no intrinsic reality. Gentile concluded his work on the mind as "pure act" with the pronouncement that "It is hardly necessary to point out that in [his idealistic conception], all the rights of individuality find satisfaction, *with the exception of those which depend on a fantastic concept of the individual among individuals.* "[18]

In effect, for Gentile, the notion that an "empirical" or "abstract" individuality is "real," is conceived a demeaning fiction.[19] Such a notion would irremediably separate individuals from each other, from their community, from nature and reality. The world around one would be intellectually and morally impenetrable.

For Gentile, "true" or "concrete" individuality is that individuality transformed in the cognitive fullness and moral realization possible only within the synthesis of liberty, learned tradition, custom, and law that, in commonsense, is the community. The express, if transient, form that community assumes is the state.[20]

As has been suggested in the discussion of his political philosophy, Gentile, like Hegel, understood the state not to be the negation of individuality, and a constraint on freedom, but their fulfillment.[21] The community and the state enjoy presumptive priority over the rights of "empirical" individuals.

As has been indicated, at the level of ordinary discourse, in the language of commonsense political philosophy, Gentile maintained that it is the totalitarian state that provides and sustains the "solid, massive structure of social life"—learning, law, morality, and custom. Within that structure, individuals define themselves. Without that self-definition, the "empirical" individual could neither know, nor reasonably govern, his own conduct. The very structure of social life, sustained by the state, is the manifest expression of the collective and reasoned consciousness in which the self of commonsense finds its true fulfillment. In that sense, and at various levels of abstraction, Gentile proceeded to identify the most fundamental cognitive and moral interests of individuals with the state.[22]

Among totalitarian systems, it is only Fascism that advances totalitarianism its ultimate, argued rationale—and Gentile is its author. It was Gentile who argued that the state is the "organization and the will of a community...." If a nation is to survive and create the vehicle for self-realization of the individuals of which it is composed, "it is necessary that the state subject all to one common will."[23] For Gentile, totalitarianism was a moral imperative.

In the official *Doctrine of Fascism*, which appeared in the mid-1930s, these conceptions, articulated before the advent of Fascism itself, are expressed in the conviction that Fascism considers individuals as one with the nation, united in moral laws that affirm a continuity with ancestors in a tradition and a mission that lifts each individual above the brief and narrow "pursuit of pleasure," and affords each a superior life freed of the limits of time and space: a life in which each individual, by the very abnegation of empirical self, the sacrifice of particular interests, can realize that entirely spiritual existence in which true human value is to be found.[24] Written by Gentile, the *Dottrina* gave expression to the rationale of totalitarianism.

For Fascism, Gentile argued, the state was a "spiritual force" that took on moral and intellectual responsibilities in informing the interior life of individuals. The Fascist state was not only the giver of laws, it was the educator and mentor of the spiritual lives of individuals. As a consequence, Gentile concluded his case with a characterization of the state that was Mussolinian: the animating principle of Fascism was "everything is in the state, and nothing human or spiritual exists, or has any value, outside the state." "In that sense," Gentile concluded, "Fascism is totalitarian."[25]

No other totalitarianism provided so complete a rationale for its behaviors. In Stalinism, totalitarianism was an affront to the Marxism out of which it putatively arose. For National Socialists, who refused to employ the concept, their racism made the concept all but indigestible.[26] For Fascism, neo-Hegelian totalitarianism was always implicit in its original ideological commitments—and it was at the center of Gentile's thought some considerable time before Fascism made its appearance.

Thus, in June 1925, when the revolutionary regime was in the process of consolidation itself, Mussolini told the Fourth Congress of the *Partito nazionale fascista* that the prevailing order of the day was "all power to all of Fascism....We wish," he went on, "to fascistize the nation." That, he maintained, constituted the goal of Fascism's "ferocious totalitarian will."[27]

In practice, totalitarianism meant for Fascism a "rigid discipline" of all the elements of a nation that found itself surrounded by threats to its survival. In the existing climate of threat, Mussolini argued, Fascism had created a state "which controlled all the forces that act within the nation, those political, moral and economic...."[28] Fascism sought to inculcate persons with "a discipline and an authority that reached down to dominate the spirit without resistance." Fascism saw itself "not only a giver of laws and the founder of institutions, but an educator and promoter of spiritual life. It [sought] to reconstruct not only the outward forms of human life, but its content, character, and faith...."[29]

In essence, that is what totalitarianism is taken to mean: the creation of a state, governed by a specific and select ruling elite, animated by a religious conviction in its mission, that seeks hegemony through the mediation of a multiplicity of formal and informal tutelary, censorial, mobilizational, economic, and political institutions.[30] Fascism's intent was explicitly totalitarian. Totalitarianism was a neo-Hegelian conception of governance that sought an unbroken spiritual unity among citizens.

Sergio Panunzio and the Fascist Interpretation of Totalitarianism

If Gentile provided totalitarianism its metaphysical rationale, it was left to other Fascist thinkers to follow the concept into the empirical world of politics. The best of the ideologues of Fascism, Sergio Panunzio principal among them,[31] attempted a comparative analysis of the concept "totalitarianism," to relate it to past and extant political systems in a manner that would illuminate something of its specific character.

For Panunzio, like other Fascist intellectuals, totalitarianism, as a complex contemporary reality, was identified as a uniquely modern phenomenon. It was the culmination of a process that commenced with the armed insurrection of an ideologically based revolutionary party that, almost immediately upon accession to power, gave rise to a revolutionary dictatorship, which once consolidated, matured into an "integral" or "totalitarian" one-party state.[32] Panunzio sought to provide an account of the dynamics of what was, for most, a static, descriptive, category.

Panunzio did not pretend to be describing a unique, peculiarly Fascist system. He understood the process he described as having not a single referent, but a class reference: all totalitarian systems.

It was argued that totalitarian systems radically distinguished themselves not only from non-totalitarian "authoritarian" systems, but from those that were predicated on the assumption of a real or fictive contract between "sovereign" individuals—presumably endowed with "natural rights"—and a government composed of temporary role-holders.[33] The obverse of the totalitarian state was the liberal, representative state.

Neither revolutions nor authoritarianism, per se, occupied Panunzio's attention. Accounts of revolution, of course, have dotted the pages of history since the beginning of recorded time.[34] There have been palace coups and military coups. There have been minoritarian revolutions from above and mass insurrections from below. There have been spontaneous peasant rebellions and revolutions involving guerrilla warfare.

For Panunzio, as a major Fascist theoretician, truly modern revolutionary parties are those, governed by a reasonably coherent ideology, that are, in principle, antiliberal and seek to fundamentally transform their societies through mass-mobilization and political inculcation. They may be Fascist, National Socialist, or Marxist-Leninist—among an indeterminate number of others.

That Panunzio insisted that the truly modern revolutionary party be antiliberal was a consequence of his conception of the liberal, contractual state as a useful fiction, contrived by the rising urban, commercial, and industrial bourgeoisie of the seventeenth and eighteenth century in order to wrest civil and economic protections from an authoritarian, and frequently despotic, political system.

The consolidation of bourgeois liberalism produced an arrangement, in which parochial and fractious groups might dominate the political life of the nation. Without ideological content and convictions, without any program that was anything other than transient and episodic, the liberal state was the battlefield of contending domestic factions, subject to the prevailing weight of any particular interest group or collection of groups at any given time.[35]

Fascist ideologues argued that the liberal state served only the interests of individuals, and aggregates of individuals, who possess wealth and power. The representative democracy of advanced industrial states compliantly satisfied the interests of those with money and influence—at the expense of the nation and its most profound interests.

Internationally, the industrialized democracies possessed the power that assured that the world trading, financial, and military systems served their common interests. Liberal democracy, Fascists maintained, was irremediably conservative, committed to the maintenance of the national and international *status quo.*

Any change in the national or international distribution of power would threaten the interests of those most powerful and wealthy. As a consequence, liberal democracy was intrinsically opposed to any redistribution of power or wealth within individual nations or among nations. For Fascist intellectuals, the advanced industrial democracies were unalterably opposed to any change in the patterns of power distribution established in the nineteenth century—and as a necessary consequence, averse to the rise of revolutionary "proletarian nations."[36]

In such circumstances, revolution, both national and international, was the only available recourse open to those nations undertaking economic development late, after the patterns of national and international power had already been established.[37] If a less-developed nation was to attain a place in the sun, it would have to undertake both national and international revolution.

What that implied for Fascist theoreticians like Panunzio was the necessity of creating a "truly modern," mass-based, elitist, redemptive national and revolutionary movement that would discipline the nation to the task of domestic and international change. That movement would be essentially "totalitarian" in intent. A "revolutionary party," possessed of a "vigorous, potent and impetuous" idea, unalterably committed to victory, disposed to "strike down, disassemble, and trash" the old order of things, would transform what had been the somnolent consciousness of passive and unresponsive masses with a new vision of the future.[38]

With political victory, the revolutionary party would impose a "revolutionary dictatorship" on masses that had been corrupted by years of bourgeois liberalism and political indifference. In Italy, Mussolini signalled the advent of the revolutionary dictatorship with his speech at the national congress of the *Partitio nazionale fascista* in June 1925 with a call for "all power to all of Fascism."[39]

Fascist theoreticians acknowledged that the mechanisms employed by the revolutionary dictatorship would initially be primitive and often unpredictable. The general population would not yet have been informed of what might constitute unacceptable behavior in the new environment. Often the dictatorship, itself, was uncertain what might constitute such behavior.

Thus, for almost a decade after the March on Rome, neither scholars nor their publics knew what the range of tolerance was in terms of political inquiry, political discussion, or political expression. Throughout the 1920s, it was not clear what could be expressed in print, published and/or distributed in Fascist Italy. No one really knew what subjects were, in fact, proscribed—nor was anyone certain what the consequences of undertaking "impolitic" activities might involve. Individuals and groups were subject to direct and indirect idiosyncratic pressure, ranging from violence to suasion, without any semblance of predictability.

Until November 1926, a number of the old political parties in Fascist Italy continued to compete for space in the emerging political order. Thereafter, the dictatorship had them abolished. In December of that same year, the Law for the Defense of the State established the political police and a Special Tribunal to deal specifically with political dissent.

In his speech to the Chamber of Deputies in May 1927, Mussolini made eminently clear the course the regime would follow. He spoke of putting together an entire organic structure of powerful institutions that would allow the Fascist state to "control the lives of all from six to sixty, in order to create the new Italian, the Fascist Italian."[40]

In the years that followed, the revolutionary dictatorship created a network of party and state agencies that were devoted to the imposition of a "harsh and military discipline" on the population of the peninsula. Having begun in the period of consolidation of the dictatorship—which Panunzio estimated to run from 1922 through 1926—the expansion and articulation of those institutions occupied the regime until the mid-1930s.

Thus, by way of illustration, during the initial period of his rule, the control of the print and broadcast media of Italy had been indifferently assigned to the Press and Information Office of Mussolini, in his capacity as Head of the Government (*Capo del governo*). By 1937, in the period Panunzio identified as that of totalitarian or party-state maturity, all the agencies of political information were systematically centralized in the Ministry of Popular Culture.

Similarly, only in the late 1920s, after the regime had made it clear that the nation was to be disciplined to Fascist purpose, were school teachers compelled to subscribe to an oath of fealty to the regime, and only in 1931 was a similar oath extracted from university professors. While there was considerable caution in attempting to implement a specifically Fascist education in the universities, by 1937, Giuseppe Bottai, as Minister of National Education, affirmed that in the Fascist state "the schools could not remain liberal in disposition."[41] There was a commitment to shaping the style, attitude, and orientation of students to better accord with the ideological purposes of the regime.[42]

Panunzio carefully described the process through which the revolutionary party became the totalitarian state in Fascist Italy by tracing the transformation of the Grand Council of Fascism. Originally the Grand Council served as an elite association of provincial, regional, and national leaders of the party. Originally composed of the elite of the *Partito nazionale fascista*, immediately after the March on Rome, the Grand Council, as the instrument of the revolutionary dictatorship, was selecting not only the leadership of the party itself, but appointing provincial prefects to exercise control over the nation itself.

In effect, and as early as 1923, the Grand Council had arrogated to itself the revolutionary right to make political decisions not only for the party, but for the nation in its entirety. By 1932, as the totalitarian state began to reach its maturity, the Grand Council was recognized, in law, as the highest governing authority in the Fascist state. The revolutionary party, through the revolutionary dictatorship, had become the embodiment of the state.

The membership of the Grand Council was selected by Mussolini as Head of the Government, and the Grand Council, as the agent of Mussolini, *Duce* of Fascism, chose the national secretaries of the *Partito nazionale fascista*. The national secretaries of the party selected the leaders of the local and provincial party organizations, who, in effect, controlled the political life of the nation. Through the national secretary, Mussolini dominated the party, and through the Grand Council, he dominated all the major activities of the state.

The national secretary of the Fascist party ultimately came to serve as secretary of the Grand Council, commander of the youth organizations, president of the associations for civil servants and teachers, as well as director of the *Dopolavoro*—the after-work recreational organization for workers. The national secretary of the party captained the party militia, controlled the workers syndicates—in which all workers were enrolled—and supervised the national sports associations, women's groups, and the national charitable institutions.

Fascism was thus fundamentally different from any other authoritarian regime in history.[43] It was an exemplar of the modern class of totalitarian regimes.

Thus, by the mid-1930s, the Fascist state had made itself responsible not only for the improvement of the nation's material conditions—to organize the collaboration of productive classes, to enhance production, and accelerate industrial development—but to shape the intellectual and moral life of its citizens.[44] That required a complex institutional infrastructure that provided totalitarianism its outward expression.

In effect, for more than a decade after the insurrectionary seizure of power, the revolutionary dictatorship had gradually constructed the infrastructure of totalitarian control—not unlike the process that characterized the years between the Bolshevik Revolution in 1917 and the creation of the Soviet totalitarian state in the 1930s. In both Fascist Italy and Stalin's Soviet Union, there was a proliferation of agencies calculated to administer the political life of the nation and to inculcate in its population the ideological principles that were advanced to legitimate single-party rule. The difference between the two was that Fascism consistently acknowledged its purposes—and advanced an ideological rationale for their implementation—while Bolshevism languished in confusion and uncertainty concerning its instrumental and intrinsic values as well as its ultimate intent.

Like the Communist Party of the Soviet Union, the *Partito nazionale fascista*, in the course of time, became the nation. Totalitarianism in Italy, as it was in the Soviet Union, was the fruit of revolution in an economically retrograde nation, competing with the advanced industrial democracies for space, resources, and international stature. The difference between the two was that Fascist intellectuals knew what the revolution was about, and what their intentions were, while Bolshevik intellectuals did not.[45]

Panunzio reminded his audience that the totalitarian state was the peculiar product of a revolutionary dictatorship secure in power. That security in power need not reflect security of purpose. Stalin's Bolshevism revealed itself to be notoriously uncertain as to its purpose. Totalitarianisms share institutional features, not ideological identity. While Fascism very early expressed its intentions in the works of Italy's neo-Hegelian, nationalist, and syndicalist authors, there was very little in the rationale left as an intellectual legacy by Karl Marx and Friedrich Engels that foreshadowed Stalin's totalitarianism.[46]

Comparative Totalitarianism

Sergio Panunzio argued that to qualify as "truly modern" and "totalitarian," a state must be involved, centralized, authoritarian, and hierarchical.[47] The state is "involved" in the sense that it is infused with a specific and comprehensive religious sense of mission.[48] It is "centralized" in so far as it attempts to "integrate" all constituents of the community into the state. It is "authoritarian" in that its "Leader," as "charismatic,"[49] exercizes more control over the entire system than any political leader in history. It is "hierarchical" in so far as power proceeds from the leader downward through essentially appointed agents in subsidiary agencies. Little, if any, initiative is expected to emanate from below.

The established totalitarian state finds its historic and inspirational source in the revolutionary party. That party charges itself with the pursuit of an urgent mission, fulfilling the requirements of a new conception of life and politics. The revolutionary party is prepared to pursue that mission and defend that conception with deadly force.

Because of its convictions, and its determined will to forcefully address what it understands to be the prevailing crises of its time, the revolutionary party, once ascendant, becomes the "single-party (*partito unico*)," in a party-dominant revolutionary dictatorship, a transitional form of the ultimate totalitarian state. The single-party, to the exclusion of all competitors, administers the revolutionary dictatorship. All political opposition is suppressed and compliance behavior is required of all citizens. Under some set of ill-defined circumstances, what ultimately emerges is the fully articulated totalitarian state.[50]

Fascist theoreticians consistently acknowledged the existence of a class of regimes identified as "totalitarian," that included, other than Fascism, at least National Socialist Germany and Stalin's Soviet Union.[51] The properties chosen to distinguish the class of totalitarianisms were those familiar to the analysts of the period that followed the end of the Second World War.

For Fascist theoreticians, totalitarianism was the product of the seizure of political power by a truly modern revolutionary party. In practice, they defined "totalitarianism" by means of properties thought to be of "generic value." Those are the properties with which we have become familiar: (1) unitary party; (2) charismatic leadership; (3) formal ideology; together with (4) state control over the economy, education, communication as well as all means of coercion.

Fascism, as a member of the class, distinguished itself from others in the same class, by virtue of its clear recognition of its revolutionary purposes. While other totalitarians spoke of "class struggle," and communist utopias, Fascism sought rapid industrialization, the restoration of national pride, and accession to "vital living space." While other totalitarians spoke of "race war" and the reconstitution of racial purity, Fascism endeavored to instill a common identity and a sustaining sentiment among all denizens of the nation.

Fascist theoreticians defined Fascism as a mass mobilizing, reactive nationalist, and developmental dictatorship with totalitarian intent, distinguished from all others by its enjoinment to national unity through class collaboration and the inculcation of a common morality.

For Panunzio, it was evident that not all single-party, elitist, developmental and reactive nationalist dictatorships would develop into totalitarianism. That would depend on all those factors that influence complex outcomes as independent variables. Panunzio reminded his audience that historical events are always conditioned by "material and objective circumstances...that operate in society."[52]

Panunzio reminded his audience that among that subset of modern revolutionary movements that sought national redemption through parties inspired by a totalistic *Weltanschauung*, committed to class collaboration and absolute national integrity, not all succeeded to totalitarian status. Either because of an ultimate lack of intent or because of circumstances, there were modern revolutionary movements that might qualify as "fascist-like," that never succeeded to a mature totalitarian form.

"Fascist-like" traits defined the modern revolutionary character of the party, but did not assure a totalitarian outcome. Panunzio reminded his audiences that the Kuomintang of China, as a single-party, had not matured into a totalitarianism.[53] In his judgment, for a great many reasons, including the lack of an effective domestic communications and transportation infrastructure, the Kuomintang was never able to fully insinuate itself into all the aspects of public and private life that would have satisfied the requirements of totalitarianism.

More than that, it was never quite clear that the ideology of the Kuomintang advocated totalitarianism.[54] Panunzio considered the Chinese Kuomintang a subspecific variant of paradigmatic Fascism. It was predicated on the Three Principles of the People of Sun Yat-sen, the first of which was the Principle of Nationalism and the third of which was the Principle of the People's Livelihood—a program for the rapid economic growth and industrial development of China. That it was not Fascism, per se, was the consequence of its commitment to representative democracy ultimately indistinguishable from that of the Western industrialized powers. Whatever its behavior, the Kuomintang was not, in the final analysis, antiliberal in principle.

The democratic commitments of the Kuomintang were qualified by a recognition that post-dynastic and nationalist China would have to be ruled, for an indeterminate period, first by the military and then under political tutelage by the revolutionary party. After the death of Sun, the charismatic *Tsungli*, Chiang Kai-shek would assume the mantle of the *Tsungtsai*, to lead the reactive nationalist and developmental unitary party.

In this context, it is interesting to note that Mussolini, himself, acknowledged that revolutionary parties in Asia were responding to many of the same conditions that gave rise to Fascism. Mussolini spoke of the common resentments to the impostures of the Western capitalist democracies that had inspired both China's revolutionaries and the first Fascists. He spoke of those "plutocracies" who persisted in using less-developed nations as "market supplements for their manufactured goods and as sources of raw materials." He told his Asian visitors that "proletarian Italy" understood full well their reactive responses—and saw in their redemptive nationalism something of its own visage.[55]

Fascist theoreticians recognized the necessary conditions for the rise of reactive, developmental, and elitist nationalist movements, and were prepared to identify at least some of those movements as "fascist" or "quasifascist." For many Fascist intellectuals, the Kuomintang qualified as "quasifascist." For Panunzio, the Spanish revolutionary party of Jose Antonio Primo de Rivera, the Falange, qualified as well.[56]

For Panunzio, all totalitarian regimes shared discernible traits. Among those regimes, Fascism distinguished itself through the possession of a coherent rationale for its totalitarian intent as well as its advocacy of a seamless, classless national unity.

Departure from the ideal type would license the employment of terms like "quasifascist," "protofascist," or "parafascist."

Among systematic zoologists and botanists, species and subspecific difference are often the consequence of employing selected features to make distinctions. Sometimes the distinctions are made for didactic reasons, for ease of identification, storage and retrieval. Sometimes, the distinctions are made for "theoretical" reasons, in order to suggest the natural relations between species or subspecies.

Fascists were to argue that all modern revolutionary movements, should they achieve maturity, evince totalitarian traits. Achieving maturity is a function of the presence in the environment of some set of determinant preconditions. Equally clear is the acknowledgment that not all totalitarianisms are fascist. Finally, not all modern revolutionary movements that qualify as fascist necessarily achieve totalitarian maturity.

In retrospect, it is clear that Panunzio was convinced that there was a generic fascism in the ideology of the Spanish Falange —and yet, in time, it was extinguished in the traditionalist, monarchial, and authoritarian dictatorship of Francisco Franco.[57]

What is important to note is that Panunzio recognized a generic fascism.

While only Mussolini's Fascism achieved totalitarian maturity, there were many other modern revolutionary movements that possessed the criterial properties of generic fascism. Such movements make reactive response to a national sense of collective humiliation, helplessness, and status deprivation. Their explicit doctrines are nationalist, statist, elitist, charismatic, mass-mobilizing, and developmental. Their typical commitments are class-collaborationist, and non-racist.[58] In ideal fascist form, the aspiration of such movements would be totalitarian. Spanish Falangism was fascist, but failed to achieve maturity.

The totalitarianism of non-fascist revolutionary movements has created classificatory problems. Over time, initially non-fascist modern revolutionary movements have sometimes transformed themselves into totalitarianism—and taken on more and more of the cardinal features of paradigmatic Fascism.

More aggressively than most theoreticians in the West, Fascist intellectuals pursued the significance of the family resemblances shared by Fascism, Stalinism, and National Socialism.[59] All were totalitarian. They all shared a resemblance that was *formal*, in terms of structural similarities, but all three differed in terms of *ideological content*.

Bolshevism pretended to be based on the theoretical lucubrations of Marx, Engels, and Lenin. The central redemptive vehicle of the revolution was not the nation, but the economic "class." The political ideal of Marxism-Leninism was the anarchosyndicalist, not the totalitarian, state. Its putative revolutionary environment was to be international and its pretended recruitment base was the proletariat.

The salvific element in Hitler's National Socialism, in turn, was not the nation, but the "race." For Hitler, race assumed ideological preeminence over both the nation and the state. In the final analysis, the National Socialist revolution was supranationalist in scope and intent. The revolution was *racial* in character, with suzerainty, ultimately, to fall to Nordics.[60] In effect, Fascist theoreticians recognized that all these revolutions were different in ideological character, with National Socialism as ideologically different from Fascism as was Stalinism. And yet, all had matured into one or another form of totalitarianism that displayed more and more features of generic fascism.

Some of the better Fascist theoreticians argued that such totalitarianisms, unlike Fascism, were incoherent and inconsistent. In all such cases, totalitarian practice, however practical to the maintenance of single party control, was radically incompatible with its legitimating ideology. Fascist theoreticians argued that Marxism-Leninism, no matter how "creatively developed," could not legitimate one party communist rule.

After acceding to power, the Bolsheviks had been compelled to make recourse to fascist political modalities. The Soviet Union as it matured into Stalinist totalitarianism, began to more and more approximate the Fascism of Mussolini. For Fascists, the history of the Bolshevik Revolution provided a confirming instance of their thesis.

While affirming the formal resemblance shared by the totalitarianism of the Soviet Union and that created by Fascism in Italy,[61] Fascist

theoreticians argued that the exigencies of rule had forced the original
Bolsheviks to abandon the anti-nationalist universalism and anarchosyndicalism of Lenin, and accept the variant of national socialism advanced by Stalin after Lenin's death. By the mid-1930s, institutional-
ized Stalinism appeared as a distorted image of Fascism.

Fascist theoreticians argued that antinationalism and antistatism were
dysfunctional in any effort to force-draft a national community from
the level of traditional agrarianism to advanced industrialization. As
early as the 1920s, Fascist theoreticians had argued that Bolshevism
would be compelled to gradually take on the institutional features of
Fascism if it was to survive in the twentieth century. If, as Fascist intellectuals argued, Bolshevism was really a reactive response to the arro-
gance of the advanced industrial nations of the West, having nothing to
do with classical Marxism, it would ultimately have to take on the attributes of developmental nationalism and gradually approximate, in
one form or another, the principal institutional features of paradigmatic
Fascism.

It is now generally recognized that Bolshevism, like Fascism, was,
in substantial part, a reactive response to the impostures of the advanced
industrial nations of the West.[62] Like the revolutionary syndicalists in
pre-Fascist Italy, the Bolsheviks initially saw revolution as class-based
and international. Only experience with revolutionary dictatorship in a
world dominated by the advanced industrial democracies, created among
them the disposition to recognize the specifically national, and "classless," character of their obligations.

In the course of transforming the revolutionary dictatorship inherited from V. I. Lenin into a totalitarianism, Josef Stalin gutted the ideology of the revolution until it was obvious to everyone that Stalinism
was essentially nationalistic in sentiment, charismatic in the person of
its *Vozhd*, hierarchic in structure, statist in character, and developmental in impetus. Mussolini, himself, saw in the emerging Stalinist totalitarianism a "cryptofascism."[63] He had early told Communists that a
"centralized and unitary state that imposes iron discipline on all persons" would have to be a necessary feature of any developmental "Marxist" state.[64] He told them they could not do without the missionary zeal,
the leadership, and the unity nationalism brought with it.

Fascists, in general, had early argued that revolution in its struggle
against the advanced industrial powers in the twentieth century would
not only necessarily have to be national in character and antiliberal in
disposition, each revolutionary power would have to take on the politi-

cal characteristics of totalitarian Fascism, as well, if it sought to effectively mobilize all domestic energies to revolutionary ends.[65]

At the very origins of Fascism, Dino Grandi and Ardengo Soffici had argued that the revolutions of the twentieth century would involve the potential and real struggle of disadvantaged nations against those that were privileged. Grandi and Soffici argued that the revolutions of our time involved the rebirth and redemption of nations, not classes—and that if Bolshevik Russia were to survive and prevail in our time, it would have to abandon Marx's internationalism, and Lenin's antistate anarchosyndicalism, restore the order and integrity of the state, and embark on a program of rapid economic growth and accelerated industrialization.[66]

All of that proved to be, in significant measure, true. It was as true for National Socialist Germany as it was for Stalin's Soviet Union. However much Hitler pursued his dream of Nordic internationalism, politically and historically defined Germany remained his recruitment and resource base. It was reactive German national sentiment that fueled Hitler's wars, just as it was Soviet national "patriotism" that sustained Stalin's "Great Patriotic War." German industrial development, after the humiliating and retrograde Weimar interlude, took place on German soil, just as Soviet efforts took place on Soviet soil. Hitler's rule was German rule, just as Stalin's rule was Soviet rule.

Giovanni Gentile, Roberto Michels, and Sergio Panunzio were among the major architects of Fascism. They produced its justificatory legitimation, its empirical rationale, and the comparative analysis that sought its place among modern political revolutions. They left a sophisticated treatment of Fascism and totalitarianism that is at once intelligent and worthy of reflection. They offered an account of Fascism that provides for its identification and the identification of its variants. They supplied a treatment of totalitarianism that is at once insightful and suggestive.

Totalitarianism and Fascism in Perspective

After the Second World War, Western scholarship attempted to deal responsibly with all these issues. There was an effort to understand totalitarianism and fascism.

For Hannah Arendt, and those she influenced, totalitarianism was studied in order to come to some understanding of the "absolute evil" it brought in its train.[67] That Mussolini's Fascism had too few victims, made its "evil" too far from absolute to allow it to be classified as totalitarian.[68]

Others argued that Fascism allowed far too much room for uncontrolled activities within the society and the economic system it dominated to qualify as totalitarian.[69] The survival of the monarchy and the Catholic Church, and the relative independence of the military in Fascist Italy, have been cited as evidence of the nontotalitarian "pluralist" features of Italian life that survived throughout Fascism's tenure.

The purpose of Fascism's totalitarianism, however, was neither to enact "absolute evil," nor to necessarily suppress all forms of pluralism. It was to foster and sustain a state- sponsored accelerated real rate of industrial development and economic growth that would provide the material foundation for the realization of the nation's redemptive "mission" in the modern world.

Dante Germino and Leonard Schapiro both argue that the surviving elements of pluralism in Fascism were not competitive, as is the case in liberal-democratic political environments, but operated in circumstances controlled by the totalitarian leader and his party.[70] Understanding totalitarianism is not learning about evil, but about ideological control in the pursuit of a political mission under some collection of determinate conditions. That evil may attend such an enterprise is a matter for separate consideration.

The "pluralism" of Fascist totalitarianism was a byproduct of the fact that major Fascist theoreticians had early argued that rapid economic growth and development required the existence of a market in order to foster and sustain a rational price structure in a rather complex economy undergoing stress—and the existence of private property was essential to the maintenance of a viable market.[71] In that sense, therefore, Fascism would be "pluralistic." It would permit the continued existence of private property, and private interests. But the pluralism that resulted would be under the constant supervision of the Fascist state.

In principal, totalitarian systems are averse to allowing free and widespread communications between social elements that might make them truly capable of aggregating and articulating their own specific interests against the overarching interests of the state.[72] Whatever pluralism resulted from the existence of private property and the market in Fascist Italy, there was an effort to confine that pluralism to limits established by the interests of the totalitarian state.[73]

All totalitarian systems seem to allow some range of uncontrolled activity. In some, unregulated market activities on the periphery of the economy serve to provide producer and consumer goods for end-users unavailable in the state-run system. In others, individual corruption functions to provide resources for economic activities otherwise starved for capital inputs.

In effect, the typical outcome of successful modern revolutionary movements is a totalitarian state. Fascism provides the most consistent and coherent rationale for such states.

In all of this, Fascism emerges with some clarity. It is now no longer necessary to rehearse the list of criterial traits that have become familiar. Given the clarity of the paradigmatic expression, the measure of "quasifascism," "parafascism" and "protofascism" can be taken. That will always involve judgment and explication, but it is evident that the empty-headed violence of soccer thugs, the stupidities of skinhead racists, the conspiracy paranoia of survivalists, or the traditional mummery of mystics, will not qualify.

Conclusions

Fascist theoreticians attempted a comprehensive analysis of the generic concept "fascism." To identify such systems, Panunzio suggests that one inspect each revolutionary movement's ideological credentials. Fascist systems are inspired by some variant of Hegelianism—that is to say some form of antipositivist and antimaterialist, ontological, epistemological, and ethical idealism that unites particulars in universals.[74]

Fascist systems emphasize will, affect, determination, and faith in the accomplishment of revolutionary goals. The state serves as a central institution and the nation as the dominant myth. Elites lead passive masses in the achievement of populist goals—and the relationship is spoken of as "spontaneous democracy."

The purpose of the revolutionary enterprise is uplift and renovate the nation and empower a people long enured to humiliation and exploitation. The enemy of the enterprise is liberalism as it has evolved in the West with its conception of a society composed of discrete individual atoms, activated only by a search for personal pleasure in an atmosphere of license.

Fascists characterized the twentieth century the century of fascism,[75] with variants of fascism to be found everywhere. They would demonstrate their affinities with the paradigm through their unitary party structure, their elitism, the presence of charismatic leaders, their mass-mobilizing practices, their irredentism, their opposition to foreign "plutocracies," their plebiscitary populism, their prescriptive moralism, and their acceptance of violence as a legitimate instrument of policy. Their economic policies would be developmental, class-collaborationist, capital-intensive, protective of domestic infant industries, and tendentially autarchic.

That any of this serves cognitive purpose depends on its didactic and heuristic utility. Whatever utility it possesses is best illustrated by applying its insights to an instantial case.

At this juncture, it is instructive to inspect a contemporary candidate for possible identification as a generic fascism. The seeming rise of just such a political phenomenon in a post-Soviet, post-totalitarian Russia, affords the occasion to apply the principles, here considered, to a present political reality.

Notes

1. The *meaning* of the concept "totalitarianism" is to be found in Gentile's early pre-Fascist works on law and philosophy. The term may have been given contemporary currency by opponents to denigrate Fascism, but that could only have effect because the concept had become reasonably well-known intellectual fare by the time Fascism came to power. See the discussion in Abbott Gleason, *Totalitarianism: The Inner History of the Cold War* (New York: Oxford University Press, 1995), chap. 1.
2. See the discussion in Domenico Fisichella, *Analisi del totalitarismo* (Florence: G. D'Anna, 1976), chap. 1.
3. Soviet intellectuals used the term "totalitarian" to refer exclusively to "oppressive and exploitative capitalist political systems," of which Fascist Italy and National Socialist Germany were held to be only the most exacerbated form. See the comments in Leonard Schapiro, *Totalitarianism* (New York: Praeger, 1972), p. 14.
4. See the discussion in Robert C. Tucker, *The Soviet Political Mind and Post-Stalin Change* (New York: W. W. Norton, 1971), p. 29.
5. See the discussion in Walter Laqueur, *The Dream That Failed: Reflections on the Soviet Union* (New York: Oxford University Press, 1994), chap. 4, and an account of the pretheoretical character of the concept "totalitarianism" in A. James Gregor, "'Totalitarianism' Revisited," in Ernest Menze (ed.), *Totalitarianism Reconsidered* (Port Washington, N.Y.: Kennikat, 1981), pp. 130–145.
6. See Carl Friedrich and Zbigniew K. Brzezinski, *Totalitarian Dictatorship and Autocracy* (New York: Praeger, 1956), pp. 3, 8, 9, and 10; and Waldemar Gurian, "The Totalitarian State," *Review of Politics*, 40, n. 4 (October 1978), pp. 516–519.
7. See Hans Buchheim, *Totalitaere Herrschaft: Wesen und Merkmale* (Munich: Koesel, 1962), pp. 11–42.
8. George Sabine, "State," in *Encyclopaedia of the Social Sciences* (New York: Macmillan, 1934), 14, p. 330.
9. "If there has ever been in history a democratic regime, that is to say a state of the people, it is ours." Mussolini, "Al popolo di Perugia," 5 April 1926, *Opera om-*

nia (Florence: La fenice, 1959–1963. Hereafter referred to as *Opera*), 22, p. 229; "The greatest and most authentic democracies that actually exist in the world are those to be found in [Fascist] Italy and [National Socialist] Germany." Mussolini, "Il discorso di Berlino," *Opera*, 28, p. 252.

10. See the discussion in Martin Greifeenhagen, "The Concept of Totalitarianism in Political Theory," in Menze, *op. cit.*, pp. 34–57.

11. Tim McDaniel, *The Agony of the Russian Idea* (Princeton, N.J.: Princeton University Press, 1996), pp. 87, 89, 93, 94.

12. Richard Pipes, *Russia Under the Bolshevik Regime* (New York: Random House, 1995), chap. 5.

13. See for example, Gentile, "L'esempio del governo," and "La crisi morale," in *Dopo la vittoria* (Rome: "La voce," 1920), pp. 65, 84–86.

14. Within the Fascist Party, there was opposition to Gentile for a variety of reasons. Some objected to his pedagogical reform; others objected to his origins in pre-Fascist liberalism. Some had objections to Gentile's "formalism," "abstractionism" and "obscurantism." See Carlo Costamagna, *Dottrina del fascismo* (Turin: UTET, 1940), pp. 9, 31, 33. Costamagna further objected to the philosophical affinities shared by classical Marxism and Gentile's neo-Hegelianism. See *ibid.*, pp. 149f. Costamagna also objected to Gentile's emphasis on individual self-realization as a moral imperative. He saw the state not as the fulfillment of the greater self for the individual, but as "an end in itself." See *ibid.*, pp. 19, 23f. The better of the theoreticians, on the other hand, recognized that Fascist doctrine required a neo-Hegelian foundation in specifically Gentilean form. See Sergio Panunzio, *Teoria generale dello stato fascista* (Padua: CEDAM, 1939), pp. 5, 21, 22–24, and 22n. Costamagna's objections, notwithstanding, he did acknowledge that some form of idealism was necessary to the rationale of the Fascist state. Whatever the case, Gentile's neo-Hegelianism had become a part of the formal ideology of Fascism with the official *Dottrina del fascismo*, published in 1932, the philosophical portion of which was written by Gentile.

15. Gentile's *Teoria generale dello spirito come atto puro* is available in an English translation as *The Theory of Mind as Pure Act* (New York: Macmillan, 1922). The *Teoria generale* appeared in its first edition in 1916. H. W. Carr's introduction to the English translation is helpful.

16. There were clear instances in which Mussolini identified himself with an epistemological and ontological idealism fully compatible with that articulated by Gentile. In 1921, for example, in the Chamber of Deputies, Mussolini affirmed that "Not only does there not exist a duality of matter and spirit, but we have annulled the antithesis in the synthesis of the spirit. Only spirit exists. Nothing else exists—not you, not this hall, not the things and objects that pass in the fantastic cinematography of the universe...." He went on to claim no reality independent of thought. See Mussolini, "Per la vera pacificazione," *Opera*, 17, p. 298.

17. See the discussion in Gentile, *Sistema di logica come teoria del conoscere* (Bari: Laterza, 1923), p. 323.

18. Gentile, *The Theory of Mind as Pure Act*, p. 274.

19. In his final work, Gentile reaffirmed what he considered to be an essential truth of his "Actualism": "The conception of the individual as a social atom is a pure fiction." Gentile, *Genesi e struttura della società* (Verona: Mondadori, 1954), p. 42.

20. See the discussion in Gentile, *I fondamenti della filosofia del diritto* (Florence: Sansoni, 1955), p. 127. The *I fondamenti* was published in its first edition in 1916.

21. See the entire discussion in *ibid.*, p. 103–120.

22. *Ibid.*, p. 118. Gentile identifies the "empirical" individual *metaphysically* with the state as well.

23. Gentile, "Le due democrazie," *Dopo la vittoria*, p. 111.

24. "It is the state which educates citizens to civil virtue, renders them aware of the mission which brings them to unity among themselves; it harmonizes their interests in justice; conveys the conquests of science, of the arts, of law, in human solidarity; lifts humankind from the elementary life of the tribe to the highest expression of human power that is empire; it consigns to the ages the names of those martyred for its integrity and to obey its laws; supplies as example and recommends to future generations those who increased its territories and the geniuses who illuminated it with glory." Mussolini, *Dottrina del fascismo*, part 2, para. 10 (part 2 of the *Dottrina* was written by Mussolini). This entire portion of the *Dottrina* is a literal repetition of remarks made in a speech, "All'Assemblea Quinquennale del regime," on 10 March 1929, *Opera*, 24, pp. 15–16.

25. Benito Mussolini, *La dottrina del fascismo* (Milano: Ulrico Hoepli, 1935), paras. 2, 7, 12, 13. The first chapter of the *Dottrina* was written by Gentile. The quote is a paraphrase of Mussolini's own affirmation: "Our formula is the following— everything in the state, nothing outside the state, and nothing against the state." Mussolini, "Per la Medaglia dei Benemeriti del Comune di Milano," *Opera*, 21, p. 425.

26. Carl Schmitt did attempt to explain the unity of the nation, and the legitimacy of National Socialist dictatorship, by alluding to a common psychology of all "Aryans." Since not all Germans were "Aryans," and the claim that all Aryans had a common psychology is dubious at best, the rationale was singularly unconvincing. See the discussion in A. James Gregor, *Contemporary Radical Ideologies: Totalitarian Thought in the Twentieth Century* (New York: Random House, 1968), chap. 5.

27. Benito Mussolini, "Intransigenza assoluta," *Opera*, 21, pp. 362, 363.

28. Mussolini, "'Se avanzo, seguitemi; se indietreggio, uccidetemi; se muoio, vendicatemi,'" *Opera*, 22, pp. 108, 109.

29. Mussolini, *Dottrina del fascismo*, part 1, para. 13.

30. See the discussion in Steven Paul Soper, *Totalitarianism: A Conceptual Approach* (New York: University Press of America, 1985).

31. See A. James Gregor (ed.), *Sergio Panunzio: Il sindacalismo ed il fondamento razionale del fascismo* (Rome: Volpe, 1978).

32. The discussion follows the account of Sergio Panunzio, "Teoria generale della dittatura," *Gerarchia*, n. 4 (April 1936), pp. 228–236, and n. 5 (May 1936), pp. 303–316.

33. See the discussion in Costamagna, *op. cit.*, pp. 153–155.

34. See the discussion in Panunzio, "Teoria generale della dittatura," *op. cit.*, pp. 228–229.

35. See, for example, a typical discussion in Alfredo Rocco, *La trasformazione dello stato* (Rome: "La Voce," 1927), pp. 12–13.

36. These convictions supplied the rationale for Fascism's entry into the Second World War. Typical of these arguments is that found in Virginio Gayda, *Perchè l'Italia è in Guerra* (Rome: Capriotti, n.d., but probably 1942) and Domenico Soprano, *Spazio vitale* (Milan: Corbaccio, 1942).

37. See in this context, Mussolini's comments in "La politica estera al Senato," *Opera*, 22, pp. 151–152.

38. Panunzio, *"Teoria generale della dittatura,"* *op. cit.*, pp. 236, 305–306.

39. *Ibid.*, p. 309.

40. Mussolini, "Il discorso dell'Ascensione," *Opera*, 22, p. 384.

41. As cited in Alexander J. De Grand, *Bottai e la cultura fascista* (Rome: Laterza, 1978), p. 190.
42. Panunzio, *Teoria generale dello stato fascista*, p. 59; see pp. 60–67.
43. *Ibid.*, pp. 67–68.
44. Rocco, "La dottrina politica del fascismo," in Rocco, *Scritti e discorsi politici* (Milan: Giuffre, 1938), 3, pp. 1103–1106.
45. See the discussion in A. James Gregor, *The Fascist Persuasion in Radical Politics* (Princeton, N.J.: Princeton University Press, 1974), chaps. 4 and 6, together with Gregor, *Marxism, China and Development* (New Brunswick, N.J.: Transaction, 1995), chap. 3.
46. Much the same could be said of the totalitarianism of Hitler's National Socialism. There is very little in Hitler's own writings that might serve as harbinger of the National Socialist totalitarian state.
47. The following account follows that provided primarily in Panunzio, *Teoria generale dello stato fascista* and *Appunti di dottrina generale dello stato* (Rome: Catellani, 1934).
48. Panunzio regularly referred to the party, and the totalitarian regime as "religious." Panunzio, *Teoria generale dello stato fascista*, pp. 7, 19, 59.
49. Panunzio, "Teoria generale della dittatura," *op. cit.*, p. 316. Panunzio cites Roberto Michels in this context; see *ibid.*, pp. 316, n. 1 and 519, n. 1. See Costamagna, *op. cit.*, p. 120.
50. See Costamagna, *op. cit.*, pp. 159–161.
51. *Ibid.*, p. 161.
52. See Panunzio's cautions in his discussion of the nationalist revolution in Spain. Panunzio, *Spagna nazionalsindacalista* (Milan: Bietti, 1942), p. 118.
53. Panunzio, *Rivoluzione e costituzione* (Milan: Treves, 1933), part 2, chap. 15, and *Teoria generale dello stato fascista*, pp. 579–580.
54. The ideology of the Kuomintang was that of Sun Yat-sen, which called for ultimate democratic rule. See Maria Hsia Chang, *The Chinese Blue Shirt Society: Fascism and Economic Development* (Berkeley: Center for Chinese Studies, 1985).
55. Mussolini, "Oriente e occidente," *Opera*, 26, p. 127.
56. See Panunzio, *Spagna nazionalsindacalista*.
57. As late as 1939, Panunzio was uncertain if the revolution of Francisco Franco in Spain had resolved itself into totalitarianism. In the last edition of his *Teoria generale dello stato fascista* in that year, Panunzio remained uncertain as to the outcome of the Spanish revolution that began with the Primo De Rivera. See *ibid.*, p. 499. In his *Spagna nazionalsindacalista*, Panunzio described Franco Spain as one that was "totalitarian, popular and authoritarian." *Ibid.*, p. 105. Whatever the case, Panunzio was convinced of the Fascist character of the Spanish Falange. See his comments in *ibid.*, pp. 46–51, 89–90, 104–105.
58. Fascist theoreticians characteristically argued that the Fascist "doctrine of race" saw the nation as a "race-cradle," with the "Italian race" the product of racial admixture and long breeding isolation. Whenever discrimination against any group was undertaken, it was not for "racial" reasons, but for "pragmatic" and "defensive" purposes. See the entire discussion devoted to "Fascist racism" in A. James Gregor, *The Ideology of Fascism: The Rationale of Totalitarianism* (New York: The Free Press, 1969), chap. 6.
59. Panunzio regularly acknowledged the formal resemblance between the three systems. See *ibid.*, p. 103.
60. See the comments in Costamagna, *op. cit.*, pp. 84–85, 185–210; Panunzio, *Teoria generale dello stato fascista*, pp. 31–36.
61. Panunzio, *Teoria generale dello stato fascista*, pp. 459–463.

62. See the entire discussion in Mikhail Agursky, *The Third Rome: National Bolshevism in the USSR* (Boulder: Westview, 1987).
63. Mussolini, "Atto quinto finora," *Opera*, 29, p. 63. See Gregor, *The Fascist Persuasion in Radical Politics*, pp. 183–188.
64. See Mussolini's comments in "Per la vera pacificazione," *Opera*, 17, p. 295.
65. See, for example, Panunzio, *Teoria generale dello stato fascista*, pp. 459–460, 513–515, 564, 566.
66. See Dino Grandi, "La guerra non risolverà nulla," "La coscienza nazionale," "La libertà comunista," and "Lettera a un socialista," *Giovani* (Bologna: Zanichelli, 1941), pp. 39–43. 85–86, 94–96, 223–228, and "Le origini e la missione del fascismo," in R. Mondolfo (ed.), *Il fascismo* (Bologna: Licinio Cappelli, 1922), pp. 51–71. See Ardengo Soffici, "Chiose," *Battaglia fra due vittorie* (Florence: "La voce," 1923), pp. 108–137.
67. Hannah Arendt, *The Origins of Totalitarianism* (New York: Harcourt, Brace and Company, 1951), p. ix.
68. See *ibid.*, pp. 256, 258, 303, and 303, n. 8.
69. See, for example, Gabriel Almond, "Comparative Political Sytems," in Heinz Eulau (ed.), *Political Behavior* (Glencoe: Free Press, 1956), especially p. 40. The most comprehensive statement of this position is Juan J. Linz, "Totalitarian and Authoritarian Regimes," in Fred I. Greenstein and Nelson W. Polsby (eds.), *The Handbook of Political Science* (Reading, Mass.: Addison-Wesley, 1975), vol. 3, and "An Authoritarian Regime: Spain," in Erik Allardt and Stein Rokkan (eds.), *Mass Politics: Studies in Political Sociology* (New York: The Free Press, 1970), particularly pp. 255–257.
70. See Dante L. Germino, *The Italian Fascist Party in Power: A Study in Totalitarian Rule* (Minneapolis: University of Minnestora, 1959), chap. 8; Schapiro, *op. cit.*, pp. 118–119. See the discussion in Fisichella, *op. cit.*, pp. 142–148.
71. See the discussion in Alfredo Rocco, "La dottrina politica del fascismo," *Scritti e discorsi politici*, 3, pp. 1103–1106.
72. See, in this context, Panunzio's comments on the issue of "social pluralism" in a "monopolitical" state. Panunzio, *Teoria generale dello stato fascista*, pp. 287–292.
73. It was the case that Mussolini lamented that he was forever beset by the necessity of wrestling with the surviving elements of pre-Fascist Italian society. See his comments in *Storia di un anno (Il tempo del bastone e della carota)*, in *Opera*, 34, pp. 301–474.
74. See, for example, the entire discussion in Panunzio, *Appunti di dottrina generale dello stato*, pp. 288–290, 326–345, and particularly *Teoria generale dello stato fascista*, pp. 21–24, and n. 1 on p. 22. In these explications, Panunzio speaks directly of the neo-Hegelianism of Gentile.
75. See Mussolini's reaffirmation of the thesis in his last testament. Mussolini, *Testamento politico* (Rome: Pedanesi, 1948), pp. 27–28.

7

Fascism and the New Russian Nationalism

That a form of fascism has arisen amid the ruins of the former Soviet Union is instructive for a number of reasons. In the first place, the similarities shared by paradigmatic Fascism and the antiliberal "national-patriotic" opposition in post-Soviet Russia are more than superficial. Arguments that share remarkable affinities with those of Roberto Michels, as an exponent of Fascist ideas, can easily be isolated in the opinions of any number of nationalist ideologues in the Russia that emerged out of the former Soviet Union.

Similarly, it is not difficult to find, in the writings of the major exponents of Russia's reactive nationalism, the high moral salience characteristic of the thought of Giovanni Gentile. Allusions to the primacy of spirit in epistemology and the significance of moral responsibility in social life dot the pages of most of the opponents of Russia's new liberalism.

The shared affinities between the belief systems of Fascism and Russia's new nationalism are neither the product of mimetism nor are they the result of foreign import. There is no evidence than any one of the Russian nationalists has read any serious Fascist literature,[1] much less any of the major works of Michels or Gentile.

None of the spokesmen for a Russian fascism give any direct evidence of a familiarity with the thought of Enrico Corradini, or that of Sergio Panunzio, or of Carlo Costagmagna—major theorists of the Fascist regime. Whatever fascist thought there is to be found in Russia, is a response to specifically, and immediately contemporary, Russian issues. Fascism in Russia is not an exercise in imitation. Russian intellectual dissidents are responding to Russian problems, not to those that prompted the responses of Italian and German thinkers after the First World War.

The advocates of Russia's nationalism appeal to what is identified as the "Russian Idea,"[2] a collection of notions about Russia and its "destiny," that originated largely in the nineteenth century, at a time when the nation was struggling to define itself against the advanced powers of the West. The authors of the Russian Idea, however different their conceptions of the nation, all anticipated a Greater Russia, one that would dispel the Western European conviction that Russia was backward and "barbarian." Russia was to fulfill its potential in a "Third Rome," a succession to glory that would afford the nation its merited place in the sun.

The Russian Idea was a reactive response to the distain with which Russians were treated by the industrialized democracies of the West. That the post-Soviet Russian nationalists should make recourse to the thoughts of those who struggled to wrest a respected place for their nation in the community of nations is instructive.

However unfamiliar they may be with Fascist literature, Russian nationalists share some of the same reactive psychological concerns that gave it rise. The Russian nationalist response to national humiliation can hardly be totally unexpected. Whatever fascism is manifest in their thought is a response to problems that beset the defeated and diminished Russia that has emerged as successor to the failed Marxist-Leninist state.

Never before has an industrialized society, on the very cusp of attaining primacy among the advanced nations of the world, disintegrated in such a dramatic fashion. The closest parallel, in our time, is Weimar Germany.

What is evident is that an abiding sense of national humiliation has settled down on a significant minority of Russians. Among them, there is a thirst for accomplishment, to expunge the sense of national failure. There is a hunger for dignity.

Like the less-developed nations of the modern world, those that have suffered catastrophic failure share a psychology of resentment. There is a sense of alienation and confusion, inefficacy and inferiority. Within the system itself, there is disillusionment and a pervasive sense of abandonment. There is a search for direction, a veritable hunger for a sense of purpose—the thirst for a restorative mission.

In post-Soviet Russia there are entire classes of persons who are demoralized. In the general malaise, the middle classes remain uncertain and long for some evidence of a restoration of steady growth and improving living circumstances. They search for any hope of renewed and sustained growth. Workers lack a sense of involvement and a disdain for the "establishment."

In all of this, the role of the Russian military remains uncertain. Faction-ridden and impoverished, the veterans of Afghanistan have been swallowed up in the disorder that now characterizes the nation for which they fought and in whose service they lost friends and comrades.

In many ways, post-Soviet Russia suffers from some of the same strains that afflict a retrograde economy in a contest with those nations that find themselves privileged by wealth, power and prestige. In the former Soviet Union, the image of the "plutocratic West" has resurfaced as the "oppressor" of nations.

It is no longer the Marxist vision of "imperialism," per se, that casts its shadow across Russia. It is the image of a vampire West that seeks to confine a wounded Russia to perpetual inferiority. The response to that kind of imagery, in a psychological environment not unlike that of Weimar Germany or pre-Fascist Italy, has been the emergence of a variant of fascism.

The thought of many of the Russian intellectuals, who articulate the resultant sense of outrage, shares many of the characteristic features of paradigmatic Fascist doctrine. Almost all the defining intellectual properties of Italian Fascist ideology are to be found in the lucubrations of Russia's national-patriots.

Any discussion of fascism outside the confines of Western Europe, and in any time other than that immediately following the end of the First World War, leaves Western academicians uncomfortable. Why that should be the case is the consequence of a variety of influences.

Identifying Fascism

In the first place, for a very long time, fascism was conceived the "creature" and the "reactionary tool" of "big business." It was understood to be a "defense of capitalism in crisis."[3]

For Marxists, and leftists of a variety of persuasions, fascism was intimately associated with advanced monopoly capitalism in its penultimate stages of decline. According to the thesis, Fascism was the "desperate defense" of late capitalism in its inexorable final decay.[4] It was capitalism's paid praetorian guard. To conceive fascism as anything else leaves many in the Western academic community discomfited.

The folk wisdom that saw fascism as the reactionary defense of capitalism leaves a great deal to be desired. There are few serious social scientists who, today, believe that a credible account of the historic phenomenon can be forthcoming using the standard Marxist treatment of fascists as the venal defenders of "class society."[5]

Since revolution in the twentieth century has been rare in advanced industrial environments, there have been few instances where "big business" has been in any position to sponsor, subventionize, and control fascist movements or fascist regimes. Revolutions have typically taken place in socioeconomic environments characterized by delayed or thwarted industrialization and economic development. In the singular instances when they have occurred in reasonably well-developed industrial environments, they have been anomalies. They have followed lost wars and collapsed economies.

By the end of the twentieth century, it has become clear that fascism cannot be identified with any general "crisis" of industrial capitalism. Unless one insists on a totally eccentric notion of fascism, fascism has appeared in marginally- or less-developed "third world nations" with singularly more frequency than it has in industrially mature economic environments.

As a result, the notion that fascism is, or was, necessarily associated with capitalism in crisis, has been, by-and-large, abandoned. The most recent scholarship no longer makes allusion to "fascism's function" as the "defense of capitalism."[6] Whatever fascism was, it is no longer understood to be intimately related to the presence of, or the conditions surrounding, mature industrial capitalism. Most contemporary scholarship speaks without hesitation of "fascism" as arising in partially or non-industrialized environments.[7]

In effect, it is no longer the case that fascism, however fascism is construed, is causally associated with advanced industrialization, or capitalism, or both. Fascism, characteristically makes its appearance in circumstances innocent of advanced industry and/or mature capitalism, where an enduring sense of deprivation and collective humiliation breeds reactive response.

There is now regular talk of "neofascism" and "fascist-like" movements and regimes in a variety of places and at a variety of times.[8] There would seem to be no compelling reason why fascism might not make an appearance anywhere and at any time—but more likely in less developed, rather than mature, economic systems. The proviso remains, that whatever the putative fascism, it displays the ideological features we have here reviewed.

While almost everyone has been prepared to grant that fascism requires certain facilitating conditions for its manifestation, few have suggested what those conditions might be other than to indicate that they be "profound." In fact, if the argument offered here has merit, it is an emphatic sense of failure and collective humiliation that ignites re-active and aggressive nationalism. That sense of failure and humilia-tion is, more often than not, associated with retarded economic growth and industrial development in a world environment of intense status competition and military challenge.

The analogue of delayed economic growth and industrial develop-ment is thwarted or failed growth and development. Thus, Weimar Germany and post-Soviet Russia share features in which serious reac-tive nationalisms and fascisms might be expected to manifest them-selves and mature. Nations suffering catastrophic social and economic collapse are afflicted with many of the same properties as those that are retrograde.

The Italy in which Fascism arose, as a case in point, was essentially a country only marginally industrialized. Its per capita income was about one-fifth that of Great Britain and France, and its inhabitants so poor that millions had been forced to emigrate to South and North America simply in order to survive.

The urgencies that afflicted Italy at the turn of the twentieth century turned on its poverty, its inferiority vis-a-vis its European neighbors, and the ineffectiveness of its government.

The humiliation felt by Italians is evidenced by the literature pro-duced in considerable abundance throughout the first two decades of the new century. The First World War only supplied the mobilizable, "alienated" young men necessary for revolution.

If one considers the circumstances that have overwhelmed Russia with the calamitous collapse of the Soviet Union, there are arresting similarities. With the disintegration of the Soviet polity, large sectors of the Russian population were thrown into devastating poverty, with some of its most gifted forced to emigrate. The immediate impression received concerning the "democratic" government that emerged from the debacle of Communist Party rule was its apparent incompetence. What all that generated among many of Russia's intellectuals was an abiding sense of failure and inferiority—anguish for the nation.

A reactive xenophobia, anti-Semitism, escape into fantasy and re-vivalist cults, the search for "traitors" who had failed the nation, all made their appearance. Vladimir Zhirinovsky surfaced out of the tur-moil. He told his conationals that their country had been betrayed and "mutilated." It had been "turned into a backward place....And today," he went on, "we're being told that we cannot manage without the help of foreigners...." Russian economic and industrial development had been allowed to decelerate until the nation found itself threatened by the hegemonic aspirations of the West—primarily the United States.[9] Zhirinovsky warned the people of a humbled Russia that they might be ultimately reduced "to the final humiliation of begging."[10]

Russia, Zhirinovsky has insisted, stripped of its language and culture, its intelligentsia driven to "depart for America, Europe, Australia, Israel," was being reduced to "a biomass," a nation of "serfs or slaves" who would be condemned to work "for foreign bosses....We have," he continued, "been insulted, humiliated, our reputation blackened.... Russia deserves to become and remain a great nation, level with our great neighbors."[11]

What was desperately required, according to Zhirinovsky, was the creation of a "strong state," capable of reconstructing industry and expanding production—stimulating economic expansion by restoring the size, integrity and capabilities of Russia's armed forces.[12] The rapid increase in production, under "an authoritarian regime that controls defense, transportation, and communications as well as...the administration of energy resources from the center" would regain Russia's "status as a superpower."[13] Only a "rejuvenated Russia," accelerating its economic expansion and industrial sophistication, possessed of a "mighty army," under the direction of a strong, centralized and authoritarian state, could fulfill the promise that would make "the twenty-first century...belong to...proud Russians."[14]

That Zhirinovsky has been unsuccessful seems to turn on the failure of a necessary response from mobilizable masses. Those attracted to Zhirinovsky have been ideological transients. His party organization has fickle membership and the response of the electorate to Zhirinovsky's appeals has been episodic and inconsistent.

In pre-Fascist Italy, the First World War sufficiently focused the attention of enough revolutionary intellectuals, and energized enough displaced and traumatized veterans, to render the first Fascism successful in three years. What seems missing in post-Soviet Russia is the lack of national organization and the availability of mobilizable masses in an environment that has degenerated into almost total anarchy.

The Crisis

For a time immediately following the disintegration of the Soviet Union, some of the features that spurred the growth and development of Fascism on the Italian peninsula seemed in evidence. Hyperinflation in post-Soviet Russia proceeded at an annual rate close to 2,000 percent. By 1994, industrial production in the former Soviet Union had contracted by about 40 percent.[15]

That was the period in which Zhirinovsky had his greatest successes. Armed with the familiar ideas of fascism, Zhirinovsky succeeded in attracting 22.8 percent of the votes cast in the elections of 1993. One report had 43 percent of Russian servicemen in Tadzhikistan voting for Zhirinovsky's party.[16] Thereafter, for whatever reason, support faltered.

All of this suggests that no one can be certain whether the political, economic, and psychological trauma that attended the catastrophic collapse of the Soviet Union might be equivalent in effect to protracted economic backwardness and war in post-World War I Italy. What does appear evident is that a form of fascism, in fact, has arisen out of the ruins of the Soviet Union—and that it features an informal logic familiar to students of generic fascism.

By the middle of 1989, it was clear that the Soviet Union had entered into mortal crisis. Public debate over political and economic reform had hollowed out the authority of the Communist Party and made transparent the impairments of the command economy.[17] In the elections for the Congress of People's Deputies in March 1989, many Communist Party officials lost to their "democratic" and "reformist" opponents, presaging the subsequent collapse of the Party itself.

By the next year, the Central Committee plenum of the Communist Party agreed to surrender the Party's monopoly on political power. In the autumn of that same year, political control by the central Union apparatus began to unravel and the components of the U.S.S.R began to reclaim sovereignty over their territories and populations.

Whatever evidence is available indicates that, by that time, the Communist Party of the Soviet Union no longer enjoyed the support of the vast majority of Soviet citizens.[18] The Party was marginalized and fragmented into factions.[19]

In August 1991, one faction, organized to arrest the rapidly increasing decay of the Party and the Union institutions, attempted an ill-considered and manifestly ill-planned coup that immediately failed. The abortive coup signalled the end of the regime and the collapse of the system.

The political dissolution and the catastrophic economic contraction that followed, not only cost the Soviet Union its international status, but its military potential as well. Very rapidly, the once vaunted Soviet armed forces dissolved into a disgruntled and diminishing company of alienated warriors, ill-equipped and increasingly humiliated.[20]

It is difficult to measure the extent of the trauma suffered by those Soviet or Russian citizens who lived through these experiences. What is known is that a number of Soviet and/or Russian citizens were prepared to identify with a manifesto, "A Word to the People," published in July 1991, that catalogued a set of anguished responses that could only count as an expression of "reactive nationalism."

Marxism and Reactive Nationalism

"A Word to the People" was written by Alexander Prokhanov and signed by Gennadi Ziuganov.[21] Its central concerns were manifest. Soviet and Russian citizens were told that "Our Motherland, our country, and our great state, which have been entrusted to us for safekeeping by history, by nature and by our glorious ancestors, are perishing,... sinking into the abyss of darkness and nonexistence."[22] The appeal was to nationalism and to statism.

Although Ziuganov, a signatory of the "A Word to the People," was leader of the Communist Party of the Russian Federation, and Prokhanov were well-schooled in Marxism-Leninism, neither felt the necessity to conjure up Marxist categories in their effort to explain either the circumstances of the catastrophe that threatened them, or invoke Marxist options in the search for a solution. Not a single Marxist insight was employed to explain why the Soviet Union or Russia, as a constituent republic, faced "bondage and submission...to all-powerful neighbors." It was clear that the twelve leading politicians, intellectuals, and generals, all schooled in Marxism, who signed "A Word to the People," were ill-disposed to make recourse to the political and ideological tradition that had hitherto informed their conscious lives.

There was no Marxism, or Marxism-Leninism, in "A Word to the People." What there was was a clarion call to representatives of all "professions and all estates," to followers of "all ideologies...and all movements" to collect themselves into "one unified, indivisible, and mighty state" that would mold them all, without regard to class provenance, into "one organism,...without which" the nation would be denied "its place in the sun" by foreign predators.

These were sentiments that have long since become familiar. They provided the impetus, three quarters of a century before, for Roberto Michels' transfer of commitment from revolutionary proletarianism to national syndicalism. They were the same sentiments that had made Fascists of revolutionary Marxists seven decades before.

Among those who contributed to the formulation of "A Word to the People," Sergei Kurginian was among the more prominent.[23] Born in Moscow in 1949, by the end of the 1980s, Kurginian, a member of the Communist Party of the Soviet Union, found that, in the face of the catastrophe facing the nation and the state, the legitimating Marxist rationale of the system was "irreparably anachronistic and stultifying...."[24]

By the turn of the decade, in 1990, Kurginian pursued the logic of his ideas in his *Postperestroika*.[25] Having abandoned Marxism and Marxism-Leninism as largely irrelevant, he maintained that the salvation of the "Motherland" would be a function of the correct analysis of society and the state and the dynamics that sustained both.

Those who signed "A Word to the People," as well as those caught up in its appeal, saw their problems in terms of "non-working enterprises," of a "defunct energy sector," and of a "desolated" agricultural economy. Like the Fascists before them, those who sought "national salvation" in a disintegrating Soviet Union, advocated a program of national "productivism" in which Marxist nostrums would play little, if any, role.

There was no call to "class warfare" in the invocations made by the former or current Marxists who were signatories to "A Word to the People." There was, rather, an appeal to classless and "organic" collaboration in the service of the diminished and threatened "national" or "imperial" community. Ziuganov, himself, rejected "the old-style dogmatism" that insisted on the formerly obligatory "class approach" to all problems. He maintained that in circumstances that required a marshalling of people "for solving the task of national salvation and survival, the class approach must be pushed to the background."[26] In all of that, commentators have not failed to detect "undeniable hints of Fascism."[27]

The authors of "A Word to the People" recognized the survival and prevalence of the nation and the state as having priority over any set of "Marxist" priorities. In fact, Ziuganov, himself, leader of the Communist Party of the Russian Federation, has renounced the "international proletarian revolution" in the service of the "Fatherland." For Ziuganov, it is the Fatherland which is held "higher than anything else in the world."[28]

Gennadi Ziuganov

Gennadi Ziuganov, a dedicated Marxist, a leader of the Communist Party of the Russian Federation, the spokesman for 500,000 Party members, has acknowledged that the notions that had served as his lodestar throughout his adult life were largely irrelevant in circumstances that found the nation threatened by the industrially advantaged "hegemonic Great Powers." For Ziuganov, the survival of the nation, in the prevailing, intensely competitive, international environment, required a productive system designed for greater efficiency, accelerated technological innovation, and unfettered growth.

The system Ziuganov has proposed would have some of the major properties of Lenin's own "New Economic Policy" of the early 1920s.[29] It would be a "deideologized developmental" program in which private property would not only be permitted, but protected. It would be an economy that would "combine economic freedom with strong state authority, ensuring that...freedom [would not] exceed the limits of necessity."[30] In effect, it would be the same kind of productive system that orthodox Marxist-Leninists, for decades, had identified with "fascist state capitalism."[31]

The fact is that the "Marxist-Leninist" response of Ziuganov to the crisis that has settled down on Russia is essentially fascist in character. It follows the logic of the fascist response to the crisis of Italian nationalism during the first decades of the twentieth century. It is embodied in the thought of Roberto Michels and any number of other heretical Italian Marxist and revolutionary ideologues of the beginning of the century.

In making response to the Russian national crisis in the middle 1990s, Ziuganov did not rummage through the abundant literature of Marxism-Leninism to search out a suitable strategy. Instead, he made appeal to the turn-of-the-twentieth-century anti-Marxist authors of *Vekhi* (*Landmarks*), to support his invocations to nationalist and statist values.[32]

In substance, Ziuganov has rejected all the "Marxist" thought that gave Bolshevism its intellectual pretensions. He has sought intellectual orientation from authors who were fundamentally anti-Marxist. It is clear that, for Ziuganov, commitment to the Marxist-Leninist tradition is subordinate to his reactive nationalism.

For our purposes, the fact that the authors of *Vekhi* were fundamentally anti-Marxist is significant. That Ziuganov, leader of the Communist Party of the Russian Federation, should make recourse to their tenets, identifies him, at best, as an "heretical" socialist.

Like the revolutionary Marxists of pre-World War I Italy, Ziuganov has sought answers to the problems of his Fatherland in nationalism, developmentalism, and statism. The "Marxism" that has emerged has all the properties of the "heretical Marxism" of the first Fascists.

In that context one can review the thought of the authors of *Vekhi* and a pattern emerges. Not only is the thought of the contributors to *Vekhi* essentially anti-Marxist, their emphasis is on "spirit" and "moral conviction."

Nikolai Berdiaev, one of the authors in the collection to which Ziuganov appeals for support, although initially Marxist in disposition, rejected all the central convictions of Marxism by 1909.[33] Like many of the Italian syndicalists who were his contemporaries, he renounced the metaphysical materialism and the egalitarianism that constituted the philosophical and normative core of classical Marxism, together with the Marxist "obsession" with class warfare, and, like them, he acknowledged the role of conviction, commitment, will, and "idealism" in overt behavior.[34]

All the authors of the seminal *Vekhi*, published at the turn of the twentieth century, had argued very much the same theses. Like Roberto Michels, the authors of *Vekhi*, almost all of whom had started their intellectual careers as Marxists,[35] insisted that Marxism failed to understand the influence of nationalist sentiment on the behaviors of "masses." Marxists had misunderstood the imperatives that govern the political orientation of "patriots" who love their nation and grieve over the impairments of its "state."[36] The "revisionist" authors of *Vekhi* followed very much the same "heretical" path as that followed by Michels and those syndicalists who were to provide much of the intellectual leadership of the first Fascism.

More interesting, perhaps, is the fact that the major spokesmen for *Vekhi*—Berdiaev, Sergei Bulgakov, Peter Struve, and Semion Frank—had all rejected the metaphysical materialism of Marxism and opted for a form of Kantian ethics, together with an epistemological and ontological idealism that shared substantial similarities with the Actualism of Giovanni Gentile.[37] They argued, as had Gentile, that whatever we know of "external reality" is known only in collective consciousness—and they conceived all human activity informed by moral imperatives.[38]

Like Michels and Gentile, the authors of *Vekhi*, to whom the present leader of Russia's communists appeals for ideological support, drew most of their intellectual substance from German social science and German idealist philosophy.[39] Like Gentile, they argued that the ultimate foundation of political life was the ethical life of those who constituted society.[40] Like Gentile, they spoke of "idealistic action" that was at the heart of "creative self-consciousness." Again, like Gentile, they understood that the "creative self-consciousness" of persons required sustaining structures: the moral training of the family, the ordered cognitive exchanges of the schools, and the relationships established in civic society, outside of which the individual would be little more than animal.[41] Like Gentile, the authors of *Vekhi* were convinced that the rejection by the individual of the "absolute" value of "state power" and "national pride" was to court personal ethical disaster.[42]

The same authors went on to argue that, as a consequence, the moral life of human beings was inextricably linked to the structures that sustained society: the rule of law, national consciousness, historical tradition, and the state.[43] They argued, as Michels and Gentilean idealists argued, that Marxism had misunderstood all of that. And like Italian syndicalists and Italian idealists, the authors of *Vekhi* deplored Marxism's appeals to "class warfare" and distributionism as inimical to the moral essence of society and the state. They advocated class harmony and productivism as critical to human purpose.[44]

In his appeal to the authors of *Vekhi*, what Ziuganov did was reaffirm the logic of the first Marxist heretics who provided Fascism its intellectual substance. Not content with that, Ziuganov has gone on to associate his doctrine of "national revival" with the advocates of "Eurasianism,"[45] an explicitly non-Marxist political conception of Russian life that anticipated Bolshevism's "transformation from Marxist, hence internationalist, to solidly nationalistic" orientation.[46] More than that, Eurasianists, in general, had early identified, and applauded, the "affinity between Soviet ideology and, in general, authoritative, fascist types of ideologies...."[47]

In their time, the principal Eurasianist authors favored authoritarianism and totalitarianism, a "nationalistic corporate dictatorship," as the regime most suitable to a "resurgent" Russia.[48] Nikolai Sergeevich Trubetskoy, one of the founders of Eurasianism, maintained that "one of the fundamental theses of Eurasians [was] that modern democracy must give way to ideocracy." He went on to indicate that the "ideology of liberalism and democracy" were "ideocracy's sworn enemies."[49]

Within that context, Trubetskoy, like Gentile, conceived personal self-realization a moral imperative that entailed an "inevitable" process in which "every individual comes to know himself as a member of a nation." By becoming self-aware, an individual becomes an increasingly "outstanding representative of his people." His or her individuality gradually comes to embody national character, spirit, and cultural attributes.[50] Within that process, the individual becomes a fully articulated person.

Like Gentile, Trubetskoy went on to insist that, given such considerations, the moral life of individuals in the modern world could only proceed within a system in which those who ruled, governed in accordance to their "faithfulness to a single common governing idea" that would "organize and control all aspects of life,"[51] the secure foundation upon which persons would erect "a moral personality." The coherence of law and the consistency of the state, ensured by the rule of an elite faithful to the common governing idea, would provide the stable environment for moral realization.

The ruling ideocracy advocated by Trubetskoy would instill in its citizens a "readiness to sacrifice...for a 'common cause,' i.e., a sacrifice justified by the welfare of the whole...." Under ideocracy "the last traces of individualism will disappear, and man will look upon himself, his class, and his nation as part of an organic whole united by a state and performing a definite function in it."[52] The system would produce "new men."

Seemingly not content with all these elements borrowed from antecedents, Ziuganov has gone on to identify the work of Lev Gumilev, "the last Eurasian," as making "highly relevant" contributions to his "national-patriotic" communism. Gumilev, who Ziuganov considers "one of the most outstanding philosophers and systematicians of the twentieth century,"[53] provided Russia's heretical Marxism a psychobiological base for its nationalistic imperialism.

Lev Gumilev and the Foundations of Nationalism

Lev Nikolaevich Gumilev, born the son of the famous Russian poets Nikolai Gumilev and Anna Akhmatova, died in 1992, but not before he had made himself the spokesman of a latter-day Eurasianism. He gave expression to his convictions in an elaborate conceptual framework he identified as "ethnogenesis"—and whatever else he imagined it to be, he was certain that it was not only fully compatible with the "dialectical and historical materialism" of traditional "Marxism-Leninism," but its theoretical culmination.[54]

The most curious fact concerning the work of Gumilev is its popularity among Russian nationalists. His major work, *Ethnogenesis and the Biosphere* is densely written and conceptually complex. It is hard to imagine political activists poring over the text in an effort to penetrate its theoretical niceties. Nonetheless, *Ethnogenesis* is enormously popular among Russian "national socialists."[55]

Part of the explanation of its popularity probably turns on the fact that traditional Marxism, and its Marxist-Leninist variant, never produced a credible "theory of nationalism."[56] For Marxists, nationalism was always an artificial product of bourgeois interests. Until the epiphany that followed the collapse of the Soviet Union, Marxists traditionally employed standard circumlocutions like "Soviet patriotism" when they were compelled to refer to the phenomena of nationalism in their own political environments.

As nationalist sentiment filled the vacuum created by the abandonment of Marxism-Leninism, the intellectuals of the communist-nationalist opposition to post-Soviet liberalism struggled to give theoretical expression to their political sentiments. The work of Gumilev satisfied their every requirement. Gumilev, although abused by the Soviet regime through much of his life because of his unorthodoxies, was finally accepted by some factions in the Communist Party of the Soviet Union, and his works were permitted publication. Moreover, however implausible, Gumilev did insist that his views, in some profound sense, were "Marxist." He had not "betrayed" the old system. He had "expanded" upon it.

Gumilev's posture allowed the theoreticians of the "new" communism to use his views as a bridge from the antinationalism of orthodox Marxism and Marxism-Leninism to the nationalism of the "National Patriotic Union" of Ziuganov. Gumilev's service to the new Russian nationalism is analogous to that discharged by Michels and the Italian national syndicalists prior to the First World War. Michels, like Gumilev, provided the theoretical grounds for abandoning the empty internationalism of Marxism for the "modern" national socialism of the twentieth century.

Both Michels and Gumilev conceive humankind to be composed of social animals that are naturally given to the formation of collectives.[57] The disposition, according to Gumilev, is "neuropsychophysically stamped" on human beings.[58] Unlike lower forms of animals, human beings do not organize themselves in simple herds, flocks, or prides, but in more complex *ethnoi*: "realities—through historical unity, and community of historical fate or destiny."[59] An *ethnos*, for Gumilev, is "a stable collective of individuals that opposes itself to all other similar collectives...."[60] The principle that governs the formation and the persistence of *ethnoi* is affinity. Each individual member of an ethnos recognizes that "we are such-and-such and all others are different"[61] reflecting some selected in-group similarities as opposed to out-group differences. The disposition on the part of aggregates of individuals to so organize is not capricious; it is "connected with the subconscious elemental psyche...."[62]

An organized community of individuals, shaped by natural disposition through the influence of geography, physiology, traditions, beliefs, language, and history, develop a sense of self, aesthetic preferences, and patterns of behavior that Gumilev calls an "ethnic stereotype,"[63] which becomes of immense significance in establishing the *ethnos* and assuring its stability and persistence in time. "...The members of an *ethnos* perceive their own stereotype as the only one worthy of a man who has the right to respect, while all others are 'barbaric' or 'savage'."[64] The "principle," we are told, "characteristic for all *ethnoi*," is "the opposing of itself to all others ('we' and 'not we')."[65]

Ethnoi are established by organized communities of "similars," sharing a sense of common destiny, who are sustained by in-group affinities measured out in traditions, rituals, ceremonies, and customs—together with historical memories and myths of heroes past and commitments to heroes present. In the process, the leaders of *ethnoi* perform essential functions. The leader can consciously set the aims for an *ethnos*.

For Gumilev, the leaders of *ethnoi* move their followers to greatness, to fashion pyramids, pantheons, and cathedrals, to embark on voyages of discovery, space flights, and scientific innovation.[66] They move *ethnoi* to self-sacrificial dedication to collective purpose, to historic enterprise, and on those occasions when the community is infused with "drive," to territorial expansion.[67] In such circumstances, "there will be found the conquistadores and explorers, the poets and heresiarchs, and finally resourceful figures like Caesar and Napoleon. As a rule there are not very many of them, but their energy enables them to develop furious activity fixed and recorded wherever there is history."[68]

In their floodtide, expanding *ethnoi* create "*superethnoi*," the grand civilizations, the historic empires of India, Greece, Rome, China, and Egypt.[69] Possessed of drive, internal discipline, an adequate material base, effective government, and gifted leadership, an *ethnos* can shape the history of the world and leave, in time, enduring evidence of its having passed.[70]

For Gumilev, an *ethnos* possessed of a state structure is a "modern nation."[71] As such, it may be composed of a variety of *subethnoi*, that may include classes, religions, extended families, and even clans and phratries. While all these *subethnoi* maintain a consciousness of themselves within the *ethnos*, in times of conflict, "all these groups [act] as a single whole...."[72]

The *ethnos*, in order to survive in an intensely competitive environment, develops social forms that provide for its defense. Those forms include the institutionalization of the authority of those who lead, together with the formulation of catalogs of duties and obligations for the general population, as well as the erection of the state and the fostering of patriotism.[73]

What is remarkable about Gumilev's exercise is its general, and sometimes specific, similarities to the account of nationalism provided by Roberto Michels. More than that, whole sections of Gumilev's discussion parallel those in some of the major Fascist literature of the inter-war years.[74]

Gumilev's work was far more comprehensive in certain respects than that found in Fascist literature, attempting, as he did, to explain the rise and fall of civilizations. And his work was inevitably influenced by half-a-hundred years of intellectual reflection by several generations of scholars. Nonetheless, the similarities with the literature of Fascism are arresting.

Gumilev has supplied the national-patriotic forces of Ziuganov with a defensible theory of nationalism, replete with masses and elites, with in-group amity and out-group enmity, with appeals to self-sacrifice and group discipline. He has made the nation and the state, as the modern expression of "ethnogenesis," the vehicles of history. He has rendered "patriotism" and "nationalism" natural "neuropsychophysical" by-products of human life. He has even tentatively advised against uncontrolled immigration and "crossbreeding" between *ethnoi*.[75]

What is eminently clear is that none of this is "racist" in any conventional sense of the term, any more than Fascist nationalist theory was "racist." Those who have found racism in Gumilev argue that he is anti-Semitic.[76] A similar charge can legitimately be lodged against Fascist nationalism, although anti-Semitism is not logically implied by either Gumilev's "ethnogenesis" or Fascist nationalist theory.

Gumilev's work accomplishes precisely the same task as that of Michels. It provides a revolutionary and reactive nationalist movement its conceptual rationale. That both Gumilev and Michels were initially Marxist in orientation, and came to revolutionary nationalism through Eurasianism and national syndicalism respectively, simply completes the impression of synchronicity.

As has been argued elsewhere, nationalism has frequently acted as a solvent of traditional Marxist internationalism.[77] Before the end of the nineteenth century, Moses Hess, the mentor of Karl Marx, had abandoned "international and proletarian" revolution for the reactive and developmental nationalism of the Jewish people.[78] Those intellectuals like Michels, and the Italian revolutionary syndicalists, were thus not the first, nor would they be the last, to make the transition from orthodox Marxism to nationalism. Gennadi Ziuganov seems to have made the transit without too much intrapsychic tension.

The National-Patriotic Ideology of Gennadi Ziuganov

By the mid-1990s, Gennadi Ziuganov had put together the ideology of the new Russian nationalism. It was inspired by the anti-Marxist authors of *Vekhi*, together with the Eurasianists of the interwar years, as well as Lev Gumilev, the "last Eurasianist." What has emerged from all that is a complex doctrine of national renewal that shares almost all the features of the first Fascism.

As though all that might not be enough to convince us of the character of his reformed communism, Ziuganov regularly cites Ivan Ilin[79] to make his points. That is the same Ivan Alexandrovich Ilin who wrote, as late as 1948, that "Fascism…was a healthy, ineluctable and inevitable phenomenon" that arose in the hour of Italy's national peril. Ilin maintained that such a response is predictable whenever such circumstances arise. "Fascism," he continued, "was right because it was coming from a healthy patriotic sentiment, without which a people can neither assert its own existence nor affirm and create its own culture."[80]

Ilin went on to add that however commendable, Fascism did commit an entire range of "deep and serious blunders" that its opponents will forever invoke in order to render it "odious." As a consequence, he suggested that "any future fascist social and political movements choose another name to identify themselves."[81]

One would not have to be a particularly astute political analyst to understand that. After the Second World War, one would have to be particularly foolish to identify with "fascism." Fascism in the contemporary world never appears as fascist. It can only be identified by its ideological pedigree, its stated program, and its manifest features.

In that sense, the ideological convictions of Gennadi Ziuganov are important. They approximate the first Fascism more faithfully than any of the "neofascists," "quasifascists," and "cryptofascists" that Western scholars pretend to have discovered in the advanced industrial democracies.

Historically, fascism has been a response to a peculiar set of political, economic, and psychological circumstances. Absent those circumstances, it is unlikely that any serious fascist movement could manifest itself. Fascism is the product of a persistent and emphatic sense of real or perceived national humiliation. It is a tortured, enraged, and passionate demand for national renewal.

Thus we find in Ziuganov a constant jeremiad that turns on the "humiliation" suffered by Russia's "national dignity." He laments the "progressive 'Americanization'" of Russia's culture and the degradation of the nation's spirit"—reducing the former Soviet Union to "a semicolony" of the advanced industrial countries.[82] He appeals to the armed forces, "who have selflessly protected our humiliated Fatherland," to collaborate in the effort to "restore the might of the Russian state and its status in the world."[83]

He went on to tell his followers that he had rejected "fantasies about 'world revolution'" in order to mobilize the domestic forces necessary to redress the humiliations to which Russia had been subjected.[84] Resurgent Russia must be a nation without "schisms."[85]

For Ziuganov, his proposed "national-patriotic union" would include "the cooperation of left and right, believers and atheists, working people and nationally oriented businessmen....Now...it is much more important to save Russia than to preserve one's ideological innocence.... The humiliating condition," he went on, "in which the citizens of a formerly great power find themselves disturbs their historical consciousness and, at the same time, awakens their national self-awareness....It must be all of us together."[86]

All of these ideas resonate with the convictions of Alexander Prokhanov. It was he who wrote the "Word to the People" in July 1991 that signalled the actual birth of the "national-patriotic" union of communists and nationalists—and it was he who was to serve as one of the Ziuganov's major advisors.[87]

Prokhanov conceives the world an arena of "unending struggle, of a huge, gigantic conflict incorporating thousands of other conflicts." At the moment, Russia finds itself "toppled, vanquished and captive," the victim of traitors within and overwhelming material power from without.

In those circumstances, Prokhanov affirmed that he would support any political strategy, "white, red, Stalinist or fascist," that would save the nation. In fact, Prokhanov candidly expressed an admiration both of Stalinism and the historic program of Benito Mussolini.[88]

All of these ideas contribute to the substance of Ziuganov's political beliefs. As a result, his convictions are spoken of as a "schizophrenic ideology," and a "nationalist-communist melange."[89] We are told that he gives vent to "authoritarianism, nationalism, revanchism and interventionism...."[90] Generally indifferent, if respectful, of Marx and Lenin, Ziuganov is said to "exude a sort of mystical nationalism," a "xenophobic" and "reactive nationalism," that has made the privileged and advantaged West the enemy of a wounded and morally debilitated Russia.[91]

Ziuganov has called upon the nation's sons and daughters to restore and protect the spiritual and cultural heritage of the Russian empire. He has called upon them not to be seduced by the "mythical" freedom of the liberals, and once again, make their own the "eternal values of the Russian character"—anti-individualistic collectivism, idealism, heroism, selfless labor, and impeccable morality.[92]

For Ziuganov, Russia is charged with a special historic mission, that of resisting the Spenglerian decadence of an "immoral and materialistic West."[93] The dominant West, like an "insatiable octopus or gigantic whirlpool," seeks to extract minerals and cheap labor from the less-developed countries in a process of exploitation calculated to condemn them to perpetual inferiority.[94] In such an environment, only Russia can assure a "balanced world" in the "geopolitical equilbrium of....Great Spaces, civilizations, and ethno-religious 'centers of force.'"[95]

To meet its geopolitical responsibilities, Russia is required to reconstruct its productive base, now inferior to those of the advanced industrial nations.[96] That reconstruction would involve class collaboration,[97] the legal protection of private property, and the state controlled use of market signals to generate a rational price-structure for the economy.[98]

In April 1994, the Communist Party of the Russian Federation committed itself to "the great idea of patriotism," calculated to produce a sense of "organicity" to the nation—a union that would finally, and without equivocation, replace "class" as the proper object of primary loyalty.[99] The organic union of all in solidarity, selflessness, and sacrifice,[100] devoted to the service of "The Russian Idea," would give the lie to the "prehistoric and failed liberalism" those under "foreign influence" were attempting to impose on the Fatherland.[101]

As opposed to liberalism, the national-patriotic union proposes that only the "closest mutual tie between the individual, society, and the state" could provide the energy and the discipline necessary for the salvation, rehabilitation, and renewal of the nation.[102] Those ties, and that discipline, could only be provided through a system of representation that would not impair the expression of the homogeneous and popular "collective will"—something that invariably happens in systems characterized by a "hollow separation of powers" that allow "traitors to the Fatherland" to carry out their "anti-national tasks."[103]

What appears perfectly evident is that whatever "democracy" Ziuganov alludes to in his discourses and publications has more to do with Panunzio's "revolutionary dictatorship" than it has with liberal representative democracy. Equally clear, and perhaps more significant, is the fact that Ziuganov continues to admire Stalin, the *Vozhd*, the architect of Soviet totalitarianism.

Ziuganov laments the "excesses" of Stalinism, primarily because those excesses weakened the state by casting Russian against Russian,[104] but he reminds his audiences that Stalin did create a modern Russia capable of defeating the most formidable armed forces in the history of the world. Furthermore, Ziuganov contends that Stalin was fully prepared to undertake a "philosophical renewal" of the official doctrine of the Soviet Union, in order to create an alternative ideology of patriotism that would supercede traditional Marxism. If death had not intervened, Ziuganov maintains, Stalin's reforms would have fully restored "the Russian spiritual-state tradition."[105]

That ideology of patriotism, dedicated to a strong state and the restoration of "Russian national pride," would unite all Russians in a common mission and a common sentiment. That new legitimating ideology would proceed to "the recognition of national values and the rejection of dogmatic utopian myths...and the shameless antichurch campaign" of the traditional Marxist past.[106]

For Ziuganov, a less homicidal and more benign Stalinism, shorn of its Marxist-Leninist trappings, infused with nationalist and statist sentiments, inspired by spiritual and moral values, developmental in intent, and clearly irredentist, constitutes a political ideal.[107] It is a political ideal that looks very much like the revolutionary dictatorship, if not the totalitarianism, of Benito Mussolini. It would seem that Veljko Vujacic is correct in arguing that in the new Russian nationalism of Gennadi Ziuganov, "the ideological circle from the communist left to the fascist right has been fully closed."[108]

The fact that it appears that few, if any, of the intellectuals in the service of Russia's new national-patriotic forces ever read anything of the works of Roberto Michels or Giovanni Gentile[109] is significant at least in the sense that it suggests that fascism arises not out of intellectual diffusion or ideological contagion, but in response to a set of situational stimulae. While it is not possible to stipulate, with any precision, what all those stimulae might be, or what their quantitative threshold levels might be that initiate the fascist response, it seems reasonably certain that high levels of felt humiliation are a major contributor.

Together with all the factors suggested by social scientists—economic crises, elite fatigue, escalation in social disorder, the alienation of intellectuals, the defection of security forces, demographic dislocation, the weakening and disintegration of stabilizing institutions—it is a sense of individual and collective humiliation that ignites a passion for national palingenesis. Aggressive minorities seek to mobilize masses to a national mission of comprehensive renewal.

What seems to emerge in such circumstances is a form of "pervasive political authoritarianism." In countries like the former Soviet Union and China, for example, a "pattern of authoritarianism and nationalism"[110] emerges at a point when both nations find themselves threatened by economic catastrophe, pervasive dysfunction, and perpetual international inferiority.

By the commencement of the 1990s, the Communist Party of the Soviet Union found itself in charge of an economy in all but total collapse.[111] Russians suddenly found themselves indigents in a world they had imagined themselves dominating. In response, they sought out authoritarianism and reactive nationalism.

Fascism

One form that pattern of authoritarianism and reactive nationalism may assume is in a variant of the historic Fascism of Mussolini. There are alternative, and internally inconsistent, forms of that pattern that have succeeded to power under very similar circumstances in the twentieth century. One can find such inconsistent forms in the redemptive nationalism of Hitlerism, Stalinism, Maoism, and the obscenity imposed on Cambodia by the homicidal Pol Pot. All were reactive responses to real or fancied humiliation and a persistent sense of national inadequacy.

With the clarity of hindsight, it is obvious that Bolshevism and Stalinism harbored multiple dysfunctions. "Class struggle" undermined the unity so necessary to rapid economic and political development. The Marxist "command economy" proved incapable of sustaining a complex economic system. Fascism, as a coherent developmental nationalism, made neither mistake.

Hitlerism was even more defective as a form of reactive and developmental nationalism. Racism divided what should have been a united German people. It alienated those powers that were ultimately to suffocate German nationalism in blood. It cost Germany domestic talent, taxed resources, divided loyalties, and plunged the nation into the horrors of genocide.

Fascism was the first explicit response to the national sense of humiliation and inefficacy. It was the first to identify Marxism, in its original form, as totally irrelevant to the problems of those communities that found themselves, for whatever reason, in the second tier of nations.

Fascism addressed its problems directly, and left a coherent and relevant, if dangerous, ideology to its followers. Fascism was unqualifiedly nationalist, redemptive, renovative, and aggressive—all given coherence of expression in a responsible body of thought.

It is extremely unlikely that "fascists" or "fascist thought" can be found among populations in the advanced industrial democracies. There will be many who will imagine themselves humiliated and exploited, but they are hardly likely to be thinkers. In all probability, they will be soccer thugs, racists, members of armed gangs, and exotic cults—but they will not be fascists.

The fascists in our future will most likely be found in post-Soviet Russia and post-Maoist China—in environments where entire peoples have suffered humiliation and massive status deprivation, where an active body of talented intellectuals give voice to pervasive sentiments, and where political leaders promise national rebirth and collective redemption.

Social science is not a particularly sophisticated enterprise. There is very little it can tell us, with any assurance, about even the proximate future of entire nations and the world. Nonetheless, a proper concern with that future prompts the hazarding of informed guesses. The ensuing discussion will undertake to do some of that, and in its course, something may be learned about the study of fascism and its political and intellectual appeal.

Notes

1. Alexander Dugin, an advocate of a form of mystic antiliberalism, has read and translated some of the works of Julius Evola. Evola, as has been argued (see chapter 1), was a reactionary most of whose ideas were antithetical to Fascism.
2. For a recent account, see Tim McDaniel, *The Agony of the Russian Idea* (Princeton, N.J.: Princeton University Press, 1996).
3. As late as 1974, Nicos Poulantzas, in his *Fascism and Dictatorship* (London: NLB, 1974) could still maintain the thesis.

4. See the discussion in A. James Gregor, *Interpretations of Fascism* (New Brunswick, N.J.: Transaction Publishers, 1997), chap. 5.

5. See the discussion in A. James Gregor, *The Faces of Janus: Marxism and Fascism in the Twentieth Century* (New Haven: Yale University Press, in press), chaps. 2, 3.

6. See the entire account in Roger Griffin, *The Nature of Fascism* (New York: Routledge, 1993).

7. See the account in Walter Laqueur, *Fascism Past Present Future* (New York: Oxford University Press, 1996), Part 3.

8. See, for example, works such as Glyn Ford (ed.), *Fascist Europe: The Rise of Racism and Xenophobia* (London: Pluto, 1991) and Peter H. Merkl and Leonard Weinbert (eds.), *The Revival of Right-Wing Extremism in the Nineties* (London: Frank Cass, 1997).

9. Vladimir Zhirinovsky, *My Struggle* (New York: Barricade, 1996), pp. 17, 24, 43.

10. *Ibid.*, p. 113.

11. *Ibid.*, pp. 65, 66, 68.

12. *Ibid.*, pp. 69, 76, 100, 103, 105.

13. *Ibid.*, p. 112.

14. *Ibid.*, p. 125.

15. See Jonathan Steele, *Eternal Russia: Yeltsin, Gorbachev, and the Mirage of Democracy* (Cambridge: Harvard University Press, 1994), chap. 12; compare Philip Hanson, *From Stagnation to Catastroika: Commentaries on the Soviet Economy, 1983–1991* (New York: Praeger, 1991).

16. Sven Gunnar Simonsen, *Politics and Personalities: Key Actors in the Russian Opposition* (Oslo: International Peace Research Institute, 1996), pp. 170–171.

17. See the account of the discussions concerning economic reform during the final years of the Soviet Union in Pekka Sutela, *Economic Thought and Economic Reform in the Soviet Union* (New York: Cambridge University Press, 1991).

18. See *Moscow News*, no. 27 (24 June 1990), pp. 8–9.

19. See the discussion in Joan Barth Urban and Valerii D. Solovei, *Russia's Communists at the Crossroads* (Boulder: Westview, 1997), chap. 1.

20. See Benjamin S. Lambeth, "Russia's Wounded Military," *Foreign Affairs* 74, no. 2 (March-April 1995), pp. 86–98.

21. Richard Sakwa, *Russian Politics and Society* (New York: Routledge, 1996), p. 14.

22. "A Word to the People" (*Slovo k narodu*), *Sovetskaia rossiia*, 23 July 1991, p. 1.

23. See the discussion of Kurginian's influence in Andrei Podkopalov, "Who's Writing Scenarios for Political Stage? Far-Right Think Tank's Aims," *Current Digest of the Soviet Press* 43, no. 14 (14 May 1991), p. 14.

24. See Sergei Kurginian, "Mekhanizm Soskalzyvaniia: #1," *Literaturnaia Rossia*, no. 26, 1989.

25. Sergei Kurginian et al, *Postperestroika: Konseptual'naya model' razvitiya nashego obshchestva, politicheskikh partii i obshchestvennykh organizatsii* (Moscow: Izdatel'stvo politicheskoi literatury, 1990).

26. Gennadi Ziuganov as cited in Veljko Vujacic, "Gennadiy Zyuganov and the 'Third Road,'" *Post-Soviet Affairs* 12, no. 2 (1996), p. 118. Compare Ziuganov's comments in *My Russia* (Armonk, N.Y.: M. E. Sharpe, 1997), p. 103.

27. Steele, *op. cit.*, p. 332.

28. Ziuganov, *My Russia*, p. 158.

29. Fascist theoreticians had cited Lenin's NEP policies as an admission that "Marxist" economic theory was a signal failure. The Fascist alternative was a mixed

economy in which market signals would provide a rational price structure with which the interventionist state would "guide" economic policy.

30. Ziuganov, *My Russia*, p. 41.
31. See the discussion in Alexander Galkin, "Capitalist Society and Fascism," *Social Sciences: USSR Academy of Sciences*, no. 2 (1970).
32. See Ziuganov, *My Russia*, p. 75.
33. See Nikolai Berdiaev, "Philosophical Verity and Intelligentsia Truth," in Marshall S. Shatz and Judith E. Zimmerman (eds.), *Vekhi (Landmarks)* (Armonk, N.Y.: M. E. Sharpe, 1994), pp. 1–16.
34. *Ibid.*, pp. 2, 4, 7, 9, 10; see Mikhail Gershenzon, "Creative Self-Consciousness," *ibid.*, pp. 51–53.
35. See the Shatz and Zimmerman introduction, *ibid.*, p. xiii.
36. See Sergei Bulgakov, "Heroism and Asceticism: Reflections on the Religious Nature of the Russian Intelligentsia," *ibid.*, pp. 18–19, 43–44.
37. See the characterization by Shatz and Zimmerman, *ibid.*, p. xix.
38. See the discussion in Berdiaev, *ibid*, pp. 1–16.
39. In the case of the authors of *Vekhi*, much of this influence was filtered through the work of Nikolai Federovich Fedorov. See the account in Stephen Lukashevich, *N. F. Fedorov (1828–1903): A Study in Russian Eupsychian and Utopian Thought* (Newark: University of Delaware Press, 1977).
40. "...The political activity of man is identical with ethical activity....Ethics may be regarded as the leaven of politics." Giovanni Gentile, *Genesis and the Structure of Society* (Urbana: University of Illinois, 1960), pp. 175, 176.
41. See Mikhail Gershenzon, "Creative Self-Consciousness," *Vekhi*, pp. 51–69.
42. Semion Frank, "The Ethic of Nihilism," in *ibid.*, p. 136.
43. See the discussion in Peter Struve, "The Intelligentsia and Revolution," *ibid.*, pp. 115–129.
44. See Frank, *ibid.*, pp. 146–148, 152; Berdiaev, *ibid.*, pp. 2, 9.
45. Zyuganov, *My Russia*, p. 71.
46. Dmitry V. Shalpentokh, "Eurasianism Past and Present," *Communism and Post-Communist Studies* 30, no. 2 (June 1997), p. 132.
47. Dmitry V. Shlapentokh, "Bolshevism, Nationalism, and Statism: Soviet Ideology in Formation," in Vladimir N. Brovkin (ed.), *The Bolsheviks in Russian Society: The Revolution and the Civil Wars* (New Haven: Yale University Press, 1996), p. 294.
48. *Ibid.*, pp. 131, 135, 136.
49. Nikolai S. Trubetskoy, *The Legacy of Genghis Khan* (Ann Arbor: University of Michigan, 1991), pp. 269, 274.
50. Trubetskoy, "On True and False Nationalism," *ibid.*, pp. 70–71.
51. Trubetskoy, "On the Idea...," *ibid.*, p. 269.
52. *Ibid.*, pp. 270, 273.
53. Ziuganov, *My Russia*, pp. 76, 100.
54. "...I must clarify how far the conception of ethnogenesis corresponds to the theory of dialectical and historical materialism. It fully corresponds to it." Lev Gumilev, *Ethnogenesis and the Biosphere* (Moscow: Progress, 1990), p. 277; see pp. 9, 29, 37, 57–58, 164, 204, 206, 207, 220, 275–276; see Gumilev's allusions to Marxist theory on pp. 76–77, 79, 146, 147, 170, 205.
55. The "national patriotic" and Communist opposition to the Yeltsin government is often spoken of as "socialist and nationalist"—the so-called "red-white" formula. See the comments of Vadim Medish, editor of Ziuganov's *My Russia*, p. vii.
56. See the discussion, Ephraim Nimni, *Marxism and Nationalism: Theoretical Origins of a Political Crisis* (London: Pluto, 1991).

57. Gumilev, *op. cit.*, p. 178–179.
58. *Ibid.*, p. 99.
59. *Ibid.*, p. 246.
60. *Ibid.*, p. 31.
61. *Ibid.*, p. 98.
62. *Ibid.*, p. 256.
63. *Ibid.*, pp. 95–98.
64. *Ibid.*, p. 96.
65. *Ibid.*, p. 248.
66. *Ibid.*, pp. 179, 225.
67. See, for example, *ibid.*, pp. 235, 259–272.
68. *Ibid.*, p. 273.
69. See the discussion in *ibid.*, pp. 106–107.
70. See *ibid.*, chap. 6, and 239.
71. *Ibid.*, p. 84.
72. *Ibid.*, p. 87.
73. *Ibid.*, pp. 109 and 177.
74. See the account of "Fascist racism" in A. James Gregor, *The Ideology of Fascism: The Rationale of Totalitarianism* (New York: The Free Press, 1969), chap. 6.
75. "In combination with endogamy, i.e., isolation from neighbors, which stabilizes the gene fund, tradition serves as a factor creating stability of the ethnic collective." Gumilev, *op. cit.*, p. 179.
76. See Alexander Yanov, *Weimar Russia and What We Can Do About It* (New York: Slovo-World, 1995), pp. 245–267.
77. See Gregor, *The Faces of Janus*, chap. 8.
78. See Moses Hess, *Rome and Jerusalem* (New York: Philosophical Library, 1958).
79. Ziuganov, *My Russia*, p. 93.
80. Ivan A. Ilin, "O Fashizme," *Nashi Zadachi: statii 1948–1954 godov* (Paris: Izdanie Russkogo Oschche-Voinskogo Soiuza, 1956), 1, p. 70.
81. Ziuganov, *My Russia*, p. 71.
82. *Ibid.*, pp. 12, 13.
83. *Ibid.*, pp. 17, 19.
84. *Ibid.*, p. 20.
85. *Ibid.*, p. 60.
86. *Ibid.*, pp. 39, 51, 64. Ziuganov has also insisted that "Only vigorous and energetic businessmen with initiative can rescue Russia today!" *Ibid.*, p. 68.
87. See James Carney, "A Communist to his Roots," *Time*, 27 May 1996, p. 61.
88. Alexander Yanov, "Political Portrait: The Empire's Last Soldier—Alexander Prokhanov, the Newspaper *Den*, and the War Party," *Novoye vremya*, no. 19 (May 1993), pp. 20–24. An English version is made available in *The Current Digest of the Post-Soviet Press* 44, no. 4 (4 November 1992), p. 13. See the comments of Jeremy Lester, *Modern Tsars and Princes: The Struggle for Hegemony in Russia* (London: Verso, 1995), p. 174.
89. David Remnick, "The War for the Kremlin," *New Yorker*, 22 July 1996, p. 44.
90. *The Economist*, 16 March 1996, p. 53.
91. M. Bivens, "Communist Party Platform is Odd Mix of 'isms'," *San Francisco Chronicle*, 11 June 1996, p. A6; A. Karatnycky, "The Real Zyuganov," *New York Times*, 5 May 1996, p. A17.
92. Ziuganov, *My Russia*, p. 97, "Rossiia I Mir," in Alexei Podberezkin (ed.), *Sovremennaia Russkaia Ideia I Gosudarstvo* (Moscow: Rau-Obozrevatel, 1995).
93. Ziuganov, *My Russia*, pp. 99–100, *Drama vlasti* (Moscow: Paleia, 1993), p. 174.

94. Ziuganov, *My Russia*, p. 108.
95. Ziuganov, *Derzhava* (Moscow: Informpechat, 1994).
96. Ziuganov, *My Russia*, p. 94, *Veriu v Rossiiu* (Vornezh: Voronezh, 1995).
97. See Ziuganov's comments in *My Russia*, p. 103.
98. *Ibid.*, pp. 9, 41, 50. See the Vadim Medish's "Editor's Note," *ibid.*, p. viii.
99. *Ibid.*, p. 99; Vujacic, *op. cit.*, pp. 140–141, 144–145.
100. Ziuganov, *Drama vlasti*, pp. 9–14.
101. Ziuganov, *My Russia*, p. 45.
102. *Ibid.*, p. 120.
103. See the discussion in *Zavtra*, 22 June 1994, as cited in Vujacic, *op.cit.*, pp. 143–144.
104. Ziuganov, *My Russia*, pp. 51, 59, 62.
105. See Ziuganov's comments on the "Russian State System," in *ibid.*, pp. 119–122.
106. *Ibid.*, p. 121.
107. This is a common theme among authors of "national patriotic" conviction. In the collection edited by Mikhail Lobanov, the argument is made that Stalin incarnated the ideas of National Bolshevism. Mikhail Lobanov (ed.), *Stalin: v vospominaniiakh sovremennikov i dokumentakh epokhi* (Moscow: Novaia kniga, 1995).

    In this context, see the argument in Yuri Belov, "Nikolai Bukharin: Sleva napravo," *Sovetskaia Rossiia*, 26 February 1998, pp. 5–6.
108. Vujacic, *op. cit.*, p. 149.
109. Gumilev cites a minor work of Gentile, see Gumilev, *op. cit.*, p. 7.
110. See Mark Lupher, *Power Restructuring in China and Russia* (Boulder: Westview, 1996), p. 287.
111. See the account in Hanson, *op. cit.*

8

Conclusions

It seems evident that there are peculiar intellectual, social, economic, and political environments in which one or another variant of reactive and developmental nationalist dictatorships may arise and flourish. We have no quantitative measures that can distinguish such environments with any testable assurance, but we have seen enough instances of the rise of reactive nationalist and developmental dictatorships among the economically less-developed, or economically impaired, nations of the world to suggest that the association is more than casual.

While reactive nationalism is more frequently associated with economic, and particularly industrial, retardation, there are clearly anomalous instances when some forms are found in communities that are reasonably well-developed economically and industrially, but which, for whatever reasons, suffer a persistent and singular sense of humiliation and corresponding resentment. National Socialist Germany was one case in point. Post-Soviet Russia may be another.

In such circumstances, a variant of reactive nationalism appeals to some intellectuals, and some political actors. It taps deeply felt sentiments among a substantial minority of those enduring assault on collective self-esteem and the feeling of political efficacy. A persistent, profound, and/or pervasive sense of humiliation generates the frustration and hostility that fuels aggressive mass movements committed to national "renewal."

In such circumstances, intellectuals make their appearance prepared to provide arguments that shape the logic of national redemption. They are the Sergei Kurginians and the Alexander Prokhanovs of a Russian fascism. Like Roberto Michels and Giovanni Gentile, they give voice to the informing sentiment of the many who find themselves incapable of articulating their anguish.

The revolutionary intellectuals of post-Soviet Russia conceive themselves as being responsible to the "true patriots" of Holy Russia, and to their dream of a "Third Rome." The West is understood to be an opponent of fabled, if decadent, power, utterly opposed to everything hallowed in traditional Russian morality and culture.

These revolutionary intellectuals represent all those Russians who no longer feel valued for their present labors, their past efforts, or their identification with their community, culture, or nation. There seems to be no future for the nation nor for those who labored, suffered, and sacrificed in its service. While post-Soviet reforms may have provided profit for many, others find themselves impoverished and resentful—as though they, and their nation, no longer have meaning at "the end of history," in the modern world of liberalism and international capitalism.

Like all reactive nationalists, Russia's fascist intellectuals speak the language of personal and collective morality in surroundings that seem devoid of both. In a system that appears mean and unworthy to them, they talk of reconsecration and renewal. They speak of intransigence to the post-communist regime that has betrayed their hopes and thwarted their aspirations. Without having read a word of Fascist literature, they are familiar with its themes, acknowledge its sense of purpose, and see a sacred mission in its prescriptions.

Animated by an irrepressible sense of in-group amity and out-group enmity,[1] revolutionary political movements have emerged in post-Soviet Russia that display, in their most emphatic form, a sense of nationalist outrage and aggressive bitterness. That they constitute a danger goes without saying. They characteristically direct their hostility against those who have "betrayed" the nation, against the "corrupt" and "unprincipled" politicians and bureaucrats, and against all those unresponsive to the clarion call to arms in defense of Mother Russia and its "thousand-year- old state."

Among reactive nationalists, in general, and fascist thinkers in particular, life is conceptualized as offering only sets of absolute alternatives between which there can be no compromise without abandoning one's moral obligations. Ultimately, one must be for or against their movement, the revolution it proposes, and the regime it anticipates. There is little latitude for shades of gray. A fateful binary moral logic emerges that permits no one to remain neutral.

The history of the twentieth century has demonstrated that it is just such movements, fascist and non-fascist alike, that mature into regimes that have been, more often than not, guilty of those crimes against humanity that darken our time. Such movements, and the regimes they create, are so charged with a sense of righteous indignation and a conviction in their own moral impeccability, they are capable of the most unspeakable offenses against their actual or imagined opponents.

Revolution and Crimes Against Humanity

Communities suffering delayed or thwarted economic and industrial growth, very often, if not uniformly, conceive themselves exposed to real or fancied threats of an order of magnitude that is traumatic. Among those reactive nationalists, who find themselves incapable of managing domestic crises or international relations, there is often a search for occult enemies.

In international relations, those enemies are characteristically foreign "imperialists," "capitalists," or "Jewish conspirators." Hegemonic powers, "plutocracies," or "international bankers," control multinational organizations, manipulate international law, exploit trade and financial relations. They overwhelm the subject nation with "reaction," "cultural imperialism," "degeneracy," and "bourgeois spiritual pollution."

Often, if not always, it is imagined that such foreign enemies have domestic collaborators. Such "traitors" may be identified as entire classes of persons—capitalists, the bourgeoisie, "capitalist roaders," landlords, compradors, kulaks, "bourgeoisified elements," "black classes," "worms (*gusanos*)," Jews, Christians, Masons, Muslims, and "antinational" subversives—the proper objects of constraint, incarceration, exile, or deadly force.

In its more pathological forms, such a response manifests itself in convictions that conceive the enemies of the nation compelled to destructive activities because of heritable "racial" traits, or because they are organized in foreign conspiracies, operating vast and intricate plots intended to exploit and destroy weak, benighted, or impaired communities. Such plots involve the complicity of venal collaborators within the threatened community. They are the suborned domestic saboteurs, the "wreckers," those who betray the salvific revolution.

In its most psychopathic form, this kind of reactive nationalism spawns mass-murder and genocide. Millions upon millions of "class enemies" perished in Soviet Russia and Maoist China. Hitler's National Socialism consumed millions of innocents in a maelstrom of violence. In Cambodia, further millions perished at the hands of Pol Pot's minions in an avalanche of bestiality unparalleled in modern times.[2]

These horrors can be legitimately associated with the exacerbated reactive nationalism that is relatively commonplace among those less-developed nations that seem to vegetate on the margins of the world system. We have seen their reemergence in the "ethnic cleansing" that accompanied the disintegration of socialist Yugoslavia.

A similar form of nationalism has appeared among those communities, reasonably well-developed, that suffer real or fancied humiliation in a world culturally, economically, and militarily dominated by those more industrially sophisticated. Thus, while mass-murder and genocidal violence tends to be identified with "fascism" among many Western scholars, it would appear that it is a lethal byproduct of a pathological reactive nationalism exhibited at least as frequently among "leftist" as "rightist" regimes.

Insofar as Mussolini's Fascism was a reactive nationalism, it shared some of the properties of the entire class. It is equally evident, however, that it did not share, in full measure, their disposition to mass-murder or genocide.

Mussolini's Fascism was a relatively benign form of reactive nationalism—in terms of the regime's treatment of its domestic population. In the years between 1926 and 1932, when Fascism was establishing its totalitarianism, the special Fascist tribunals for political offenders pronounced only 7 death sentences.[3] Throughout the years of Fascist rule, most political offenders were sentenced to incarceration or, alternatively, house arrest in the more rural parts of Italy. Most commentators have agreed that "measured by the standards of Germany and Russia, Fascist Italy was almost a humanitarian society."[4]

The Fascist regime in Italy employed incarceration and exile, rather than mass-murder and genocide, to suppress "antinational" dissidence and prompt compliance behavior. Mussolini's political police were a pale reflection of the Gestapo, the Cheka, the NKVD, or the KGB. There was no one in Italy who could serve as the equivalent of Heinrich Himmler, Genrikh Yagoda, or Kang Sheng—Mao's "evil genius"—who kept most of China in terror for a generation.[5]

Every population counts an indeterminate number of moral and intellectual defectives in its number. In revolutionary circumstances, such elements have greater opportunities for rising to positions of authority. The history of National Socialist Germany is too well known to require review here. What is more instructive, perhaps, is the recognition that all these movements of reactive nationalism host those who seek out the presumed domestic enemies of their humiliated nation with an unrelenting passion. In the twentieth century, they have left millions of corpses in their wake.

Lenin and Mussolini both recognized that moral indigents, lunatics, and sociopaths had collected in the interstices of their respective movements. Lenin—who was, himself, part-Jewish—tolerated the anti-Semitic outbursts of the young Josef Dzhugashvili because Stalin was "useful to the movement."[6]

The vagaries of history made Stalin, an anti-Semite all his life, the leader of the Soviet Union. The price paid by Soviet Jews is now well established.[7]

One finds a similar collection of defectives around Fascism. Giovanni Preziosi, two years Mussolini's senior, was an early adherent of Fascism. A defrocked priest—and probably clinically disturbed—he early became Italy's foremost anti-Semite.

Found repugnant by Mussolini, Preziosi remained politically marginal throughout the entire period before the Second World War. As Fascist Italy's rapprochement with Hitler's Germany drew Italy into assuming more and more anti-Jewish postures, Preziosi, using allies within the system, urged anti-Semitism on Mussolini.

With the catastrophic collapse of the Italian armed forces, and the final attempt of Fascism to preserve some semblance of serious purpose with the establishment of the rump Republic of Salò in the north of Italy, Preziosi surfaced to become the head of the General Directorate of Demography and Race. While his every enterprise was obstructed by Fascists, including Mussolini, German support afforded him the opportunity to vent his pathological hatred, and he succeeded in making Fascism, in its final months, complicit in the murder of Italian Jews.[8]

The entire atmosphere of reactive and developmental nationalist dictatorships, as totalitarianisms, contributes to the occurrence of such enormities. The very notion that one has a moral warrant to incarcerate, exile, or kill opponents is a product of the passions that enflame revolutionary nationalists. In its time, totalitarianism is host to the most extravagant form of those passions.

By the end of the century, the long pretense that "fascism," alone, was culpable of all the "crimes against humanity" that have burdened our time, has been abandoned.[9] The estimates are that the number of unnatural deaths, on four continents, attributable to "communism" since 1917, ranges from 85 million to 100 million.[10] The dead include all those who "conspired" with "imperialists" to undo the "socialist" and "world proletarian" revolution, and obstruct the renewal and uplift of Russia, China, North Korea, Vietnam, Kampuchea, or "Marxist-Leninist" Ethiopia.

It is impossible to fully grasp the enormity of so many deaths, much less attempt to explain the dynamics that led to them. Moreover, it remains unclear why so few such political murders can be charged to Fascist Italy. None of the explanations thus far attempted are very persuasive. There is one possibility, offered here only as a suggestion, that may have some merit.

Ideology and Mass Murder

The principal feature that distinguishes Mussolini's totalitarianism, from that of Stalin and Hitler, is the coherence of its ideology. Even before its accession to power, Fascism had articulated a consistent and relevant ideology of national renewal and development, predicated on the presumption that only an "organic" unity of *all* elements of the community could serve the purposes of a "proletarian" nation in its unequal international contest with "plutocracies." Fascist thought committed Fascism to the tutelary inclusion of all members of the community, without distinction, in the effort to construct a self-sustaining and mutually reinforcing totalitarian unity.

Obversely, Marxist-Leninists forever remained confused about the purpose of their revolution. Possessed of that Marxist intellectual legacy so much admired by Western scholarship, Bolsheviks conceived "class warfare" an essential part of their revolution. Other than make war on the bourgeoisie in the cause of the "proletarian" revolution, they had not the least notion of what they were required to do upon seizing power in post-tzarist Russia.

Lenin clearly understood the Bolshevik revolution to be a war against the bourgeoisie. Beyond that, the revolution became a holding action until the proletariat of the advanced industrial nations might rise up in universal rebellion. When the world revolution failed to materialize, Lenin scrambled to restore the ravaged domestic economy of a post-revolutionary Russia. At the same time, he was compelled, by virtue of his ideological confusion, to continue his struggle against domestic "class enemies." The mayhem that resulted compromised not only the restoration of the domestic economy, but the very future of the revolution.

It was Stalin, Lenin's unnatural heir, who "in the early 1930s...injected the adrenalin of Russian nationalism into the Soviet political bloodstream"[11] in an effort to restore some vitality to what gave every appearance of a failed revolution. At the same time, in contravention to the most elementary precepts of nationalism, Stalin continued the "class war" that divided the nation and impaired its efforts.

It was Stalin who abandoned Marxist internationalism and settled on the formula of "socialism in one country," that was to make of Marxism-Leninism a rationale for developmental national socialism. At the same time, Stalin spoke of "international proletarian revolution" and its betrayal by domestic "bourgeois elements."

It was Stalin who understood that only overall economic growth and industrial development could save Russia from being overwhelmed by the advanced industrial West—and whatever "international proletarian revolution" meant to him, it was always subordinate to the defense of the Soviet Union. And yet, it was Stalin, who at the very commencement of his reign, reinvoked the elemental forces of the "Marxist" revolution: "Class war to the death!"[12]

While there was an emphasis on "Soviet patriotism" in the service of the "Soviet Fatherland"—there was still the lethal insistence on counterproductive "class warfare" within the nation. "Class enemies" were found everywhere and death was swift to follow.

Among the leadership, confusion was pandemic. Trotsky and Bukharin both recognized that what Stalin had jerry-built was an inconsistent fascism, committed specifically to national rebirth and rapid industrial development—while, at the same time, he persisted in the hunt for domestic enemies and in the pursuit of international revolution. Trotsky and Bukharin were both soon to be swallowed up in the revolutionary terror.

Under Stalin, as the Soviet Union struggled to industrialize itself, the notion of a class-riven society undermined the sense of unity and cooperation central to collective labor, sacrifice, and flawless commitment. Economic development, under a "proletarian" dictatorship lacked all coherence. The system had no sustaining logic. It was captive to a higher, ideologically defined, class-based, system of priorities that drove it from one contradiction to another.

The system itself, in the course of its development, continuously created "bourgeois elements." Those in authority, of whatever class provenance, succumbed to "bourgeois" thinking and became, by definition, enemies of the "proletarian" state. Those who failed to understand the class nature of Stalin's "socialism in one country" immediately became enemies of the "proletarian" state.

Throughout the early 1930s, arrests in the Soviet Union continued without interruption. Hundreds of thousands, perhaps millions, perished in those years. At one time or another, peasants, managers, and skilled workers were not only "bourgeois" elements, but mortal "enemies" of the "proletariat." The "logic" of the revolution required their destruction.

Western intellectuals, like Lion Feuchtwanger, H. G. Wells, Henri Barbusse, and Romain Rolland, who approved of Stalinism, but not its nationalism, were convinced, by some quaint logic, that class warfare and the liberation of the "proletariat" were the only hope for the future. What they failed to appreciate was the fact that rapid economic development and industrialization required the collaborative effort of all elements of a society in transition. War between the elements of such a society was a symptom, not of hope for the future, but of a profound disorder.

The Soviet revolutionary dictatorship, and the subsequent totalitarianism it created, rested on a "proletarian" base. Ideally, the "proletariat"— the "promethean class"—separated itself out of all other "classes" in society. Only "proletarians" contributed to the historic mission of the Soviet fatherland. Other "classes" would be tolerated, but only if they could be compelled to contribute to the "proletarian" enterprise.

In response to what he perceived as the flagging loyalty, and "bourgeoisification" of the Party, Stalin proceeded to destroy almost the entire Communist leadership of the Soviet Union when they found themselves incapable of penetrating the tortured "dialectical logic" that made Marxist internationalism and class warfare an inextricable part of a program for nationalistic rapid industrialization and *etatization* of the economy.

Confusion and disillusion made many, if not all, Communist Party members potential "enemies of the state." Since there were no clear criteria of what might count as antistate or anti-Party activity in a developmental nationalism that was both class-based and internationalist, everyone in the Soviet Union lived under the pall of mortal peril.

Few of the faithful Marxists of the October revolution survived Stalin's purges. Baffled and uncertain, they went to their deaths as "class enemies" at the hands of a regime that had embroiled itself in multiple contradictions. That, together with Stalin's apparent paranoia,[13] created an environment in which murder by the state seemed to be a perverse inevitability.

As contradictions mounted between the system and its legitimating Marxist ideology, more and more found themselves potentially criminal "deviationists" and "bourgeois sectarians." While there was talk of "proletarian democracy," Stalin constructed an antidemocratic and elitist "sacral state." While there was talk of the elimination of "class" distinctions and the cultivation of equity, the reality was a form of inflexible political superordination characterized by invidious distinctions between the elite who ruled and the those who were ruled.

Stalin's commitment to class warfare, to the persistence of "class struggle," even after the abolition of private property in the Soviet Union, created the circumstances in which anyone who resisted the national plan, or performed badly in its fulfillment, was considered a "class enemy." Marxism had taught Stalin to expect no less.

Stalin expected to find "class enemies" everywhere—and they were everywhere found. "Class enemies" had early become the proper objects of state violence, and untold millions perished as a consequence.

While Fascists spoke of nationalism, the collaboration of classes, and the primacy of the state, Marxist-Leninists pretended to "proletarian internationalism," class warfare, and the "withering away" of the state. While Fascism spoke of accelerated economic and industrial development, the assimilation of all into the collective identity of the nation-state, Marxist-Leninists spoke of inheriting the abundance of "monopoly capitalism," the persistence of violent class struggle, and "international proletarian revolution."

Half a world away, in China, the rule of Mao Zedong was afflicted with very much the same confusion. Mao was perhaps even more uncertain than Stalin about the nature and intent of the revolution he undertook. Throughout his revolutionary struggles, during the post-dynastic republican period, Mao insisted that the ideology that informed the Chinese Communist Party was essentially that of Sun Yat-sen's "Three Principles of the People."[14]

While always insisting on his Marxism, Mao maintained, with equal insistence, that the Communist Party sought the "complete realization" of Sun's Three Principles, the first of which was nationalism—and the third—rapid economic growth and industrial development.[15] Thus, while he identified himself as an internationalist "proletarian" on the one hand, Mao insisted that he was a developmental nationalist on the other.

While he granted that the Party's *ultimate* program was "more comprehensive" than that of Sun, Mao insisted that his commitment to the "Three Principles of the People" was very real. Before 1949, Mao maintained that, like Sun, he intended to unite all Chinese, irrespective of class origins, in a nationalist program of renewal, that would remain "unchanged...for several decades."[16] Until 1949, Mao maintained that the purpose of his "new democracy," with its class collaboration and private enterprise, was to "build a powerful national defense force and a powerful economy"[17]—the specific revolutionary, developmental, and nationalist intentions of Sun Yat-sen.

Before his succession to power in China, Mao appealed to the nationalist and developmental sentiments of the Chinese people. Those sentiments were predicated on the "organic union" of all the Chinese people, irrespective of class or category distinction. It was common knowledge that Sun had abjured class warfare and sought "a reconciliation of the interests of capitalists and workers, rather than a conflict between them,"[18] in order to foster and sustain economic expansion and industrial growth.[19]

Sun had emphatically rejected the notion of class warfare. He understood it to be inimical to rapid economic development and violative of the unifying principle of nationalism.

Until his accession to power, Mao pretended to be the true defender of Sun's nationalist and developmental principles.[20] Once in power, however, he imposed his dysfunctional convictions about intense and perpetual "class struggle" on the nation. That alone was to consume millions of lives.

At the very commencement of his rule, Mao discovered "class enemies" everywhere. Ultimately, "class enemies" and "capitalist roaders" were to be found even in the highest echelons of the Communist Party itself. Communist China was, as a consequence, to be caught up in a frenzy of "class" violence and mass murder until the "Great Proletarian Cultural Revolution" brought the entire nation to the very brink of catastrophe.[21]

In retrospect, the evidence indicates that the "capitalist roaders" in China's Communist Party were those, like Liu Shaoqi and Deng Xiaoping, who continued to hold fast to some of the essentials of Sun's class-collaborationist and developmental program. Mao's Stalinist aberrancies were to make them "counter-revolutionary bourgeois elements." They, and hundreds of thousands of lesser revolutionaries, were to be subsequently caught up in the vortex of confusion, betrayal, and murder.

Only after Mao's death were the leaders of the Chinese Communist Party free to identify his failures. Mao had led the nation on an ineffectual and self-destructive course.[22] Mao's class warfare, and "proletarian internationalism," had consumed resources and labor, and destroyed the lives of perhaps as many as 40 million Chinese.

Almost immediately after Mao's death, Deng Xiaoping denounced class warfare and allowed the reappearance, among the peasantry, of qualified private property rights. Foreign capitalists were invited to invest in joint ventures in "socialist" China, and new domestic classes of enterprisory and skilled personnel were cultivated in order to foster and sustain the profit-fueled growth of industry and commerce. The purpose of the revolution was no longer the seizure of power by the international proletariat, or making "class struggle" its "key link."

The purpose of the revolution was redefined as the "Four Modernizations"—the "modernization in this century of agriculture, industry, defense, as well as science and technology, in order to promote [China] to a position among the most advanced countries in the world."[23] The unceasing and cataclysmic class warfare of Marxism, Stalinism, and Maoism was abandoned. By 1981, Deng Xiaoping had restored the nationalist and developmental core to the ideology of the Chinese revolution.[24]

A case can be made that the failure of "Marxist-Leninist" systems to understand the nature of the revolution upon which they had embarked contributed to the death of millions. Conceiving the revolution as "proletarian" and internationalist, Marxist-Leninists were never really certain what their economic and political responsibilities were. Faced with the task of reconstructing economies devastated by war and revolution, they often alienated or destroyed those very "bourgeois and nationalist elements" most essential to the restoration of productive systems. Having defined the "bourgeoisie" as class enemies, they were surprised to find that the "bourgeoisie" failed to freely contribute to the growth and stability of "socialism." "Class warfare" became a self-fulfilling prophecy of devastating consequence.

Because Marxist-Leninists had convinced themselves that it was class warfare that rendered history dynamic, they used every opportunity to employ the notion to defeat internal enemies. The enemies of Stalin and Mao were always "bourgeois counter-revolutionaries"—and could be dealt with as though they were the enemies of the nation, the unitary party, and the totalitarian state.

Conceiving their revolutions to be class-based, with the concept "class" ill-defined and mercurial, Marxist-Leninists created an environment of domestic tension and free-floating hostility that not only cost the lives of millions, but impaired necessary economic growth and industrial development. The failure to achieve anticipated growth rates not only contributed to the burgeoning death rate through starvation, malnutrition, and the absence of adequate health care, but increased the frequency with which violence was employed as redress.

As a consequence of Mao's attempted "Great Leap Forward," for example, perhaps as many as twenty-five million Chinese died in the famine that resulted from the flawed attempt to force-draught China's peasants and simple workers into the twentieth century using "anti-bourgeois" and "Marxist" methods. Enemies appeared everywhere, even in the highest ranks of the Party. There was an ever tightening cycle of "class" violence. During the "Great Proletarian Cultural Revolution" alone, it is estimated that "Mao's Red Guards" killed over a million "class enemies."

A very similar argument might be made, with appropriate amendations, with respect to Hitler's Germany. While many, many Germans enlisted in the ranks of National Socialism with the conviction that they were embarked on a nationalist program of renewal and vindication, it soon became evident that National Socialism was not nationalist, but racist.

It was not only the Jews who were perceived as enemies of the nation. It soon became evident that many non-Jewish Germans, as "racially inferior," were to be victims as well.

In his *Table Talks*, Hitler spoke of the eventual "elimination" of those Germans who did not meet "Nordic" criteria of racial purity. The fact was that according to Hans Guenther, Nazi Germany's "racial scientist," ninety-five percent of Germans did not meet those criteria.[25] It was no longer clear who would suffer in the serious implementation of National Socialist policy.

Uncertain racial criteria threatened almost everyone subject to Hitler's rule. Hitler, himself, was never really quite sure who his "racial enemies" were. There were Jews, but then there were "half-Jews," those with "some Jewish blood in their veins," and those who had been "Jewified." And then there were "Alpines" and "Mediterraneans" as well as those "less-than-worthy racial and individual types." For Hitler, there were real or potential enemies everywhere.

To compound all this confusion, it very quickly became evident what the implications of a consistent racist policy meant for the German nation. During National Socialist Germany's very struggle for survival, Hitler committed rolling stock and resources to the transportation and murder of millions of Jews and hundreds of thousands of non-Jews, Gypsies, homosexuals, and other "less worthy" peoples. While involved in an unequal struggle with the nation's enemies, Hitler was prepared to jeopardize the nation's defense in order to pursue the "racial enemies" of his revolution.

What Hitler had done was what Stalin had done, and Mao and Pol Pot were to do in their own time. They all betrayed the nation, and nationalism, in order to destroy imagined class or racial opponents. Hitler, like Stalin or Mao, misunderstood the character of the revolution of the twentieth century—and that certainly contributed to the wholesale destruction of the nation's innocents, who could have well served in any program of nationalist development and renewal.

Fascists, on the other hand, had committed themselves to a totalitarian nationalism in which all classes, sects, and distinctions were to disappear. Political opponents of the regime were individuals and groups that were in "error"—they were not entire classes or races that could be dealt with collectively.

When Fascism embarked upon its official anti-Semitism, in the forlorn effort to impress Hitler with its "seriousness," a significant number in the hierarchy resisted—and the population of Fascist Italy responded with little interest or enthusiasm. As has been suggested, Gentile did not comply and, at considerable personal risk, refused to tarnish the memory of his Jewish teachers or abandon his Jewish colleagues. Fascism aspired to a totalitarian union of all Italians; its ideology left little space for racism or class struggle.

Revolution and Ideology

It took a very long time for academics to fully appreciate the role ideology played in the most destructive revolutions of our time. For decades we were told that "Marxist-Leninist" systems distinguished themselves in the possession of profound intellectual credentials. The masters of the Soviet Union, or Communist China, were supposed to be guided by the deep philosophical, political, and economic thought of Karl Marx, Friedrich Engels, and V. I. Lenin. That was somehow imagined to enlist them in the service of humanity.

National Socialists, on the other hand, were inhumane and barbaric because they simply had no philosophical, economic, or moral principles. They were all clinically deranged. Fascists were little better. They were simply thoughtless thugs.

Authors who wrote entire volumes concerning "fascist" thought often devoted only the most fleeting allusions to the extensive primary sources of fascist ideology, at least partly because the effort was considered misplaced. Unlike Marxism, Fascist thought was rarely seriously considered. It was thought to be devoid of intellectual substance and could only be understood exclusively in terms of the psychosexual dynamics of its practitioners. Fascist thought was usually "reconstructed" out of subconscious feelings, affective drives, Jungian archetypes, and Freudian curiosities.

Largely because of these prejudices, Western analysts have sought and found "fascists," "neofascists," "parafascists," and "cryptofascists" only among those who are sexually deviant, disposed to excess, Reagan Republicans, Christian fundamentalists, homophobes, conspiracy theorists, or members of male fraternities. None of these notions has served us well.

From the vantage point of the end of the twentieth century, it seems that our time has witnessed not intellectually profound leftist, and irrational rightist, revolution, but variants of an inclusive class of revolutions of reactive, antidemocratic, and developmental nationalisms. And it is not the thought of Marx, Engels, and Lenin that illuminates those revolutions. It is the thought of theoreticians like Roberto Michels, Giovanni Gentile, and Sergio Panunzio.

The intellectuals of Mussolini's Fascism provided the most consistent, coherent, and relevant doctrinal rationale for the reactive nationalist and developmental revolutions of our time. Departures from the coherence of that rationale, and the prescriptions and proscriptions it entailed, contributed, at least in part, to the destructiveness and inhumanity that settled down on more than half the world that has experienced revolution in the twentieth century.

The class of reactive, antidemocratic, and developmental nationalisms is a family of modern revolutionary movements and regimes, with totalitarianism a subfamily or genus, of which Mussolini's Fascism may be considered a species or variety. Mussolini's revolution, in fact, represented the entire class in a fashion that illuminates the rest.[26] In a nonspecific sense, one might say that almost all the other antiliberal, reactive nationalist and developmental revolutions in our century were deviant forms of paradigmatic Fascism—the more deviant, the more destructive.[27]

Such a notion is neither morally nor cognitively gratifying. For taxonomists, it produces an unmanageably large number of revolutionary movements and regimes as potential members of the family, and requires, in each case, extended scrutiny of both ideology and behaviors before heuristic classification can be attempted. Such movements have been found almost everywhere,[28] and nothing logically precludes the possibility that such movements might be found, given unique circumstances, in advanced industrial democracies—although after the Second World War no credible candidates have been unearthed.

The "fascists" that have been identified by some scholars in advanced industrial democracies prove to be not fascists, but defectives of all kinds,[29] organized in small groups that pursue hopelessly unrealistic agendas, that have nothing to do with national renewal, accelerated industrial growth, opposition to foreign "plutocracies," or securing their nation a place in the sun.

The properties of Mussolini's Fascism, as the paradigmatic instantial case, provide the criteria for entry into the class of "fascisms"—criteria now too familiar to warrant rehearsal. At the end of the twentieth century there are at least two important candidates that would seem to qualify for inclusion: a Russian, and a Chinese "fascism." The one, as has been suggested, has made its ideological posture and intent transparent. The other, by "reforming" Maoism, has produced an antidemocratic, elitist, nationalistic, and rapidly industrializing China featuring hegemonic party control, ritualized charismatic and ideocratic rule, an interventionist state, an assertive "anti-imperialist" foreign policy, class collaboration, qualified private property, and a mixed economy governed, in part, by market signals. The authorities in Beijing call the post-Maoist system they have fabricated a "socialism with Chinese characteristics." It looks very much like fascism.

The Fascisms in Our Future

There is little doubt that a Chinese fascism will impact on Western policy throughout the early years of the twentyfirst century. Less certain is what will transpire in post-Soviet Russia. So chaotic are the conditions in the Russia of the late 1990s, that it is almost impossible to anticipate the future of the federation. Given the reality of Russia's circumstances, a fascist future for post-Soviet Russia is perhaps too sanguine a projection.

The Russia of the late 1990s has been so devastated by economic collapse and political disintegration, that the possibility of a military dictatorship, much less an authoritarian and developmental system like that of Fascist Italy or "communist" China assuming control of the ruins, appears to be nothing less than an aspiration devoutly to be wished. All that acknowledged, granting the advent of a Russian and a Chinese fascism, several possibilities suggest themselves.

The fascisms in our future may confine themselves to putting together variants of Panunzio's "revolutionary dictatorships"—and they may never attain totalitarian "maturity." It may be that a Russian and a Chinese fascism may remain, for an indeterminate time, administrative dictatorships no more threatening to their populations than Mussolini's Fascism was to Italians.

The international behaviors of those future fascisms might very well share features with the original Fascism. All were, or are, animated by an insistent irredentism, a restoration of "lost territories," and an insistence on a "living space" adequate to the needs of a "Great Nation."[30]

Should there be a fascist Russia, it would turn its gaze toward what Russians now call the "near afar," all those regions that fell away from the Soviet Union upon its collapse and which now exercise varying degrees of independence. Quite other than the fact that an entire catalog of resource, political, and security interests tie Russia to its near abroad, and thus engage everyone's considerations, the nationalists, more than any of the others, recognize that for half a millennium, Russia has dominated Eurasia. To surrender that dominance would be to acknowledge Russia's loss of its historical position as a major influence in the Asian and Western geostrategic balance of power. Mother Russia would lose her place in the sun.

As recently as 1994, two Russian generals signed a memorandum entitled, "National Doctrine of Russia: Problems and Priorities" that foresaw the rehabilitation of the military with the intention of making the "21st century...the century of Russia."[31] That could hardly be accomplished until the most critical issues of the relationship of Russia to the near abroad were resolved.

Any such effort would involve the authoritarian restoration of the national economy and the reconstruction of the shambles that were once the Soviet armed forces. A Russian fascism would devote its energies to reconstructing its military, now little more than a shadow of its former self.[32]

The intentions of a Russian fascism have been made very clear. Ziuganov has warned the rest of the world that Russia "will not accept the humiliating role being imposed on it and will restore its natural position as a great power....Moscow," he went on, "does not have the right to abandon [its] traditional role of 'gatherer of the lands'...."[33] As a "gatherer of lands," Russia would seek the eventual irredentist restoration of all the boundary lands of the former Soviet Union and the immediate protection of ethnic Russians in all the non-Russian regions of the near abroad.

The case of a fascist China is very much the same. The reactive nationalist China that has emerged from the reform of Maoism, is a China that still bears irrepressible resentments against the "imperialist" West. It is a China that has, in effect, repudiated Marxism—a China that both Western Marxists and China's own dissidents have identified as a "typical social-fascist dictatorship."[34]

By the middle of the 1990s, in fact, the government of the People's Republic of China made little pretense that "socialism with Chinese characteristics" was really Marxist in inspiration or in application. By that time, most serious Western thinkers acknowledged that the "global collapse of communism" had left the authorities in Beijing "ideologically bereft."[35] Their response had been the invocation of a "visceral nationalism" to legitimate their rule.[36]

The Chinese military has welcomed the emphatic nationalism that now undergirds the reactive nationalist dictatorship in China.[37] It recognizes that nationalism provides the ideological foundation for the unity of all Chinese in their reactive response to a "century of shame." A reactive and developmental nationalism,[38] not unlike the reactive nationalisms that gave us the fascisms and the totalitarianisms of the interwar years now serves as a surrogate for whatever Marxism-Leninism survived the Mao years.

The China of Jiang Zemin is nationalistic, anti-Western, statist, ideocratic, elitist, and messianic. More than that, it is the inflexible enemy of Western "imperialism," and committed to the irredentist restoration of the nation's "lost territories" all along the land and maritime borders of continental China.[39]

Jiang Zemin has committed China to a "state nationalism (*guojia minzu zhuyi*)," predicated on a "group consciousness" that will instill in the domestic population a sacrificial readiness to serve the national community.[40] Together with that state-patriotism, the theoreticians of Chinese nationalism now define the national "spirit" as loyalty, selflessness, sacrifice, dedication, and courage. These properties, which are the conditions of moral self-fulfillment, are elevated to the formal rank of "communist sentiments and principles."[41] National rebirth requires nothing less. The nation must be economically and industrially modernized, with the population "organized and disciplined" under "strong centralized leadership."[42]

What any of this augurs for the future of the industrialized democracies is very difficult to say. One of the principal dangers that a Russian fascism carries with it is the possibility that it would be captured by the host of anti-Semites, mystics, and cultists of every psychopathic variety that have collected around its "national patriotism."[43] A fascist developmental dictatorship, in itself, while not the best of all possible alternatives, would be vastly preferable to an anti-Semitic and racist Russia.

A fascist China would resemble Kuomintang China in many ways. That it would develop into a totalitarian China seems unlikely. It would display many of the traits industrializing democracies deplore, but it probably would be a manageable international actor—even should it grow into the world's second largest economy in the twenty-first century.

Whether China continues the remarkable economic growth and the industrial expansion of the 1980s and the 1990s is not assured. Neither is the successful modernization of its armed forces.[44]

Jiang Zemin's China will be afflicted with major economic problems for the foreseeable future, and the upgrading of the Chinese armed forces to the level at which they might be a peer competitor of the United States will require both time and a great deal of money. It is not certain that Communist China has enough of either.

Current U.S. policy toward China is predicated on the conviction that "constructive engagement" between the industrialized democracies and the People's Republic of China will foster increasing liberalization on the mainland of China, defuse the possibilities of military misadventure, and preclude any return to totalitarian rule. That together with a decline in reactive nationalism that may follow a steady increase in domestic personal welfare and international status, may weaken or dissipate Beijing's disposition to embark on any adventure. Given all the inscrutables that might influence China's political and economic future, as well as U.S.-China relations, very little can be predicted with any confident probability.

Whatever happens over the next few decades, past experience with reactive nationalisms suggests that they are relatively fragile systems with a correspondingly short life-span. One of the reasons is their impulse to embark on very risky programs of international "greatness."

National Socialist Germany destroyed itself in a war that ultimately pitted it against almost every major industrial power in the world. Fascist Italy involved a desperately inadequate military in a war that far exceeded its capabilities—which not only cost the nation hundreds of thousands of unnecessary deaths, but destroyed the regime as well.

Reactive nationalist regimes have a tendency to dissipate young lives in the pursuit of irredentist goals and some obscure notion of national grandeur. Even when the prospects of success seem remote by any rational calculation, reactive nationalists have been prepared to embark on very hazardous ventures.

It is not certain that a fascist China would avoid such temptations in the South or East China seas. As militarily ill-equipped as China will be well into the twenty-first century, there remains the nationalist and irredentist temptation to remove alien domination from its surrounding "living space." The twentieth century is filled with instances of such miscalculation.

The Fascist Phoenix

Western scholarship has, in general, failed to understand Mussolini's Fascism. It was a paradigm instance of revolution in our time. Some or all of its features have appeared and reappeared in some or all the revolutionary dictatorships and totalitarianisms of the twentieth century.

In that regard, the study of Fascism, and particularly the thought that provided its rationale, is not an exotic and arcane concern among Western intellectuals. Fascist thought, as it found expression in Mussolini's Italy, is of immediate political and international relevance. If nothing more, it provides a guide to the reappearance of a phenomenon most Western thinkers have simply misunderstood.

Non-Western intellectuals have been attracted to fascism because it resonates with their concerns—concerns that have become entirely alien to those enjoying the abundance and status of the West. One only need read the passionate arguments put together by contemporary Russians—so traumatically bereft of a sense of purpose, an identity, and a respected place in the world, by the catastrophic collapse of the Soviet Union—to understand why the nationalism, the statism, and the "masculine protest" of Fascist Italy, is appealing.

Russian or Chinese reactive nationalists need never have read a word of Michels or Gentile, to echo their sentiments. The reactive nationalism of the Chinese, so long humiliated by the West, is as natural as life itself. They have reconstructed almost the entire logic of Fascism in their very long quest to redeem their old-new nation.

To understand something of the thought of Roberto Michels, Giovanni Gentile, and Sergio Panunzio, is to understand something of all this. The revolutions of our time have a logic that had earlier escaped us.

With the insights of Michels, Gentile, and Panunzio, we understand something of the appeal of fascism. We also intuit some of the profound risks fascist convictions entail. We understand something of the passion and the intensity that easily lapse into massive violence. We understand something of revolutionary movements, revolutionary dictatorships, and the totalitarianisms they sometimes create.

There may come a time when the study of fascist thought is no longer necessary—when it will be of only antiquarian interest. Reactive nationalisms generally have a short life-cycle. They can, on occasion, grow into totalitarianisms, or, perhaps, into representative democracies—as has the Republic of China on Taiwan. Or they implode, as did the Soviet Union. Or they can self-destruct, as did National Socialist Germany and Fascist Italy.

It may even be that some time in the next century, we will see the end of fascism. Perhaps the world, with its international and transnational organizations and multilateral constraints, has outgrown reactive nationalisms, revolutionary dictatorships, and totalitarianisms. An integrated "global economy" may have no place for nationalist developmental dictatorships. Nationalism, itself, may no longer command the emotions it once did—and if that is the case, reactive nationalism will have no host, and gradually disappear.

Any and all of that may be true. Russian fascism and Chinese fascism may be the last fascisms—and then again, they may not.

Notes

1. See the discussion in Carl Schmitt, "Das Begriff des Politischen," *Positionen und Begriffe im Kampf mit Weimar-Genf-Versailles 1923–1939* (Hamburg: Hanseatische Verlaganstalt, 1940), pp. 67–74.
2. See Israel Charny (ed.), *The Widening Circle of Genocide* (New Brunswick, N.J.: Transaction Publishers, 1994); R. J. Rummel, *Death by Government: Genocide and Mass Murder since 1900)* (New Brunswick, N.J.: Transaction Publishers, 1994); and Irving Louis Horowitz, *Taking Lives: Genocide and State Power* (New Brunswick, N.J.: Transaction Publishers, 1997).
3. See Hannah Arendt, *The Origins of Totalitarianism* (New York: Harcourt, Brace and Company, 1951), p. 303, n. 8.
4. Walter Laqueur, *The Dream that Failed: Reflections on the Soviet Union* (New York: Oxford University Press, 1994), p. 131.
5. John Byron and Robert Pack, *The Claws of the Dragon: Kang Sheng, the Evil Genius Behind Mao—and His Legacy of Terror in People's China* (New York: Simon and Schuster, 1992).
6. Edvard Radzinsky, *Stalin* (New York: Doubleday, 1996), p. 55.
7. See Arkady Vaksberg, *Stalin Against the Jews* (New York: Alfred A. Knopf, 1994) and Gennadi Kostyrchenko, *Out of the Red Shadows: Anti-Semitism in Stalin's Russia* (Amherst: Prometheus, 1995).
8. The Italian Jews who were murdered in the Second World War were murdered by Nazi forces, but the fact that Italian Jews were herded into concentration camps

on the orders of authorities exposed them to easy capture by the Nazis. In that sense, the Fascist forces were inextricably complicit. See Silvio Bertoldi, *Salò: vita e morte della Repubblica Sociale Italiana* (Milan: Rizzoli, 1976), chap. 19.

9. In Soviet Russia, "the figure of 681,000 executed in 1937–1938 compares with a few dozen (at most) of political executions in Italy from the beginning of fascist rule to Mussolini's fall." Laqueur, *op. cit.*, p. 141.

10. See John-Thor Dahlburg, "Historians Count Communist Crimes," *San Francisco Sunday Examiner and Chronicle*, 30 November 1997, p. A19.

11. Frederick C. Barghoorn, "Russian Nationalism in Historical Perspective," in Robert Conquest (ed.), *The Last Empire: Nationality and the Soviet Future* (Stanford: Hoover Institution, 1986), p. 35.

12. See Radzinsky, *op. cit.*, p. 232.

13. See the discussion of Soviet specialists in Anatoly Butenko, Gavriil Popov, Boris Bolotin, and Dmitry Volkogonov, *The Stalin Phenomenon* (Moscow: Novosti, 1988). Their principal objections turned on Stalin's insistence that the "class struggle" must intensify in the course of the "building of socialism," a prescription for the mass murder of citizens.

14. The best English translation of Sun's *Three Principles of the People* is available as *The Triple Demism of Sun Yat-sen,* translated by Paschal M. D'Elia, S.J. (Wuchang: The Franciscan Press, 1931, reprinted in 1974 by AMS press, New York).

15. See the discussion in A. James Gregor, *Ideology and Development: Sun Yat-sen and the Economic History of Taiwan* (Berkeley: Institute of East Asian Studies, 1981), chap. 1.

16. Mao Zedong, "On Coalition Government," *Selected Works* (Beijing: Foreign Languages, 1965), 3, pp. 283–285.

17. Mao, "You are Models for the Whole Nation," *ibid.*, 5, p. 41.

18. Sun Yat-sen, *Sanmin chui: The Three Principles of the People* (Taipei: China Publishing, n.d.), pp. 160–161.

19. As late as 1947, Mao insisted that his program corresponded to that of Sun. Until December of that year, Mao insisted that his "new democracy" would protect the "bourgeoisie" and "their industry and commerce." Because of China's backwardness, he would continue to support *capitalist* development and ensure that both public and private, capital and labor, interests would benefit from the revolution. Mao, "The Present Situation and Our Tasks," *Selected Works*, 4, pp. 167–169.

20. See Mao's discussion in "On a Statement by Chiang Kai-shek's Spokesman," *Selected Works*, 4, p. 42.

21. See A. James Gregor, *Marxism, China and Development: Reflections on Theory and Reality* (New Brunswick, N.J.: Transaction Publishers, 1995), chaps. 2, 4 and 5.

22. See the entire discussion in the Chinese Communist Party's assessment of its own history and the leadership of Mao, in *Resolution on CPC History* (Beijing: Foreign Languages, 1981).

23. As cited, Uli Franz, *Deng Xiaoping* (New York: Harcourt Brace Janovich, 1988), p. 261.

24. Maria Hsia Chang, *The Labors of Sisyphus: The Economic Development of Communist China* (New Brunswick, N.J.: Transaction Publishers, 1998), chap. 4.

25. See the discussion in A. James Gregor, *Contemporary Radical Ideologies: Totalitarian Thought in the Twentieth Century* (New York: Random House, 1968), chap. 5.

26. Days before his death, Mussolini insisted that Fascism was the only form of "socialism" appropriate to the "proletarian nations" of the twentieth century. See Benito Mussolini, *Testamento politico di Mussolini* (Rome: Pedanesi, 1948).

27. See the discussion in A. James Gregor, *The Fascist Persuasion in Radical Politics* (Princeton, N.J.: Princeton University Press, 1974).
28. For a period following decolonization, variants of fascism where found in Africa, but they quickly gave way to simple kleptocracies or military dictatorships.
29. See, for example, Ingo Hasselbach, *Fuehrer-Ex* (New York: Random House, 1996).
30. See the discussion in C. Terracciano, G. Roletto, and E. Masi, *Geopolitica fascista: Antologia di scritti* (Milan: Barbarossa, 1993).
31. See Richard F. Staar, *The New Military in Russia: Ten Myths That Shape the Image* (Annapolis: Naval Institute Press, 1996), chap. 10.
32. See Benjamin S. Lambeth, "Russia's Wounded Military," *Foreign Affairs*, 72, no. 2 (March/April 1995), pp. 86–98.
33. Gennadi Ziuganov, "Essay in Russian Geopolitics: The Merits of Rus," *Sovietskya Rossiia*, 26 February 1994; an English language translation is available in J. L. Black (ed.), *Russia and Eurasia Documents Annual 1994: The Russian Federation* (New York: Academic International press, 1995), pp. 112, 114.
34. Charles Bettelheim was convinced that the post-Maoist leadership in China had fulfilled Mao's prediction that the Chinese Communist Party might "change into its opposite and become counter-revolutionary and fascist." Charles Bettelheim, in Charles Bettelheim and Neil Burton, *China Since Mao* (New York: Monthly Review, 1978), p. 112; see p. 72. See Wang Xizhe, "Mao Zedong and the Cultural Revolution," in Anita Chan, Stanley Rosen, and Jonathan Unger (eds), *On Socialist Democracy and the Chinese Legal System* (Armonk: M. E. Sharpe, 1985), p. 180 and Chen Erjin, *China: Crossroads Socialism* (London: Verso, 1984), p. 226.
35. Nayan Chanda and Kari Huus, "China: The New Nationalism," *Far Eastern Economic Review*, 9 November 1995, p. 20.
36. "Chinese nationalism is emerging as an important issue for reassessment. Under Mao, nationalism was one of the core sources of loyalty to the state, but its salience was shrouded by an overlay of revolutionary ideology. With the demise of Maoist ideology over the past two decades a vacuum in commitment to public goals has become obvious among the people of China in what Chinese newspapers have called a 'crisis of faith'." In these circumstances, nationalism remains the one bedrock of political belief shared by most Chinese." Jonathan Unger, "Introduction," in Jonathan Unger (ed.), *Chinese Nationalism* (Armonk, N.Y.: M. E. Sharpe, 1996), p. xi. See also "China: Saying No," and "Stay Back: China," in *The Economist*, 20 July 1996, p. 30 and 16 March 1996, p. 15.
37. See Li Honjun and Zheng Shan, "Greatly Promote the Spirit of Chinese Nationalism," *Guofang* (*National Defense*) no. 9 (1993), particularly pp. 15–16.
38. See Marcus W. Brauchli and Kathy Chen, "Nationalist Fervor," *Wall Street Journal*, 23 June 1995, pp. A1, A5.
39. See Maria Hsia Chang, "Chinese Irredentist Nationalism: The Magician's Last Trick," *Comparative Strategy* 17, no. 1 (January-March 1998), pp. 83–100.
40. Li Xing, "On the Concept of State-Nationalism," *Minzu yanjiu* (*Nationality Studies*) no. 4 (1995), pp. 10–14.
41. See Yao Bolin, "A Careful Study of the Morality of Communists," *Jiefang junbao* (*People's Liberation Daily*), 20 November 1996, p. 4.
42. See Deng Xiaoping, "Uphold the Four Cardinal Principles," *Selected Works (1975–1982)* (Beijing: Foreign Languages, 1984), p. 170.
43. See the discussion in Walter Laqueur, *Black Hundred: The Rise of the Extreme Right in Russia* (New York: Harper, 1993).
44. See the discussion in Don Flamm, "Impact of China's Military Modernisation in the Pacific Region," *Asian Defence Journal*, February 1997, pp. 16–21.

Index